Religion as a Chain of Memory

Translator's Note

I should like to thank Grace Davie for the generosity she showed me and the help and encouragement she gave me during the time that I was working on this book.

Religion as a Chain of Memory

DANIÈLE HERVIEU-LÉGER

Translated by Simon Lee

Polity Press

This translation © Polity Press 2000

First published in France as *La Religion pour Mémoire* © Éditions du Cerf, Paris 1993

First published in 2000 by Polity Press
in association with Blackwell Publishers Ltd

Published with the assistance of the French Ministry of Culture – Centre National du Livre

Editorial office:
Polity Press
65 Bridge Street
Cambridge CB2 1UR, UK

Marketing and production:
Blackwell Publishers Ltd
108 Cowley Road
Oxford OX4 1JF, UK

ISBN 0–7456–2046–9
ISBN 0–7456–2047–7 (pbk)

A catalogue record for this book is available from the British Library.

Typeset in 10.5 on 12 pt Sabon
by Ace Filmsetting Ltd, Frome Somerset
Printed in Great Britain by MPG Books Ltd, Bodmin, Cornwall

This book is printed on acid-free paper.

Contents

Foreword

I am delighted to introduce this book to an English-speaking audience. Danièle Hervieu-Léger is a leading figure in the sociology of religion in the francophone world, but too little known outside this. This is so for a number of reasons. The first (obvious but in some ways superficial) is the language barrier. Whilst most French-speaking scholars can read English, at least to a certain extent, the reverse is seldom the case, a situation which results in a one-sided exchange of ideas. The more fundamental difficulty lies, however, in the very different training – or *formation* to use their own term – of the French scholar both in sociology itself and, more specifically, in the sociology of religion. The sources on which French sociologists are likely to draw in coming to their conclusions are markedly different from those that prevail in the English-speaking world; so, too, the assumptions they are likely to make.

With this in mind, the English edition of Hervieu-Léger's *Religion as a Chain of Memory* makes a double contribution: it permits the English-speaking reader to access the stimulating, and at times provocative, ideas of the author herself; more deeply, however, the text offers insights into the way in which French sociologists approach the subject of religion in modern societies. An excellent example lies in the concept of memory itself – the *fil conducteur* of Hervieu-Léger's analysis. Durkheimian in inspiration, this evolves through the work of Maurice Halbwachs – a writer little known outside France – to offer Hervieu-Léger the key to her understanding of religion in the modern world.

Why then is the concept of memory so central to Hervieu-Léger's work? An obvious link can be found in the notion of tradition – that is, in the perception of religion as a *shared* understanding or perspective, mediated by particular individuals or groups of individuals, themselves situated in an almost infinite variety of social contexts. Hervieu-Léger, however, goes deeper than this and uses the concept of memory in order to confront one of the most thorny problems of the discipline itself: the sociological definition of religion.

The first chapters of the book deal with this issue in particular, looking for a constructive way out of the ongoing, and increasingly fruitless, confrontation between relatively narrow, substantive definitions of religion and more inclusive (but difficult to limit) functional approaches. An answer gradually emerges in the definition of religion as a specific mode of believing. The crucial points to grasp in this analysis are (a) the *chain* which makes the individual believer a member of a community, a community which gathers past, present and future members, and (b) the tradition (or collective memory) which becomes the basis of that community's existence. Hervieu-Léger goes further than this: she argues that modern societies (and especially modern European societies) are less religious not because they are increasingly rational, but because they are less and less capable of maintaining the memory which lies at the heart of their religious existence. They are, to use her own term, amnesic societies. This is a rather different situation from one which assumes, uncritically, that modern societies have found satisfactory alternatives to the traditional forms of religion so crucial in their historical formation. Manifestly, they have not.

Indeed in an earlier book, *Vers un nouveau christianisme*, Hervieu-Léger argues that modern societies are by their very nature corrosive of the traditional forms of religious life, and exemplifies this argument with the kind of data commonly presented in support of the secularization thesis, notably the fall in the hard indicators of religious activity. But this is only half the story. Modern societies may well corrode their traditional religious base; at one and the same time, however, the same societies open up spaces or sectors that only religion can fill. These, Hervieu-Léger refers to as 'utopian' spaces. Modern individuals are encouraged to seek answers, to find solutions and to make progress, in other words to move forwards. Such aspirations become an increasingly normal part of human experience. But their realization is, and must remain, infinitely problematic, for the horizon will always recede. The image of utopia must always exceed reality and the more successful the projects of modernity, the greater the mismatch becomes. Hence the paradox of modernity which in its historical forms removes the need for and sense of religion (the amnesia), but in its utopian forms cannot but stay in touch with the religious (the need for a religious future). Through what mechanisms, then, can modern societies overcome their amnesia and stay in touch with the forms of religion that are necessary to sustain their identity? That is the challenge set by Hervieu-Léger's analysis.

In setting out this challenge and in working with the concept of memory to provide at least a partial answer, Hervieu-Léger's text forms a distinctive contribution to one of the most central debates in the sociology of religion in western societies. All of us are perplexed by the place of religion in the modern world, as we become increasingly aware of the ambiguity and ambivalence by means of which late modern people express their religiousness. The cross-fertilization of ideas between the English- and French-speaking worlds – made possible by a translation such as this – can only enhance our understanding. The fact that Hervieu-Léger uses primarily French data to illustrate her points simply enriches the text further for those more familiar with the Anglo-Saxon world.

A final word of thanks must go to the translator, who faced the unenviable task of rendering in clear English some fiendishly difficult rhetorical French. Simon Lee is to be warmly congratulated on the result.

Grace Davie
University of Exeter

Introduction

Initiation into the sociology of religion twenty years ago or so essentially meant embarking upon an analysis of the reasons explaining the decline of religion, a decline considered as a defining feature of the modern world. A reading of the founding fathers of sociology afforded a theoretical basis for such analysis. The process of rationalization which informed the advance of modernity went hand in hand with the process of 'dismantling the gods', and the triumph of autonomy – both of the individual and of society – implied the ineluctable disintegration of the religion-bound societies of the past. This theoretical position found itself largely confirmed by empirical studies of the changes undergone by the major religions in all developed countries. It was equally apparent that the crisis in observance, the decline in the political and cultural influence of religious institutions and the dislocation in belief did not reflect the same intensity or assume the same form in every national context. But there was ample evidence to sustain the hypothesis that, in all so-called secularized societies, religion survived purely as a private option, as essentially discretionary. Consequently, the question of the transformation of religion under the impact of modernity tended to merge into that of the gradual dissolution of different religious traditions in the societies and cultures which they had helped to model but in which they could no longer reasonably hope to play an active or significant role.

Twenty years on, the entire research landscape is astonishingly changed. The rising political strength of fundamentalist currents all over the world, the several demonstrations of Islam's mobilizing po-

tential, the religious explosion accompanying the ongoing reconstruction in eastern Europe, the multiform development of new religious
movements and the vitality of new communities which in the west are
transforming the appearance of religious institutions themselves, sup-
posedly the most affected by the process of secularization – all this has
provoked a wave of questioning and new involvement. Religion, which
was deemed to have been relegated to the margins of modern society,
has every appearance of displaying its capacity to take on new social,
political and cultural relevance in the crisis of modernity. This cultural
reversal has not merely rehabilitated religion as a subject of scientific
investigation; it also favours theoretical forms of revision which are as
agonizing as they are ambivalent. Indeed, faced with current religious
revivalism, there are signs that some exponents would be prepared to
jettison the whole conceptual achievement that the theorists of
secularization have built up over long years.

The discussion which this transformed intellectual climate has provoked has taken different forms in different countries. The significance
of current reaffirmations of religion does not awaken the same response in France, where the sociology of religion has long been concerned with the dislocation of a historically dominant Catholic culture,
as it does in the United States, where the processes of secularization
and revivalism, in a pluralist setting, have followed an entirely different course. But however much research may differ in tone in each
national context, the principal question confronting the sociology of
religion at the present time has to do with the intellectual approach
required to grasp both the dimension by which modernity continually
undermines the plausibility structures of all religious systems and that
by which it gives rise to new forms of religious belief.

To move forward along this path, one needs to look beyond the
convenient but short-term view which associates the revival of religion with the crisis affecting modernity, namely its inability to deliver
what it promises. More fundamentally, one needs to amend the social,
cultural and symbolic rationale that lies at the heart of what I have
ventured to call the religious products of modernity. A first step in this
endeavour was a critical renewal of the concept of secularization itself, which was the main purpose of a book published in 1986 by Les
Éditions du Cerf with the title: *Vers un nouveau christianisme? Introduction à la sociologie du christianisme occidental* (Towards a New
Christianity? Introduction to the the Sociology of Western Christianity). But it was no more than a first step, and I knew when the book
was published that the task was far from over. It is not enough, in fact,
to point to the limits of the standard paradigm of the loss of religion in
the modern world. It is not even enough, as I proposed at the time, to

establish the link between the permanent redeployment of religious belief (even up to the present) and the utopian credulity of rationally disenchanted societies; societies in which one discerns the affinity that modernity has retained with a set of religious themes to do with fulfilment and salvation, but from which it continually seeks to distance itself in order to exist as such. The process has to be extended to the analysis of structures and the dynamics of modern religious belief and must include (as did Michel de Certeau when he examined the 'anthropology of belief') not merely the beliefs, which are the supreme objects of individual and collective convictions, but the body of practices, behaviour and institutions in which these beliefs find expression. If one submits, as I did in the above publication, that the process of secularization is above all a process of reconstructing belief, it immediately follows that one must ask by what form of reasoning such reconstruction takes place, what elements it brings into play and what dynamics of belief it generates in its turn.

And it very soon became clear that by following this path in the search for a coherent approach to the religious dilemma of modernity – loss *and* reconstruction – I could not avoid a direct confrontation with the problem that has beset the sociology of religion since its origins, the problem of the definition of religion. The starting point of my reflections in this context was the observation that, in order to redefine the notion of secularization, I should have to make use of two definitions of religion. A first, extremely wide, definition would, under the designation of religious representations, include all constructs of the imagination by which society, groups within society, and individuals within such groups, endeavour to assimilate the gap experienced between the limitations and definitions of the everyday and those aspirations to fulfilment for which the secular promises of modernity, replacing the religious promises of salvation, constitute the reference. A second definition comes into play when designating, within such products of conscience, those that explicitly call upon the constituent traditions of the historic religions. These function as a stock of symbols, capable of being mobilized especially when the secular projections of historical fulfilment (modernist ideologies of progress, in their several variants) are called into question.

How far did I need to expand my study of the symbolic productions of modernity so as to grasp in sociological terms the modern processes of the reconstruction of religious belief? This expedient enabled me to link up with a set of questions also raised in the course of research into the development of the new religious movements (to what extent can one still describe them as religious?) and in particular in the course of studies bearing on the secular, analogical or metaphorical religions.

The growth – observable everywhere in societies that are known as
secularized – of invisible or diffuse religiosity dispensing with the mediation of specialized religious institutions constantly reopens the question of the limits of the term 'religious'. But the issue regularly comes
to naught in the conflict that cannot be resolved between those who
choose to be all-inclusive and those who choose to concentrate their
attention only on religions which are socially identified as such.

My goal in this book is to establish an analytical method which,
while enabling the circle to be broken, will also enable religion in
modernity to be considered the subject matter of sociology. With this
in mind, the first requirement has been to give a precise outline of the
problems posed in the sociology of religion by the determination of
the subject matter. This is the theme of the first part. The second part,
which provides a pivot for the whole, is devoted to settling on a definition of religion as a particular form of belief and one that specifically
implies reference to the authority of a tradition. In the third part, I
attempt to apply this definition in the context of modern societies, one
of whose chief characteristics is to be no longer collective depositories
– custodians – of memory. This last section proposes one sociological
approach (among other possible ones) to transformations in religion
within a modernity that rejects the notion of a necessary continuity
between past and present; a modernity that devalues the forms in which
such continuity is supposed to impress itself upon individuals and
groups, but that also gives rise – though in new forms – to a social and
individual need to have recourse to the security of such continuity.

At each stage of the journey, I shall insist on the essentially hypo-
thetical nature of the propositions made. Never at any point is one
drawn to making a definitive statement about the place of religion in
the context of modernity; all that can be done is to try to find means of
imposing some shape and meaning on the profusion of empirically
observable phenomena. Such a prospect will in all probability arouse
debate. A likely criticism will be that it is overdidactic and takes little
account of the common-sense distinctions between religious and non-
religious matters, which as such have to do with defining the subject
matter. To this objection the only reply can be that the definition settled upon has in fact to serve as a measure of the distinctions provided
by general evidence, distinctions through which in fact the forms of
reconstruction we seek to identify function. Very probably the point
will be made that the process of conceptualization would be more
secure – richer certainly – were it backed up with a socio-historical
perspective, cross-cultural comparisons (denominational and religious),
close empirical surveys, and the like. It is also necessary to admit that
the present undertaking is open to the very contradiction it has made

it its purpose to resolve. Theories of secularization encounter the charge of aligning the analysis of modern religion with the evolution of the established religions of western societies in which modernity has developed, that is, Judaism and Christianity. But more often than not it is to Christianity and to Judaism that one returns, when reconsidering the question of institutionalized religion in these same modern societies. Is this limitation attributable to a flaw in the approach, the fragmentary nature of the author's abilities, or the partiality of her interests? To all three probably, and it will only be overcome insofar as others, demonstrating different abilities and different interests, are prepared to make use of the same approach.

The objective pursued in this study is at once extremely ambitious and extremely modest: extremely ambitious because it attempts – not always successfully – to untangle a number of highly intractable theoretical knots: the definition of modernity, the problem of belief, an explanation of the concept of tradition, an elucidation of the question of collective memory, and so on. At the same time, it is modest, as befits any project that consists in opening up discussion on the whys and wherefores of a point of view which establishes a particular manner of presenting a certain range of social phenomena.

This stage would never have been reached had not discussion already begun with several French and foreign colleagues who, by their comments, criticisms and suggestions, helped me to bring the present undertaking to its provisional conclusion. Since I cannot include them all individually in this acknowledgement, I would simply stress what I owe to the kindness and critical attention shown me by Régine Azria and by Patrick Michel, who have been closely connected with the different phases of the enterprise; also to the constant and crucial involvement of Bertrand Hervieu. Nor do I forget that most of the questions touched upon grew from the group seminar led by Jean Séguy at the École des Hautes Études en Sciences Sociales and from the work of the DIFREL[1] team within the CNRS[2] Sociology of Religion section. Hence this book is dedicated to him especially.

Paris, November 1992

[1] Différenciations religieuses.
[2] Centre National de la Recherche Scientifique (supervisory and funding body for academic research).

I

Doubt about the subject matter

1

Sociology in Opposition to Religion? Preliminary Considerations

Determining the subject matter, as everyone knows, constitutes the initial operation in any sociological endeavour. Yet when it has to do with religion, a presentiment of uncertainty is pardonable. What if there was nothing to define? Or if the sociology of religion simply lacked a subject? On the face of it such questions may appear absurd. After all, research institutions, international gatherings, symposiums, teaching and publications provide sufficient evidence that this branch of sociology is thriving. Religion is the subject matter of sociological investigation, treated as a social phenomenon and explained in terms of other social phenomena. What more can be asked?

From religious sociology to the sociology of religion

However, things are not that straightforward. And the debate which, not so long ago, marked the designation of the discipline – should it be religious sociology, sociology of religion, sociology of religions? – was already proof of this.

It is more than thirty years now since French and French-speaking sociologists gradually gave up using the term religious sociology, suspected of implicitly invoking Christian – even Catholic – sociology which the ecclesiastical establishment could use as a pastoral instrument and consider to be a branch of moral theology. Current demarcation disputes between pure and applied sociology, settled as each occasion arises without threat to the discipline as a whole, render such issues even further outdated. Retrospectively, one may wonder whether terminological nicety has not been overdone in this context. After all, rural sociology was never suspected of being angled towards farmers nor political sociology of being partisan. How come then that the sociology of religious phenomena makes of its terminology an academic issue in itself?

Manifestly, historical and political circumstances peculiar to France serve to account for such scruples. The climate of conflict – or, at least, of suspicion – which hung for so long over relations between the universities, the intelligentsia and the world of research on the one hand, and the Catholic Church, its hierarchy and its theologians, on the other, played a part here.[1] One would merely add that the choice of words to some extent still symbolically echoed an affirmation of independence on the part of a university discipline breaking free from the various enterprises in self-interpretation which the Church, however much it claims to revere science, invariably maintains to be the last word in knowledge about religion. Evoking the need for collaboration between the different specialities – sociology, history, cultural anthropology, and so on – that together form the 'unique caravan of scientific discovery', Gabriel Le Bras in the first number of *Archives de Sciences Sociales des Religions* in 1956 celebrated a non-religious approach to religious phenomena, as the necessary condition of research independence, whatever the personal commitments of those involved. 'Let belief and unbelief go side by side in the enterprise, private feelings have no relevance here. This journal serves no doctrine, sectarian or non-sectarian, its single concern being to serve science.'[2]

Sociologists of religion have dwelt at length upon the difficulties of this emancipation,[3] which led to the abandonment of the term religious sociology. The introduction of the reference not to religion in general but to the plurality of religions received briefer comment, though it merits equal attention. The scientific study of religious phenomena was established as an academic discipline in France in the mid-1950s, under the aegis of the Centre National de la Recherche Scientifique; and by placing emphasis on the plural, those who founded the French sociology of religion explicitly recognized how fragmented, how confused, was their field of investigation. The same recognition of the plurality of territory and of approach prompted Henri Desroche to insist on the title *Sociologies religieuses* for his book published in 1968, prior notice of which had had the title in the singular. The diversification of research projects and the high probability of an ever-widening research field, in the view of Gabriel Le Bras, virtually ruled out a unified discipline, in the foreseeable future at least; how could one thus talk of a sociology of religion in the singular? 'To suppose that all sociologists embarked on the study of religions should ever see eye to eye as to the field, the aims and the methods of their research', he noted in the same programme, 'suggests naive optimism or else senile resignation.'[4]

After all, was it not sufficient for there to be near-unanimity among researchers for a minimal designation of the subject matter? In the absence of finding it possible to identify a common subject, sociologists of religion could – in Le Bras's opinion still – identify a common aim, 'the structure and nature of organized groups for whom the sacred provides both the principle and the purpose'.[5] That the social nature of such an enterprise might in fact pose too many problems for a consensus to emerge among those involved did not worry him unduly. To the extent that sociology should, in his view, restrict its scope to the community and refrain from exploring 'the mysteries of the supernatural or the *maquis* of the terrestrial city', the difficulties inherent in a definition of religion in terms of the sacred could easily be avoided. The question of the definition of religion as such was in fact left to others, to philosophers, for instance, who were properly concerned with general theories. Sociologists, Le Bras recommended, should be modest and make do with the observation of social groups, in the most ordinary expression of their rapport with the sacred, so as to construct the 'pyramid whose base is at the level of tribes and of parishes, of legend and the boundaries of magic'.

> The sociologist should move forward prudently, by degrees, applying himself to the most humble tasks – collecting accounts, conversing with elders, consulting treaties, interpreting ceremonial; then observing reality – a methodical count of buildings and documents, cartography and monographs, semiology and psychology among representative samples of the faithful. Study of the community will reveal the place of the religious group within it – confusion in Islam, intimacy in Christian countries, diaspora among secularized people. The relationship between the two visible communities, and the pull of the invisible will suggest a typology, an aetiology and a discreet nomology whose perfection will form the apex of the intrepid pyramid.[6]

This plea, inimitable for a descriptive sociology of the assemblies of disciples, gave considerable momentum to the empirical sociology of religious phenomena, setting it clearly apart from the social philosophy which French sociology was slowly distancing itself from. In proposing so vast yet modest a programme for sociologists of religion, Gabriel Le Bras without question succeeded in circumventing the problem he confronted, as a practising Catholic, of engaging in an enterprise which could well have struck at the very roots of Christian belief. In fact, he signified elsewhere his refusal to take as the subject matter of sociology the substance of faith and Christian dogma. But, however equivocal, the proposal met with the determination of sociologists engaged in research into religious phenomena to mark a distance, both with regard to phenomenological attempts to arrive at the essence of religion by way of manifestations of the religious and with regard to enterprises which, in order to make of sociology a general science of societies, reduced religion either to the materiality of its emergence or to a collective consciousness through which society affirms itself.

In constructing an empirical sociology at the level of groups and institutions, which were thereby observed in the specificity of their structures and modes of functioning, sociologists ran the risk of giving unique significance to the manifold expressions of religious experience.[7] At the same time, they enabled a notion to be formed of what constitutes religion, which in itself could not entirely undermine the positivist critique of religious ideologies. There one encounters – they said, in effect – a concrete body of reality which is not an optical illusion. It is made up of human groups, social actors and power systems that need to be studied in their specificity. Certainly, the cognitive, cultural, social, economic and political issues of religious phenomena need to be constantly stressed; there being no doubt that, in specific historical contexts, they serve to express views about the world, collective aspirations or social concerns which have no other outlet or else choose this one. Yet there are no grounds for maintaining that this task of elucidation explains away the significance of religious manifestations; except insofar as they are considered uniquely as representing an inchoate form of politics or an invalid form of science, a reductive point of view, which the more positivistic sociologists would now hardly find tenable.

In adopting the empirical study of the diversity of groups, beliefs and practices, and in developing a (plural) sociology of the plurality of religion, French sociologists of religion avoided the pitfalls of a philosophical debate on the nature of religion, at the same time steering clear of any ideological controversy as to the 'reality' of religious phenomena. This perhaps explains, in part at least, their long-held dislike of the grander theories, for which many of their colleagues – in particular, British and American – showed a fondness. Such reservations about theory, somewhat surprising given the mainstream of classical sociology in France, was perhaps a means of preserving their discipline from the ideological contagion which was especially threatening in a culture indelibly marked by the conflict between Church and state. Furthermore, it enabled them, to a degree at least, to hold off suspicions of connivance with the subject matter which inevitably attached itself to their interest in religion as a dimension of social reality.

Science opposed to religion

Until recently, the sociology of religion met with some misgivings on the part of colleagues working in the field of the social sciences, as if the will to objectify religion was in itself a contradictory aspiration, revealing the personal concerns of those who exercised it. Even now it is quite normal for a sociologist of religion on declaring his or her identity to evoke the response 'Oh, so you're Catholic' or 'Yes, of course, you're Protestant.' Almost invariably, in the course of conversation, the remark occurs, 'But are you yourself a believer?' And most of the time such conjectures are right. Those who choose research in the social sciences of religion have seldom done so by chance or by a purely intellectual choice unaffected by any non-academic consideration. But a degree of personal investment in choosing an area of research is common to all who work in the social sciences, whether or not they admit to it. Yet it would not occur to anyone, in assessing the output of a sociologist of the family, to enquire whether he or she were married, or how they related to their father. How come that the critical detachment characteristic of a scientific attitude in the social sciences is thought to be more difficult, if not impossible, to attain when the subject matter is religion?

Pierre Bourdieu has given a vigorous, indeed conclusive, reply to the question. For him the problem has to do with the nature of the subject studied, and the association with belief compounds it. 'The field of religion, like all fields, is a realm of belief, but one in which belief has the active role. The belief that is systematized by the institution (belief in God, in dogma and so on) tends to mask belief in the institution, the *obsequium*, and every concern associated with the reproduction of the institution.'[8]

The explanation is valid, but only on condition that religious belief is allowed to have a far stronger force of penetration than beliefs which apply in other social fields. Following Bourdieu's line of thought, there is no need to know whether or not the sociologist believes in God. What frustrates the task of objectification is belief in the institution, belief which lives on even after it is openly repudiated. The sociologist who belongs to the institution is clearly disqualified; the sociologist who once belonged, who is 'unfrocked', even more so, since the dishonesty 'with which the science of religion is instantly tarred' is aggravated. Since anyone who has never belonged has little chance of ever becoming interested in the subject matter of religion and/or a good chance of missing out on useful information, there are few let-outs for a sociology of religion. The fact that the text quoted above is reproduced from a speech given by Pierre Bourdieu at the Association Française de Sociologie Religieuse very probably accounts for its bluntness. Assuming his awareness of the doctrinal origins of this body and of the 'unfrocked' condition of a majority of its members (a condition applying to anyone exchanging adherence for analysis), Bourdieu struck a note familiar to his audience in order to exhort them not to 'save themselves the suffering implicit in renouncing membership'. The demonstration is nonetheless strange in allowing it to be supposed that belief in the institution contains less of a threat to a scientific attitude (or else is more plausibly brought under control) when dealing with the central institutions of secularized society – schools, political institutions, universities and so on – than when dealing with religious institutions. In fact, the presumption of compromising with the subject matter is only given such aggressive expression here because religion is implicated. What this text is saying is not that the sociology of religion is (a) very difficult, so difficult as to be virtually impossible, or (b) condemned to be no more than an 'edifying science, destined to serve as a foundation for scholarly religiosity, enabling the advantages both of scientific lucidity and of religious loyalty to be combined',[9] but that religion as such is the obstacle that continues to stand in the way of the process of unimpeded critical rationalization which, in Bourdieu's mind, is the aim of sociology.

In order to understand the issues which are presented with particular intensity in this text, one needs to recall the debates surrounding the birth of sociology which make it clear that the question of religion is historically inseparable from the subject matter of the social sciences. As such it was an essential feature in the minds of the founding fathers of sociology and a major element in their attempts to determine to what extent a science of society was possible. As we are reminded by Raymond Boudon, sociology was conceived by its founders as a 'general nomothetic science of societies'. On the basis of very different paradigms – the search for evolutionary laws of society, with Comte, Marx, Spencer and the early Durkheim; the search for functional relations between social phenomena in the later Durkheim; the establishment of historical patterns in Weber; the rationale of non-rational action in Pareto; the recognition of social forms that originate in the interaction of individuals, with Tönnies and Simmel – on the basis of all this, the quest common to all is that of establishing the laws and conventions which rule society.[10]

The enterprise of imposing order on a social entity which by common experience is perceived as inextricably chaotic comes up against the aspiration present in every religion, considered as a system of meanings, namely to make complete sense of the world and to condense the infinite multiplicity of human experience. The clash between the unifying venture of emergent social sciences and the unifying vision of religious systems took the form in the field of sociology of rationally deconstructing the attempt by religion to embrace the whole of reality, which in turn consigned religion to the multiplicity of religious phenomena it embodies. And by so doing, sociology met with the resistance of religious systems to an interpretation from outside which emptied them of their substance and undermined from within the scheme nurtured by such as Burnouf to constitute a pre-eminent unified science of religion, which could be set up against self-interpreting systems of religion: 'Before the century ends we shall see a unified science established which is as yet fragmentary, a science unknown to previous centuries, which is still undefined and which perhaps for the first time we name the science of religion.'[11]

The whole debate seems to belong to the prehistory of the discipline. The programme, which Henri Desroche sees as an ambition of the nineteenth century, to 'define and fully account for the fact of religion in terms of society', considering it as a unique and quite specific order of social phenomena, gave way before the advance of a science of society which on principle rejected any specific treatment of religious phenomena. The majestic initial paradigms of this science of society in turn collapsed, giving way to a descriptive sociology that was built up gradually on the basis of empirically identified subject matter. In France the sociology of religion tried to rid itself of its associations with religious society by energetically embracing the empirical method. With the meticulous enumeration of the faithful and with the scrupulous attention given to the social history of institutions, the intellectual probity of those undertaking research seemed assured. But this empirical, descriptive façade afforded them no protection from the ever-insistent question of whether sociology can, with the conceptual tools available to it, recognize the essentially religious ingredient in the social manifestations it appropriates.

In order to appreciate what is at stake here, one needs to look further into the thought given to the subject matter of sociology. Sociology is defined less by its content than by the critique it implies, itself defined by Alain Touraine as 'a refusal to give credence to all interpretations, from the rationalization with which an actor accompanies an action to the meaning embodied in administrative categories which seem furthest removed from expressing intention'.[12] The generalized wariness which underlies every aspect of what social praxis has to say about itself is no more than a systemization of the first requirement advanced by Durkheim in *The Rules of Sociological Method*, around the notion according to which life in society must be explained 'not by the conception which those who participate in it have, but by profound causation which eludes consciousness'.[13] It is necessary to dissipate the smokescreen of the terminology commonly used, rescue the subject matter from its social demonstration, extricate it from inhibiting preconceptions, continually reconstruct it by updating presuppositions to accommodate the discourse as it changes.[14]

This ongoing critique which confers legitimacy on the comprehension of society by way of social phenomena, according to procedures and methods which are those of science, defines the task of sociology. The critique of spontaneous, naive experiences and expressions in the realm of society is inseparable from the close examination of the metasocial conceptions of society, and especially those which allow and invoke some sort of extra-human intervention in history.

In these two areas, inevitably, sociology, being an analytical enterprise, collides with religion. The initial impact occurs inasmuch as religion is a mode of imposing a social construction on reality, a system of references to which actors spontaneously have recourse in order to conceive the universe in which they live. As such, the critique of religion is an integral part of the scrutiny of the data of social experience in which sociological phenomena are embedded. It was – and it remains – the obligatory passageway in the process of their objectivization. But sociology also meets religion inasmuch as religion itself is a formalized explanation of the social world which, however far it may go in recognizing the freedom of human action, can only conceive autonomy within limits set by the divine purpose. Protestant, and more specifically Calvinist, theology of salvation constitutes the exemplary religious formalization of this dependent autonomy. The encounter between sociology and theology thus – and irrespective of the occasional ecumenicism attempted between one and the other – cannot but give rise to altercation, to conflict even.

What is at issue for sociology is whether it is able to conceive itself. Recognition of this state of conflict between sociology and theology – and first and foremost Christian theology, of course – does not mean that the conflict in itself is inescapable. Or rather, it is inescapable only on account of the path which has led to the conflict and which developed historically in the course of the relationship between science and religion in the west. One hardly needs to be reminded that at the birth of modern science, at any rate until the seventeenth century, the conflict did not exist, nor did it occur to those such as Pascal, Newton or Descartes who initiated the scientific revolution. Descartes, in fact, did not so much as imagine that an atheist could be a geometrist. The altered perspective occurred as a result of confrontation between the Church, fighting to preserve its social ascendancy on the pretext of defending Aristotelian authority, and the scientists wresting scientific experimentation from the control of religious institutions. The struggle continued over several centuries, whilst scientific investigation, which began at the extremities of the universe with astronomy and the Copernican revolution (anticipated by the school of Pythagoras), grew closer to humankind and to its physical and psychic functioning.

The story is familiar enough,[15] but one cannot help but call to mind the initial conflict once mention is made of the circumstances in which science took possession of religion. Because, before becoming one subject among others, religion was the adversary; and in the struggle for the secular autonomy of knowledge the common consciousness of the scientific community took shape across the differences, particularly with regard to social theory, which divide scientists. And it is by reference to this struggle that the legitimacy of the scientific quest is still secured. A scientist who is a believer is tolerated provided he never mentions his belief unless it be that the weight of honours and of years gives him *carte blanche* for confidences. The sociologist engaged in research must avoid communion with his subject, however self-denying the cost; so much at least is accepted by a conception of professionalism in sociology that is dominant and indeed legitimate. How much more then will this rigour apply to those who choose as their field the systems of religious belief and observance against which such legitimacy was established in the first place! Western science defines itself in terms of its historical rift with religion, and this is the abiding context in which the sociology of religion is obliged to define its own aspirations. In asserting its separateness from pastoral sociology, the sociology of religion in France has at times appeared trapped in an empirical positivism which other branches of sociology, and in particular the sociology of knowledge, have long ago left behind. Among other reasons, this is probably because the risk of connivance with the subject, which must mobilize the epistemological vigilance of any researcher in the social sciences, is doubly present in this field. For if complaisance towards social actors continues to disqualify sociological effort, it contains the further risk, in the case of the sociology of religion, that it may suggest an avenue to religious belief which is presumed to invalidate sociology itself.

Undermining the subject?

However, the project of the sociology of religion can be put quite simply – to treat religious phenomena in the way that sociology treats any
social phenomena, by collating them, classifying and comparing them,
and treating them in terms of relationship and conflict. The status of
the sociology of religion can admit of no more exceptions than can
that of sociology in general.

At the same time, one wonders – taking things to their extreme –
whether the sociologist of religion can escape the destruction of his or
her subject matter by the very act of exposing it to the process of
analysis required by the discipline. To say as much is blunt and deliberately provocative, and it hardly represents the conscious objective of
the sociology of religion. No professional would be so presumptuous
as to claim to be able, with working tools alone, to grasp religious
phenomena (any more than any other social phenomena) *as they are*,
in all their complexity. Still less would he or she dare claim that they
can be explained out or away. What sociology acquired, above all
from the school of Simmel and of Weber, was the stamina to renounce
the claim to restore reality as such or empirically to actualize the universal laws of history and society. Its claim to be scientific is based on
its appreciation of the abstract, relative and revisable nature of the
conceptual tools – forms, ideal types or models – with which it sets
about ordering the boundless profusion of reality.

Even so, in the very act of recognizing its limits, indeed because of
doing so, the objective of a unified, all-inclusive explanation continues
to shape a vision (or fantasy), which is constantly rejected only to
reappear, of a process of illumination which by its nature cannot accept self-limitation. The more exacting and rigorous the sociological
quest looks to be, the more it has *both* to relativize its immediate project
and broaden its driving objective. In the latter case, it is bound to
assume that its subject matter can and must, in principle, be reduced
to the elements to which it relates. The proposition brings about a
methodical reductionism, a necessary phase in critical initiative, which
applies to sociology as a whole. But in the context of the historical rift
between science and religion, it takes on both theoretical and normative meaning. It implies first that religion is inseparable from the social, political, cultural and symbolic meanings and functions that it
has in any given society. It further suggests that actualizing these meanings and functions corresponds to the dynamics of scientific knowledge, prevailing day by day over the illusions of the primitive or
spontaneous, in other words over religion itself. Hence it is not a case

simply of repressing the illusions of spontaneous self-explanation, by relating, for instance, messianic expectations to real, extant misery, or the force of mysticism to the social and political frustration of *déclassé* intellectuals, but a case of breaking up the subject matter itself, insofar as it is of its nature illusory.

What remains of such fervour when subjected to the critique proposed by sociology but subjective forms of resistance to exogenous explanation which can be decoded in the same terms? How can the sociologist of religion take the claim to be scientific for granted, the field of sociology and its historical context being what they are? He or she can only do so, if at the same time making the assumption – as does the psychologist or the linguist in their respective disciplines – that the explanation of religious phenomena in the social context is one where there is nothing left to explain, any element unaccounted for now being incapable of withstanding whatever future refinement sociology will bring to its equipment.

There is no point in rushing to say that, so put, the problem is grossly oversimplified, that the plurality of the scientific approach is a safeguard against the temptation to explain everything on the part of one single discipline, or again that such a view is a product of a now outdated positivism. It may well offer little insight for the routine social history of institutions, but the matter is one of urgency when one moves into the field of belief and systems of meaning and symbolic constructs. The question of the sociological reduction of religion can still create a storm. One only has to think of the bitter controversy set off early in the 1970s in the United States by propositions made by Robert Bellah questioning the reductionism of those who sought to account for religious symbols by tracing their origin to empirically apprehensible events, thus giving them greater authenticity. According to Bellah, who invoked Durkheim as a witness, the reality of these spiritual symbols is thereby lost:

> The canons of empirical science apply primarily to symbols that attempt to express the nature of objects, but there are non-objective symbols that express the feelings, values and hopes of subjects, or that organise and regulate the flow of interaction between subjects and objects, or that attempt to sum up the whole subject–object complex, or even point to the context or ground of that whole. The symbols, too, express reality and are not reducible to empirical propositions. This is the position of symbolic realism.[16]

Such symbolic realism has been vigorously contested by those who, like Anthony and Robbins, straightway saw in it a theological plot at work in the social sciences.[17] The point here is not to discuss in detail the issues in a theoretical argument in which, as it happens, French sociologists took no part, but merely to note the discussion which the understanding of the critical function of sociology applied to religion gave rise to in the sociological community itself.

Let it be clear, however, that the need to destroy religion in order to clear a space for a scientific explanation of society (as well as for nature, history, the human psyche and so on) has seldom been formulated within the discipline itself as an explicit requirement for the practice of science in general, and for the social sciences in particular. Nor was it necessary, given the general view that religion was in terminal decline, a decline which the founding fathers of sociology all made use of as the fulcrum of their analysis of modernity. Their assessment of the significance of this process of decline for the future of humanity might differ, just as did the explanations they offered, without the assertion so clearly expressed by Emile Durkheim in *The Division of Labour in Society* being challenged, namely that religion encompasses an ever-decreasing portion of social time:

> Originally, it extended to everything; everything social was religious – the two words were synonymous. Then gradually political, economic and scientific functions broke free from the religious function, becoming separate entities and taking on more and more a markedly temporal character. God, if we may express it in such a way, from being at first present in every human relationship, has progressively withdrawn. He leaves the world to men and their quarrels. At least, if he continues to rule it, it is from on high and afar off.[18]

The developing social contraction of religion, which, according to Durkheim, coalesces with human history, is the exact counterpart of the process of expansion in science, with science annexing even the development of the scientific intelligence of religious phenomena. Even so, the manner of comprehending the historical path taken by humanity varies greatly with the cultural context of study. The divergence between American and French research tradition in this respect is glaring. Arthur Vidich and Stanford Lyman have clearly shown (even if the somewhat systematic character of their approach has been criticized) what social science in America owed to the Puritan tradition in which it is rooted. For the early American sociologists, religion was so fundamental a source of inspiration that for a long time they abstained from taking it as a research subject. Only by degrees in the early years of the twentieth century did American sociology distance itself from its early religious leanings. During this process of secularization, social science, in a novel departure, took over the Protestant ambition of social improvement through rational management. 'Sociodicy' took the place of theodicy, thanks to the special affinity existing between puritanical Protestantism and sociological positivism in their common belief in the perfectibility of society.[19] This course of action went naturally with the social and cultural attitudes of American democracy, in which religion is given a decisive role.

In the case of France, a tradition of confrontation between the world of religion and the world of political and cultural modernity very soon gave substance to the conviction – accepted as a hypothesis by the social sciences – of the inevitable eclipse of religion in the modern world. Moreover, it is clear that surveys conducted in the 1930s into the state of Catholicism in France strongly endorsed this hypothesis with its evidence of the collapse of religious practice and observance, the startling drop in the numbers of those entering the priesthood or choosing the monastic life, and the break-up of traditional communities with the movement to cities and into industry. The gradual reduction of religion, seen as the likely intellectual and cultural outcome of modernity, acquired observable and quantifiable substance across these surveys. This meant that sociologists of religion were spared having to engage in a philosophical and/or epistemological debate on the cultural significance of the equivalence, established by western scientific modernity, between the contracting space occupied by religion in society and the expansion of their discipline. Analysis of the reduction of the field occupied by religion eliminated the need to examine sociological reductionism as such. The matter of the 'fight against religion' was thus consigned to the area of outdated scientistic notions. Progress required independence in exercising one's profession as a sociologist.

For sociologists of Catholicism such independence in the first place implied keeping out of the way of ecclesiastical influence. Nowhere else but in France was there so rigorous an insistence on the need to 'establish a barrier between the *condominium* [of the sciences of religion] and the applied sciences which exploit it'.[20] A determination to avoid pressure from the Catholic hierarchy or being taken over by pastors and theologians constituted the preliminary and initial requirement for all sociology of religious phenomena. And its reiteration, quite out of proportion – or so it seems retrospectively – to any concrete threat to the intellectual autonomy of scholars who enjoyed full academic status, can be interpreted (but the point clearly merits discussion) as a way of being seen to possess academic respectability, this time *vis-à-vis* the sociological community for whom religion remains – or remained until recently – suspect as subject matter. Was such highlighting of the relations between scientists and religious institutions a means of deflecting attention from the subject itself? Was it for those concerned a way of exhibiting their scientific credentials before their peers during a period, the 1960s and 1970s, when any attempt to question sociological reductionism might well have been received by their colleagues (and even in their own ranks) as an unacceptable concession to the illusion of religion and/or their personal involvement? One cannot be certain. One can do no more than suggest that the pressures that come from science were (and are) no less of a problem in the matter of constituting the field of a sociology of religion than those that come from religion. However that may be, it remains the case that the community of sociologists of religion has been deeply marked by the contradiction variously experienced by each of its members: that of having to assume the rationalist tradition linking the end of religion with the advance of science and the scientific attitude, and the properly scientific need to treat the subject matter seriously and in all its irreducible complexity.

2

The Fragmentation of Religion in Modern Societies

Historical change since the early 1970s has profoundly altered the situation. For one thing it has challenged the rationalist assumption previously taken for granted that religion would inevitably succumb to modernity along with the perception that religious institutions had established a mechanism of domination over society. The steady advance of the new religious movements, the spread of integralist or neo-integralist churches, and the vociferous reaffirmation of the legitimacy of religion both in western society and beyond have led to a major reassessment of the initial assumptions of the discipline; this at the price perhaps of a new eclipse of the fundamental problem posed by religion as the subject matter for sociological investigation. To say that 'religion exists, we have seen it manifest itself' is no less empty a proposition than that which, thirty years ago, consisted in saying, more or less: 'religion is an ideological phantom, proof of which is that it continues to dissolve in our rationalist society.'

However this may be, the intellectual issue now presents itself more or less thus: given a scientific attitude which is based on religion being incompatible with modernity, how is one to acquire the means whereby to analyse the continued importance of religion outside western society as well as the changes it has undergone – its revival even – in the west? To imagine that this involves no more than recent misgivings about rationalism or the side-effects on science of the manifold demonstrations of what is mistakenly seen as a return to religion is to misconstrue the situation. 'The critical period for a religion', observed Gabriel Le Bras in his introductory note in the first number of *Archives de Sociologie des Religions*,[1]

> is when it is subjected to action from civil society rather than inspiring it. But religious society does not lose all its strength by this reversal. It applies itself to the task of persuasion and recovery. Recent surveys on politics, the family, city and country life, all find that religion occupies an often essential place. And this is true not merely of Islamic countries, where the disbelief of some intellectuals, the effect of urban living on observance and the slackening of discipline are insufficient to divide political and religious society, but also of western democracies and of eastern Europe too. The increasing disregard of religion, as much a class as a cultural phenomenon, also calls for attention. It too may induce dogmas and forms of observance and morality and acquire temporal status.

These lines, written in 1956, in their way sum up the central dilemma of the sociology of religion. The subject, even in the act of disintegrating, shows astonishing resistance; it re-emerges, revives, shifts ground, becomes diffuse. How in this era of science and in terms of a critique are these changes to be accounted for?

The future of religion in the modern world: the classical sociological approaches

The question touches on the same fundamental issues as those raised in the early days of sociology, issues to do mainly with Christianity given its intermediate position – and intermediary role – between the age of religion and the age of modernity, namely of science and of politics. The analysis developed by Max Weber of the unfolding 'disenchantment of the world' turns on the central question of the function of Judaism, then of Christianity, in this process. The theme was subsequently taken up and developed, more recently by Marcel Gauchet, with his conception of Christianity as the 'religion that offers a way out of religion'.[2]

Even with Marx and Engels, for whom the withering away of religion was incontrovertible, there is a case for arguing that there is no clear call for the suppression of religion just as there is no pronouncement of its approaching end. The Marxist analysis of the decline of religion develops the theory of its gradual and painful exclusion inasmuch as it is the 'general theory of this world, its encyclopedic compendium, its logic in popular form'.[3] In any event, the progress of knowledge by itself is not sufficient to rid mankind of the illusions offered by religion, so long as the material foundations of alienation are not swept away in the social movement of liberation by which humanity recovers possession of its rightful world. But, other than that the stages and outcome of this long-term process are not prede-termined, the question of imagination, or dreams, hence of religious feeling, cannot be settled until all forms of exploitation and aliena-tion, whether social or psychological, are finally eradicated.[4]

The problem of the end of religion, which is inseparable from that of the complete realization of communism, is thus incorporated in the secular eschatology of Marxism – a promise more than a prediction, an expectation rather than a sociological prospect. Besides, this theo-logical uncertainty has had historical repercussions. While it was re-sponsible for short-term strategic considerations, such as the concern that there should not be religious martyrs and that the energy mobi-lized by religious dissent should be geared to the Bolshevik Revolu-tion, it contributed to the political uncertainty of the Russian revolutionaries with regard to religious sects, at least until the end of the 1920s, whereas the fight against the Orthodox Church which rep-resented the old order they saw as an immediate political objective.[5]

Durkheim gives precedence to the sociological view in noting the many forms taken by the decline of religion in modern societies – the Church's loss of temporal power, its separation from the state, the restriction of religious groups to the voluntary sector, the inability of these same groups to make the civil authorities enforce their moral teaching, and, more generally, their inability to regulate the lives of individuals, the disaffection felt towards them by the intelligentsia and their failure to produce their own intellectual elite, and so on. Religion itself has become a subject for scientific and historical research. But the dwindling of religion in its social dimension is not merely an effect of the triumph of science as a superior form of knowledge. After all, as Pickering remarks, if society had had need of religion, religion would have absorbed science.[6]

Alongside the principle of the secularization of modern societies, there is the dislocation of the social fabric which was itself held to-gether by religion. The disintegration of past forms of interdepend-ence and the social erosion of religious ideals are countervailing processes: religion is in decline because social change wears down the collective ability to set up ideals; the crisis of ideals loosens social bonds. However, what emerges from this twofold movement is not the end but the metamorphosis of religion. Science in effect is powerless to take over those functions of religion which lie outside the realm of knowledge. It has no unfailing answer for ever-recurring questions about human nature and its place in the universe. It throws no light on the moral issues confronting individuals and the community. It cannot respond to the need for ritual inherent in society. Hence, if religion in modern society has ceased to be the unqualified language of human experience, it continues to be a vital element in modern society, a paradox which Durkheim escapes by proposing what a 'religion of mankind' might be, a 'functional alternative to traditional religion', according to Pickering, through which the relations between the individual and society and within society could continue to find symbolic and metaphorical expression.[7]

This new religion which would convey the highest values of humanism calls for no church, no rigid orthodoxy and no organization; but as an ethical ideal it provides a ground for devotion, sacrifice and renewed scope for individuals to transcend their instincts and their self-absorption. As François-André Isambert urges, one should take care not to take the parallel between traditional religion and Durkheim's 'religion of mankind' too far, for, contrary to a commonly held oversimplification, Durkheim does not simply substitute society for God. By making society the basis of morality and so filling the gap left by religion, he invokes an order of reality which is accessible to a positive science. Durkheim's purpose, as a moralist as much as a sociologist, is to define a possible science of morality.[8] Whatever the precise nature of this 'religion of mankind', it is witness to the fact that, in Durkheim's view, the question of religion continues to be posed, over and beyond analysis of the loss of religion in modern societies.

With Max Weber, the problem of the future of religion within modernity differs widely from the evolutionary optimism which characterizes Durkheim's view of the religion of mankind. However, in an entirely different perspective, it raises, at least implicitly, with regard to the disenchantment of the world, the question of substitute religions or replacement religions, those taking the place of the historic religions in a world where reference to the supernatural increasingly loses credibility. Certainly, and in spite of regarding it as a fairly improbable hypothesis, Weber does not entirely rule out the possibility that strictly religious prophecy may return; but he is more particularly concerned with the shifts produced by religiosity and the metaphorizations of religion, as well as by the institutional reordering this leads to within historic religions. Alongside the principle of the 'polytheism of values' which, according to Weber, occupies the centre of the modern religious landscape, there are the shifts in belief that occur in societies where the disappearance of the gods does not signify a concomitant disappearance of the need for meaning or of the concern that moral imperatives should have a transcendent basis.

In modernity, it is towards art, politics, physical and sexual fulfilment or science itself, spheres which through the process of rationalization have been gradually weaned away from the hold of traditional religions (and to which one might now add information technology), that the thirst for meaning is turned.[9] These spheres call forth endurance and asceticism, the exercise of ritual, devotion and ecstasy, just as does traditional religious belief. As Jean Séguy recalls in a new reading of Weber's approach to religious phenomena,[10] the disenchantment of the world does not signify the end of religion or even of traditional religious institutions; rather, just when these are contracting, new forms of religiosity make their appearance and take the place they occupied. The point should be made here, to be returned to later, that Max Weber does not give a clear definition of these substitute forms of religion any more than of religion in the full sense of the term. It is indeed a mark of his ambiguity with regard to defining religion as such. In the opening lines of his chapter on the sociology of religion, he declares that such a definition will be kept in reserve until the conclusion of his study. In fact he never returns to it but allows himself to make use of several working definitions.[11]

The Marxist view of the withering away of religion as a function of the realization of a communist society, at the same time postponing its extinction to the end of time, and the view of Durkheim whereby in the religion of mankind the social necessity of faith is maintained in spite of the triumph of science – both views, in totally different, even contradictory, ways recognized the impossibility of treating the rationalist hypothesis of the end of religion in sociological terms – the first, to a certain degree, against its own presuppositions; the second, explicitly and according to the logic of the definition given of religion as the very expression of society. The Weberian problem of the disenchantment of the world, by divorcing analysis of the marginalization of religion from any prophecy to do with the meaning of history, in theory made it possible to separate the empirical study of the loosening hold of traditional religions from the positivist forecast of the death of the divine in modern society. At the same time the problem requires the question of the religious productions of modernity to be tackled head on.

Constructing a new perspective

Substitute religions, replacement religions, analogical religions, surrogate religions (the preferred term of English-speakers), all of which fill the place of religions – these terms convey the intangibility of the religious products of modernity. Research in the field is boosted by the renewed interest shown in religion, with widespread evidence in the press and elsewhere – and against the tide of secularization – of new forms which religion is taking and of a spiritual need induced by the uncertainties of modernity. For some this has to be seen in proportion, representing little more than an irrational, regressive impulse familiar enough among the culturally deprived in periods of uncertainty; while for others it is proof of an irreducible religious dimension in humankind and the failure of positivism to explain away ultimate causes.

Between these extremes there are various attempts made to point out that the trend is neither reliable nor ground-breaking, as well as to rationalize the hypothesis of reversion to a need for religion in societies that were less secularized than had been thought or hoped. And enlightenment is on occasion sought from sociologists of religion, who are somewhat bewildered to find themselves thus invited in from the cold.

Contrary to what one might imagine, the newly awakened interest in religion, not simply among those who thrive on media-driven sensation but among those in a position to be directly concerned by the future of modernity, does not work entirely to the advantage of sociologists of religion. Until recently they had the often difficult task of upholding the social significance of religion within a largely secularized culture in which their discipline played a part.[12] Now they are faced with having to defend their critical function in circumstances where reflection on the irreducible element in religion is readily ascribed to the abdication of reason. Hence they may be no better off than before. Certainly the change from a climate where religion was absent to one where it is hard to avoid it confronts research with a new challenge. For it is evident that the current research interest in the new religious phenomena only partially corresponds to the more refined scientific approach to manifestations of religious belief in modern societies, but is itself part of the phenomenon that attracts sociological inquiry. Renewed academic interest in religion is also an aspect of the new awareness in society as a whole of manifestations that no one now dares to think of as residual or strictly private. This is an ambiguity peculiar to the social sciences which touches particularly on their critical nature.

In this context, one which calls for extra epistemological vigilance on the part of those engaged in research, the sociology of religion in modern societies has two analytical concerns to keep in mind. One is to give ever more careful consideration to the social reasons for religion no longer playing a central part in the societies under study. The other is to trace the limits of contemporary manifestations of religion, which itself is decidedly more alive than had been supposed.

The problem stems from the fact that this complex religious climate reflects the fragmented, shifting and diffuse nature of the modern imagination – an awkward conglomeration of beliefs cobbled together, indefinable bric-à-brac of dreams and reminiscences which anyone may assemble, privately and subjectively, as the situation demands,[13] its impact on society being at the very least problematic. In the field of Christianity, the atomization of systems of meaning is in direct proportion to the breach in the stable link between beliefs and practices, a breach which Michel de Certeau places in the centre of his analysis of the implosion of contemporary Christianity.[14] Christian belief, he remarks, is less and less anchored in specific groups and attitudes; it is less and less a determining factor in associations and practices.[15] The fragmented character of modern manifestations of belief, on the one hand; on the other, the disappearance of the link between society and religion, itself the foundation of a religious culture which affected every aspect of social life in western society – these are the two sides of the process of secularization which is historically one with that of modernity itself. The implications of this will continue to affect our treatment of religious phenomena as the argument develops.

Nonetheless, for all the evidence of the fragmentation of religion in modern society, it has to be recognized that religion still makes itself heard, though not always where one expects to hear it. It makes its presence felt implicitly or invisibly throughout the gamut of human expression. Thus instead of thinking of a dwindling religious domain (the institutions of traditional religion) set against the domains of politics, aesthetics, therapy and so on, one should look for covert signs of religion in every sphere of human activity. The problem is to know how far to conduct the investigation. Does one limit it to identifying the unobtrusive influence of recognized religions where one does not expect to find them? Or to pursuing different sorts of religious manifestation outside a conventionally religious context? Or to concentrating upon 'undeniably' religious phenomena and so shut one's eyes to the social evidence that proclaims them to be such? Or should one broaden the horizon in order to display the (invisible) religious argument of modernity and run the risk of seeing the particular nature of the subject matter dissolve, running the risk also of allowing the scholar too much subjectivity in the selection of material?

The sociology of religion is not finding it easy to position itself between these two courses. But it is not alone in this. The recent development of a symbolic history, whose objective is to throw light on the mechanism of politics, not in the places where power is officially exercised but in 'places – or realms – of memory' where politics has the appearance of being in some manner suspended,[16] poses the same problems as does the deployment of a sociology of diffuse or implicit reli-

gion.[17] In both cases it is the erosion of structured systems of representation (political in the one, religious in the other) linked to precise
social practices and developed by clearly identifiable social groups which
justifies the research interest in the dispersion of these representations
and practices outside their proper sphere. At the same time, evidence
of a systematic conception of institutional differentiation has to be re-
examined. The individualization and subjectivization of belief on the
one hand, the individualization and subjectivization of the relationship with the past on the other (hence of the vision of the future nurtured by the past), oblige those engaged in research to question a
sector-by-sector approach to social questions, which appears to respond to the differentiation and specialization of social fields.

Certainly one may wonder whether the new interest in the religious
as distinct from religions is not a means whereby specialists in religion
may save a subject that is disappearing and/or take on the responsibility of the social sciences in the process of disenchantment which, among
other consequences, has led to the implosion of belief. However this
may be, the problem today in the social sciences seems to be not so
much that of setting the rules applicable in each of the clearly differentiated fields as that of taking stock of the disruption that now affects
compartmentalization and interdisciplinary relations on account of
the pluralization, subjectivization and individualization of systems of
meaning. Indeed the function of these systems is to re-establish coherence now that it has become dislocated by institutional specialization.

For a sociology of religious modernity, this is the real significance of
the review of the concept of secularization which is chiefly occupying
research at the present time,[18] with the aim of refining further the analysis of the contraction and expansion of the place occupied by religion
in society. But the first question to be addressed is why the sociology
of secularization, fluctuating as it does between the problem of loss
and that of dispersion, produces a variable-geometry of the religious.

Introducing this question inevitably means putting the question of
the sociological definition of religion back into the centre of research.
Definition of the subject matter is one of the first principles in the
practice of sociology as a profession, and there can be no exception in
the case of religion. How then is this principle to be implemented in
research?

Defining religion: a new look at an old debate

It is precisely here that problems appear, problems drawn attention to
some years ago by Émile Poulat in a summary of the state of religious

sciences in France. If the concept of religion is particularly impervious
to definition, it is because

> religion in itself is not an empirical observable reality. All we can grasp
> are expressions and carriers: gesture, word, text, edifice, institution,
> assembly, ceremony, belief, place, time, person, group – anything may
> designate it, but it is not to be pinned down. Religion is by nature a
> composite, inseparable from the design that animates it, not uniformly
> stable; when it is broken down, only the objectifiable element remains,
> the one that manifested it.[19]

And the problem in defining the scope of religion and picking out
indicators to distinguish it from other phenomena may seem to place
the sociology of religion in a particular position in relation to other
disciplines.[20] Yet it could be said that politics, ethics and aesthetics
among other disciplines cut across the totality of human experience
and that the arguable marginality of the sociology of religion could
well arise not from particularity of subject matter but from the special
status claimed for it in submitting that it is beyond definition.

However, it has to be stressed that the sociology of religion is exceptional in that its subject matter is determined by the definition it
gives of itself. Religion knows and, in a formalized manner, says what
religion is. In a sense, the entire subject is apparent in the discourse it
conducts with itself, and in the encounter between this discourse and
the space assigned to religion in a differentiated society. Thus would
Émile Poulat's position be justified. In recognizing that uncertainty is
the structural condition of the sociology of religion, he proposes to
restrict definition, not to religion itself, but to the 'field each religion
appropriates'.[21] Clearly such an approach poses an epistemological
problem, namely the obligation to subordinate definition of the field
of sociological investigation to the divisions the subject itself prescribes
and/or that society advocates. But it must be said that it presents considerable practical advantages, so long as it is confined to traditional
religions, whose designation as 'religions' is not socially contested.

Even so, problems remain. The transformation of these religions in
the course of history raises the question of whether one is still dealing
with the same subject. 'Does it make sense', Jean-Paul Willaime, an
authority on Protestantism, recently asked, 'to think of Protestantism
as being sufficiently unified to constitute a subject in itself, with the
evident differences between the Protestantism of sixteenth-century
Germany, nineteenth-century Sweden and twentieth-century North
America?' In this instance, an acceptable definition of Protestantism
as a subject would need to take in these different historical realities.

But once one is faced with manifestations that raise doubts as to their inclusion among the major religions, the problem of defining the subject matter continues to recur – there is no way out.

Indeed, since the birth of sociology, the problem has been there continuously, without those who hold to a substantive – or substantial – definition (associated with the substance of belief) and those who favour a functional one (which takes account of the functions of religion in social life) being able to agree and so transcend or resolve the difficulty.[22] The core of the argument was already present in Durkheim's criticism (in *The Elementary Forms of Religious Life*) of the Tylorian substantive definition,[23] for which he substituted a definition of religion in terms of the sacred. This – and I shall return to the point – merely had the effect of transferring the inquiry in a different direction.

In research practice, the increasingly clear trend towards descriptive and factual sociology, where the main concern is to plot the process of change in traditional religions, has long inhibited questioning that is held to be pointlessly abstract. The more traditional debate continues only in the sociology of secularization in America and Britain with its predilection for the study of the future of religion in present-day society; but it too comes up against the same dilemma – whether to select a set of substantive criteria with a view to composing an exclusive definition of religion (but then how would these be compiled so as to avoid the risk of ethnocentrism?); or else to treat as religious phenomena whatever in our society is productive of a social sense or a social bond (but then where would one draw the line?). In asking himself whether one should 'include in a definition of religion all the beliefs and values that are fundamental to society', Roland Robertson has tried to focus on the theoretical issues of the debate which divides those who uphold an exclusive definition from those who uphold an inclusive definition of religion. He has dwelt interestingly on differences in the conception of the social which might determine the choice of one or other approach to religious phenomena. And his investigation inclines him, mainly for methodological reasons, to prefer an exclusive definition.[24] But it cannot provide a way out of the blinkered, unending dialogue between those who opt for the functional and those who opt for the substantive (or substantial) approach.

It is no coincidence that the question has resurfaced in a concrete form, first in the American and then in the European sociological debate, in connection with the developing new religious movements (NRMs). The term is an umbrella for a wide range of phenomena: cults and sects that have recently come into competition with traditional churches (dominant or the historic minorities), eastern-inspired syncretism, movements aiming to renew institutionalized religions; then, the various and amorphous components of a 'mystico-esoteric cluster' which show a marked ability to assimilate and recycle available knowledge, be it 'scientific' or marginal and fragmentary with roots in ancient learning, and which purpose and promise individual self-transformation.[25] These very diverse groups and systems may 'attach themselves to major eastern religions, attempt to reconcile different forms of ancient esoteric belief or seek a fusion between religion and psychology or else provide for the practice of divination through astrology, tarot, Yi Ching and so on'. They foster and maintain contact with journals, publishers, bookshops, and initiate talks, exhibitions, weekend courses and so on in order to draw a following. Their adepts go the rounds, displaying a 'cultural self-service, which is rich, flexible and personalized in what it offers'.[26] To a large degree it is they who have occasioned the question as to the limits of religion and the increasingly divisive debate between an intensive sociology of religious groups and an extensive sociology of systems of belief.

Religion and systems of meaning: an inclusive approach

A first analysis might take NRMs as the most significant element in a much wider process at work in reconstructing the field of religion, or even as revealing the gradual emergence of a new form of religion which would succeed Christianity in the west. At the end of the 1960s when observance of NRMs had not yet assumed the importance it now does in discussions on the future of religion, Thomas Luckmann had already suggestively outlined the 'sacred cosmos of modern industrial societies', incorporating a multitude of meanings assembled by modern symbolic consumers so as to respond to ultimate questions which they have addressed in order to give shape and thought to their experience.[27] From the moment that contrasting modern societies no longer asked established religion to provide a framework for social organization, religion has become fragmented across an array of specialized spheres and institutions. Individuals, in groups or on their own, hence are free to construct a universe of meaning on the basis of a chosen dimension of their experience – family, sexuality, aesthetics and so on. The constitution and expansion of the modern sacred is a consequence of the direct access individuals have to the stock of cultural symbols available. An invisible religion indeed has no need of the mediation of any institution, whether religious or public. It gives free play to a combination of the themes inherited from traditional religions and the modern themes of free expression, self-realization and mobility which correspond with the advent of individualism. In such combining, a shift operates, according to Thomas Luckmann, from the greater transcendencies associated with the vision of another world to medium transcendencies (of a political nature) and, more particularly, to micro-transcendencies directed towards the individual and investing the modern culture of selfhood with a sacred character.[28]

The view of religion as an envelope for a host of fundamental and endlessly proliferating meaning systems which enable human beings to live, and to live in society, is not restricted to Luckmann. It is the culminating point of the functional, Durkheimian sociology[29] which has had a marked influence in North American tradition and is to be found in a number of writers who give a loose religious interpretation to whatever in society has to do with ultimate preoccupations (Talcott Parsons) or ultimate problems (J. Milton Yinger) or fundamental meanings (Peter Berger). It owes a great deal also to the influence of Max Weber and to his insistence on the need to grasp religion as a galaxy of meanings. The crossing of the functional questions that Durkheim raises about religion with Weber's systems of meanings is very evident and explicit in Robert Bellah and even more so in Talcott Parsons, who develops the concept of grounds of meaning, an 'existential conception, of the universe, and within it the human condition in which human action is to be carried out'.[30] Religion is understood as the mechanism of meaning which enables humanity to transcend the deceptions, uncertainties and frustrations of everyday life. This transcendentality occurs by reference to the vision of an ordered world which surpasses reality.[31] There is a clear link, especially in Yinger[32] (and less explicitly in several others), with the theology of Reinhold Niebuhr, defining religion as a 'citadel of hope built at the edge of despair', and especially with the work of Paul Tillich.[33]

 If Luckmann's approach is of particular significance here, it is due to the objective he sets himself (taking Durkheim's notion to its logical conclusion) of returning 'to the general source that gives rise to the historically differentiated social forms of religion', to the anthropological base where the individualization of conscience comes into play.

> The organism – in isolation, nothing but a separate pole of meaningless processes – becomes a self by embarking with others upon the construction of an 'objective' and moral universe of meaning. Thereby the organism transcends its biological nature. It is in keeping with an elementary sense of the concept of religion to call the transcendence of biological nature by the human organism a religious phenomenon. . . . This phenomenon rests upon the functional relation of self and society.

We may therefore regard the social processes that lead to the {
of self as fundamentally religious.[34]

This anthropological conception of religion, which precludes its ~~~
confused with any of the historical forms it may have taken, allows all
kinds of ideological combinations as well as social phenomena corresponding to this basic function to be encompassed; and this is particularly so in the analysis of its modern manifestations. Pushed to an
extreme, everything in humanity which lies outside biological survival
taken in its most narrowly material sense has to do with religion. By
the same token, the terms customarily associated with the word religion to designate religious forms (in the sense used by Luckmann)
which are not within the province of traditional religions – secular
religions, parareligions, analogical religions, political religions and so
on – should strictly no longer have grounds for existing. Nothing further should stand in the way of analysing, as religion in the full sense
of the term, manifestations in which scholars empirically recognize a
functional relationship with the dominant religions, even if they do
not invariably warrant the theoretical assumption which this relationship justifies.

In contrast: a much more restrictive framework

The indefinitely inclusive implication of the functionalist approach to
religious phenomena is precisely what a restrictive position that advocates the need for a substantive criterion rejects in an operative definition of religion. The animated discussion occasioned by Thomas
Luckmann's book dealt chiefly with the limits of its heuristic impact.
In company with Roland Robertson, one of the more constant and
severe critics of an excessively extensive approach to the field of religion in modern society is Bryan Wilson.[35] When tackling a classic problem of secularization as a process of continuously restricting the social
influence of religion in the modern world (a problem which the theory
of invisible religion rids of any content), Wilson constructs an ideal
type of religion which enables him to exclude much of the NRM population from the field of analysis. This ideal type combines two main
features – appeal to the supernatural and effective social utopianism,
the ability to create and legitimate projects and action with the aim of
transforming society. The former is frequently present (though in highly
diverse forms) in the new religious manifestations, the notion of possible human participation in the potential of supernatural or personal
or, more often, impersonal forces being very much part of the NRMs.

But the latter is generally absent, since the NRMs strive to bring about individual regeneration and fulfilment, rarely to change the world. This process of selection enables Wilson to eliminate from religion most of the so-called human potential movements, and in particular those influenced by the New Age. It also enables him to rescue the definition of modernity which lies at the source of his analysis of contemporary religion, whereby the characteristic of modernity is to allow individuals to stand aside from nature so that they may confront it with their own potential. This is impossible to combine with recognition of the power of supernatural forces in nature and in history, which according to Wilson is a constituent part of all religion.[36] In his plea for a substantive definition of religion, which takes account of the content of belief, he roundly impugns the inconsistency in the functionalist approach which, by embracing all systematized responses to ultimate questions on the meaning of life and death and one's presence on earth, turns religion into a nebulous and indefinable entity.[37]

A false opposition

Nevertheless, leaving aside the declared conflict of theory between them, it is not entirely clear that the inclusive and exclusive positions are as opposed as they outwardly claim to be.

In Luckmann's view, which I shall continue to see as representing the most extensive conception of religion, it would appear that the now so characteristic fragmentation of meanings assembled by the individual conscience excludes their being incorporated into systems of belief, thus investing combined action with coherence, initiative and imaginative resources. In the absence of these elements which manifest the exteriorization and projection of meaning constructed by the individual in the world as it is, and in the absence of any likely systemization of these individually assembled meanings, it is difficult to see that anything remains of the process by which these fragments of belief might constitute a modern sacred cosmos.[38] Thomas Luckmann himself considers it highly unlikely that the social objectivization of such themes as self-realization or personal accomplishment, which originate in the private sphere, could usher in a coherent closed sacred cosmos and the specialization of new religious institutions. He observes, however, that inside this multitude of individual expectations and aspirations images which he describes as specifically religious may possibly survive. These images have their source in historic religious traditions and relate to the dominant religions. According to Luckmann, their survival hangs on their ability to function, that is to assure the subjective satisfaction of individuals. Survival is made possible, in a social climate where competition between official models of religion and subjective systems of meaning no longer exists, because of the free availability to private consumers of the reservoir of meanings which make up the historical religious traditions. But the mere fact of designating the traditional representations that survive in the modern sacred as specifically religious shows both what little substance Luckmann himself accords to invisible religion and the implicit importance of substantive criteria which mean that only the historic religions may be considered to represent religion in the full sense of the term.

One discerns a similar ambiguity with Robert Bellah and others when they discuss values that are held in common and constitute the fabric of civil religion.[39] John Coleman defines the term as the 'set of beliefs, rites and symbols which relates an individual's role as citizen and his or her society's place in space, time, and history to the conditions of ultimate existence and meaning'.[40] Is this to be taken as religion in the full meaning of the term or as an analogy? Bellah sees it as a religion so long as one accepts, as he does, that one of the functions of religion is to furnish a meaningful core of ultimate values on which to base social morality.[41] But whether or not these values may come to constitute the substantive core of a religion, in the way that the values underlying Christianity, Judaism, Islam and so on have done, remains inconclusive. Paradoxically, there is a constant pull towards the substantive definition of religion for those who mean to discard the limitations it puts on empirical research as well as on theoretical construction.

In fact the gap is narrower than one might think between the view of a modern sacred cosmos which comes across as an indistinct cluster of atomized meanings and the restrictive approach personified by Bryan Wilson. Wilson declines to apply the term 'religious' to associations and professionals whose one function is selectively to improvise or orchestrate and make more explicit a set of meanings to suit the individual. Thomas Luckmann would probably not decline to do so, at the same time implying that religion thus understood can reach no further than the individuals concerned and their subjective satisfaction. And most probably he would decline, as would Bryan Wilson, to see as religious the ritual gesture of washing one's car on Sunday mornings!

In both cases, the problem is that of differentiating between the multitude of religious meanings within the modern and rapidly changing kaleidoscope available.[42] To reduce yet again to their essentials the terms of the divide between Luckmann and Wilson, with Luckmann one may say the difficulty is caused by the fugitive continuity between

the modern system of meanings and religion introduced by the ultimate reference to the sacred cosmos; whereas with Wilson, it is due to
the discontinuity introduced by the reference to the supernatural and
utopia. If one allows that the religious construction of meaning forms
part of a system of meaning as constituted by a society, the definition
cannot be settled in a substantive way once and for all, except by
reifying the (premodern) historical state which produced (western) religious belief by appealing to the supernatural and the utopia of the
Kingdom.

The same objection could be made to the definition proposed by
Yves Lambert, with a view to averting the disintegration of the concept of religion in the whole host of responses to ultimate questions.
His definition is based on three separate characteristics, whose association is expressly required for one to be able, he says, to talk of
religion. The first is the 'assumed existence of beings, forces or entities
surpassing the objective limits of the human condition, yet relating to
human beings'. The second is the existence of 'symbolic means of communication with them – prayer, rites, worship and sacrifice'. The third
is the existence of 'communalization, whether within churches or elsewhere'.[43] This comes down to constructing a formal model of religion
through the identification of features that represent the smallest common denominator of traditional religions. In the perspective of a comparative sociology of traditional religions, which concerns Yves
Lambert, this definition may turn out to be admirably effective; but it
imposes a considerable limitation on the possibilities of exploring, in
the context of religious modernity, the phenomena of recomposition,
displacement and innovation which develop from the decreasing social and cultural plausibility of the major established religions in the
modern world.

If functional definitions of religion prove incapable of containing,
as they claim to do, the unlimited growth of phenomena, and thereby
lose all heuristic relevance, substantive definitions of religion, constructed in fact by reference only to traditional religions, paradoxically condemn sociological thought to the role of guardian of the
authentic religion that major religions see themselves as incarnating.
Functional definitions can only testify to the dispersion – intellectually
beyond control – of religious symbols in contemporary societies; while
substantive definitions can do no more than reiterate analysis of the
loss of religion in the modern world. Both constitute a partial, yet
radically limited, response to the question of the location of religion in
modernity. Religion is nowhere, or else it is everywhere, which in the
end comes to the same thing.

One way out of the dilemma?

Among the more convincing attempts to find a way out of the dilemma, the theoretical construction proposed by Roland Campiche and Claude Bovay, in their study of religion in Switzerland, referred to above, deserves a special place.[44] The prime interest of the undertaking is epistemological and methodological. Campiche expressly insists on the contingent and provisional character of the proposed definition, which he constructs not so as to embrace the universal reality of religion but to order an empirical situation shaped by a particular history and which he sees as 'revealing something of the relationship between observer and subject matter'. The intention is to refine an instrument of analysis that can prove equal to the research aims. A useful call to order, which is in singular contrast to the definitive propositions regularly made about the nature of religion by those who hold exclusively to one or other opinion. The value of the enterprise lies in the attempt to go beyond the substantivist and functional positions by bringing them together and finding in one a solution to the drawbacks of the other. Thereby the substantive definition of religion, which is in principle restrictive, is widened by being made to contain 'any body of more or less organized beliefs and practices relating to a transcendent supra-empirical reality'.

At the same time, however, the authors firmly reject the tautological circularity of a definition of religion by transcendence. As a counter to this circular reasoning, they associate the first notion of religion with a set of restrictively defined functions ('integration, identification, interpretation of collective experience, response to the structurally uncertain character of individual and social life'). Hence one is led to understand that it is the identification of these functions at a given moment and in a given cultural space that enables one to determine what set of beliefs and practices in relation to a transcendent reality may be considered to be religious. But a problem immediately arises, pointed to by the authors themselves, which is that these functions are not universal. They relate to a given society, but 'religion can perfectly well fulfil other functions in other social and cultural circumstances.'

The argument here comes up against a purely logical restriction: either one calls upon the characteristic functions of religion in order to determine what sets of beliefs and practices in relation to a transcendent reality can be called religious, which assumes, at least on heuristic grounds, that these functions are acknowledged to have, if not a universal character, at least a permanent character in the context of their investigation; or else the highly variable character of these functions in both space and time is recognized, and then, in order to account for these variations, one needs to be able to call on another indicator to determine that which, within the multitude of beliefs and practices relating to a transcendent supra-empirical reality, pertains to religion. For Campiche and Bovay, such an indicator unequivocally remains that of institutionalized religion, which responds, by definition one might say, to the ideal type presented. The point is made with particular clarity when, in the paragraph following their general definition of religion, the authors stress that in Switzerland 'in different epochs religion has played a cohesive role or has generated conflict because of the denominational split which has characterized the country since the Reformation.' Thus in the further acceptation of the term, religion merges with the socio-symbolico-cultural apparatus which has been historically constituted around (and in the relationship between) the two 'poles' of Protestantism and Catholicism.

This is not to say that the prior attempt at definition, with the methodological and theoretical significance given it by Campiche, is no more than a formal one. The importance of the book lies in the constant correspondence between two levels of analysis: analysis of the processes of disintegration and reintegration of belief under the influence of individualization, pluralization and uncertainty, all of which mark modernity; and analysis of the processes of demolition and reconstruction of the social and cultural apparatus of denominational identification. The meeting point of these two types of phenomena produces a sphere for religion operating (ideally) between two 'poles': one where the transcendental and the denominational references are in theory fully superimposed (traditional religions) and one where the transcendental reference is completely separate from any denominational reference, although fulfilling the same social functions (integration, identification and so on) as those carried out at the same time by these same traditional religions. The definition proposed by Campiche and Bovay allows this 'pole' to be designated and it is clear that its role as marker for the redistribution of religion only comes into effect because the functional relationship with the more clearly differentiated 'pole' of institutionalized religion has been established. That being the case, the relevance of the project to an analysis of the transformations undergone by religion applies best within a social and cultural milieu in which the structures of institutionalized religions, though no longer directly and exclusively arranging for individual and collective access to a state of transcendence, still offer major symbolic references and at the very least define the social functions of such a reference. Switzerland, whose culture is permeated by religious tradition and the part played by religion in its history, affords an instance of this.

It is doubtful whether the same instrument would serve to analyse situations where the split between traditional culture and religion is more complete. Clearly, however, the definition of religion proposed by Campiche and Bovay loses relevance if it is removed from the instrument of analysis (the dialectical relationship between institutional and non-institutional forms of religion) within which it may avoid the risk of simultaneously incurring the disadvantages of the substantive and functional definitions. This limitation – intentional on the part of the authors – requires one to search yet further in order to resolve the theoretical dilemma posed by the definition of religion, of which the characteristic in modernity is to be fragmented.

3

The Elusive Sacred

Scholars have frequently had recourse to the notion of the sacred in seeking to account both for the decline of institutionalized religions and for the dispersion of religious symbols in modern society. Since the end of the 1970s the sacred has been the subject of widely different approaches, heralding its return or renewal, or setting out the deviations or transformations it has undergone.[1] The aim of this chapter is not examine these in detail, but to try in a very broad way to account for the confusion that characterizes them. It would seem as if each attempt to clarify the relationship between religion and the sacred in modernity further tangles the threads it sets out to untangle. Indeed, the following reflections in part spring from uncertainties I myself felt during the preparation of an earlier book about retaining the traditional contrast between the sacred and the profane in order to describe the ideal constructions developed within the utopian sphere of modernity as 'religious in the broad meaning of the term'.[2]

The sacred: an impossible concept

 For many writers, reference to the sacred merely provides an occasion to rehearse the functional argument by extending it to encompass every sphere of meaning engendered by modern societies. Taken to its extreme, whatever has the slightest association with mystery, or with the search for significance or reference to the transcendent, or with the absolute nature of certain values, is sacred. The unifying factor in this mosaic is that it fills the space relinquished by the institutionalized religions; for the process of differentiation and individualization, which has marked the advance of modernity, has deprived them of the monopoly they once enjoyed in responding to fundamental questions about existence. How are death and adversity to be faced? How are the duties of the individual towards the group to be established? And so on.

If one allows that the substance of these responses constituted the sphere of the sacred in traditional societies, an expression such as the sacred cosmos of industrialized societies, or the coupling of modern, diffuse or informal with the notion of the sacred will serve as a response to these same questions in the context of modernity.[3] Manifestly, however, these replacement terms would gain by being clarified. Can one readily acknowledge that the process of rationalization and institutional differentiation which has broken the monopoly once held by established religions[4] has no concurrent effect on the need and the ability within modern societies to generate these substitute meanings? Here one comes back to the question already mentioned of the assumed continuity between traditional religious systems and the modern sacred.

Daniel Bell's article of 1977 on the return of the sacred illustrates the difficulty perfectly. Bell starts by stressing at length the extent of the process of profanation that has developed in the cultural sphere (and relatively independently of the process of secularization which, in his view, is of a specifically institutional nature). One might expect that such considerations would incline him to leave aside the problem of the modern sacred. Yet the insistence on the twin principles of secularization and profanation at work in the modern world does not stop him – while taking note of the failure of religions and the proliferation of new cults – from pronouncing the likelihood of the return of religion, as identified with the supposed return of the sacred.[5] Bryan Wilson has rightly – and cogently – pointed to the weaknesses inherent in this view, and its inability to reveal clearly what may be at the source of such a return (always supposing this to be what it implies).[6] This functional approach to the sacred – sacred by default, if it can be so put – is hardly questionable, since it does not of itself imply a need to clarify the possibility of a common principle informing the whole, above and beyond the human need for meaning. Yet, even so, it is as ineffective – because as inclusive – as the functional definition of religion to which it is closely linked.

But perhaps, more ambitiously, the notion of the sacred may serve to cover a structure of meanings common both to traditional religions and to new forms of response to the ultimate questions about existence, extending beyond the beliefs developed on each side. With the awareness that the term 'religious' is likely to retain the attraction that traditional models of conventional religion exercise on the analyses of modern systems of meaning, those whose research leads in this direction generally plead for a clear distinction between the notion of the sacred, thus understood, and that of religion. The sacred swamps and envelops the definitions provided by traditional religions and long imposed on society. It further swamps the new forms of institutionalized religion perceived in the new religious movements. Above and beyond every systematization to which it will give substance as it has done in the past, it refers to a specific reality which is exhausted in none of the social forms it takes.

Similarly, reference to the sacred, by assuming the existence of an innate structure, common to all its forms of expression, allows what constitutes the domain of the sacred to be differentiated within the shifting and diffuse mass of collective representations. Most often one will have in mind representations within this domain that have to do with the fundamental contrast between two quite distinct orders of reality and the set of practices that go with social management of the irreducible tension between the profane and the sacred. On the basis of this strictly Durkheimian criterion, it is possible to distinguish – but also to determine – the contemporary recurrences, renewals and resurgences of this property of the sacred, given a universal anthropological dimension.

The enterprise – and its anthropological considerations – necessarily reopens a debate, which is in one aspect philosophical and sociological and whose intricacies need not concern us here;[7] but it bears also on religious modernity, and here the debate has been stifled by the never-ending skirmishing between exclusivists and inclusivists. It may be that reference to the sacred will present a way out of the impasse. In effect, all attempts to apply this approach meet with the same problem: they are captive to the way that sacredness and religiousness (or the domain of the sacred and religiosity) become mirror-images of each other – which is what such terminology was intended to prevent.

In a recent article, which is better argued than much else on the subject, Liliane Voyé demonstrates the difficulty. She begins by noting the combinations and transactions by means of which the construction of meaning systems endlessly proliferates in modern societies. These combinations develop as a direct function of the social and cultural reversal of institutionalized religion. They marry 'elements which characterize modernity, such as the centrality of the individual, borrowings from past situations – more particularly, from the reservoir of rites and practices, symbols and signs which churches have compiled in the course of their history – with a wide variety of elements not necessarily of religious origin'.[8] In such assortments which are invested with meaning, Liliane Voyé discovers the upsurge of an inherent sacred quality which she identifies, along with Abraham Molès, as 'a residue (in Pareto's meaning of the term) of the sum pattern of human behaviour with regard to an environment in which causation is beyond control'. The collapse of the institutionalized and religious monopoly over the sacred thus liberates the capability of humankind to produce sacredness. Such capability is seen as inherent in the human condition and in the inability, even for scientifically and technologically advanced society, to master the material and immaterial conditions of existence.

Can this free-floating sacredness within modern society be said to define a new religious system that develops outside and in the place of traditional religions? Liliane Voyé argues forcibly that 'the sacred should not be reduced to the religious.' And she shows with some cogency that the sacred is not to be confused with definitions given to it by traditional religions, and especially by Catholicism. But when her argument broadens out from institutionalized religions to religion, to ways of being religious, it becomes unconvincing and the coupling of the sacred with religion (or with the religious) is re-established. Religion remains defined as the means by which sacredness is given form, sacredness as the raw material of religion. The inquiry then veers away (and this is indicated by the title given to the article) from the 'inherent sacred' to the 'ineluctable religious' sense, which doubtless is not to be confused with institutionalized religion, but which in definition remains pegged to the notion of the sacred. The same remark, with minor variations, might apply to a whole range of studies that set out to heighten the specificity of modern sacredness by criticizing the assimilation of sacredness and religion. By insisting that the sacred is what is institutionalized in the name of religion, they manage to invalidate the distinction they recommend.[9]

The source of the difficulty seems to lie in the fact that as soon as scholars address the notion of sacredness, they often unwittingly become caught up in an analogical circle from which it is virtually impossible to escape. To simplify somewhat, it is as if, after making the assumption that the notion of the sacred enables the core of an experience transcending the contingent forms of traditional religions to be identified, they were irresistibly tempted to measure the possible manifestations of this experience against these same traditional religions, still considered as the supreme imprint of the sacred within the social. The problem arises from the need to have more than a clear awareness of the inadequacies of the analogical approach in order to escape from the circle. The real difficulty lies elsewhere, in the genealogy of the very notion of sacredness.

Before taking up the point, let us illustrate the above remark from the evidence provided by Albert Piette's contribution in the book he co-edited with Claude Rivière on the unexpected anomalies of sacredness in the modern world.[10] Far from providing an instance of the kind of blatant conceptual ambiguity one is seeking to expose, the point here is that the author goes out of his way to stress the problems inherent in making use of the notion of sacredness in order to identify modern religion. At the very start, Albert Piette clearly states his intention to question the reasoning by analogy which prevails in most of the studies dealing with the contemporary marginalization of religion. In order to avoid this, he proposes 'two classifying notions': *religiosity*, which points to 'the presence of characteristic elements of religion in the different secular fields' and *sacrality*, which concerns 'the construction of a sacred dimension, based on contemporary values which are productive of meaning'.[11] In order to operate, the distinction implies that the two dimensions – the religious and the sacred – correspond to distinct social and symbolic forms of reasoning, whose intersection and/or tensions are to be empirically identified later. But when, after considering a series of possible approaches, Piette seeks to define the features comprising the framework of his particular concrete type of religion, he reactivates the ineradicable reference to the sacred:

> Thus, in line with the objective of fixing the boundaries of religion and identifying the referents, we pose five essential elements of religion as a type of activity: . . .
>
> The fact of death, a constituent element of the religious and inherent in human nature;
> Two necessary conditions for the exercise of religious activity and at the same time a principle for its structuring: the transcendent–immanent relationship – its representation situates the transcendent outside earthly experience and assumes different expressions (supernatural/natural, 'up above'/'here below'); the sacred–profane relationship, setting up two radically separated registers;
> The quest for the Absolute, as a finality for which religious authority is exercised, in the face of the relativity of everyday existence;
> A set of specific means, a complex of myth and ritual, containing specific elements, such as prayers, offices, processions, celebrations; but also asceticism, chastity, ecstasy, rapture and so on.[12]

Albert Piette is then led to remark that 'this definition applies more closely to religious activity exercised by Christianity than to others.' The limitation appears acceptable to him insofar as his intention is to 'comprehend how the religious *habitus* in the west has exploded and partially infiltrated so-called secular activities'. In other words, the characterization he offers us is of a particular type of religion whose presence – shattered, diffracted and metamorphosed – he means to apprehend within a cultural domain where religion has become an option for the individual.

So defined, the undertaking is perfectly legitimate, but it diverges markedly from its original intention. Does it not in effect signify that the problem of secular religions amounts to no more than that of identifying traces of the Christian religion in activities which no longer refer to Christianity, or to any other traditional religion, for their authority? Nothing in the author's intention or in the book itself initially appeared to substantiate this view, which implies limiting investigation to identifying degrees of proximity or distance in the manifestations observed in relation to the concrete type defined above.[13] The initial theoretical aim rather suggested disaggregating religion from one particular religion (reduced even to the features of a concrete type), in order to allow the identification of a potential religious functioning of secular activities as such.

Yet in this more ambitious perspective,[14] the definition adopted is more than likely to be ineffectual. The proposition was to inquire whether religion as a productive instrument of meaning (the motivating force, according to Piette, being the problem of death) is not present in modernity emancipated from the control of traditional religions; what in reality is identified is still religion as a carrier for meaning, organized entirely on the basis of the separation between the sacred and the profane, which commands all the other oppositions (transcendence/immanence, supernatural/natural, absolute/relative, etc.) that provide a structure for religious activity. By so tying religion to a particular structure of meaning whose special affinity with the traditional Christian model he recognizes, Piette shuts off the avenue he had opened up. If religion is a mode of production of meaning ordered for the production of sacredness and if in the end sacredness refers back to the Christian version of the sacred, the debate is over before it is begun.

One talks of religion in connection with the secular order, that is to say outside the field of institutionalized religion, merely in a figurative sense, and the application of secular to the sacred is never more than approximate or derivative. But the deviation parallels that of the problem itself, entrapped by the kind of evidence which in our mind-set creates an indissoluble affinity between the concept of the sacred and that of religion, itself constructed on the Christian model. The deviation is in this case all the more apparent because Piette had himself suggestively outlined the path which he finally abandoned. Or to put the same point in a different way, what is at issue here is not primarily the reasoning in a particular research project, but what it reveals – in the problems it encounters – about the extreme ambiguity of the notion of the sacred and of the difficulties it poses when it is a matter of distinguishing the symbolic productions of modernity.

Albert Piette himself recognizes the problem since, in a more recent book on the same theme, he has made a deliberate effort to avoid the circularity of his own argument. Accordingly, he proposes to distinguish the existing religions, which present the overall features set out in the definition[15] (but allowing the possibility of there being exceptions – the case, for instance, of Buddhism), and secular religiosity, essentially syncretic religiosity, which, he comments, corresponds to the presence, within a secular activity, of features perceptible in recognized existing religions and which might in reasonable probability characterize other future religious forms. This severely reductive revision of the initial perspective removes most of the criticisms advanced above; but the notion of secular religion virtually disappears (in spite of the book's title) behind the treatment of religiosity 'in a minor mode' which continues to exercise a non-religious world. The problems posed by the necessary link which Piette continues to assume between sacredness and religion remain effectively unchanged.

The genealogy of the sacred: Isambert's contribution

What explains the fixed adherence of the notion of sacredness to conventional religion, given that it is invoked to escape the pressure applied to the idea of religion by the model of traditional religions? The key to the problem lies in the genealogy of the notion of sacredness. One can do no better than refer to the conclusive analysis applied by François-André Isambert to the process whereby the notion became a compulsory stage in reflecting on the religious, when in fact it had no precise substance before Robertson Smith, and subsequently Durkheim and his followers, gave it their attention.[16] So far as I am aware, the deconstruction of the notion has not been taken further or treated more systematically. Given the depth of his analysis it is essential to refer to Isambert at this point.

Isambert begins by reaffirming that the Durkheimians 'had no other aim in mind than to set out, refine and define a notion which they held to be common to all peoples';[17] and this is precisely why they played a decisive role as semantic producers. By transforming a notion that was held to be common into a concept, they enabled ordinary language to embody the evidence that the sacred constitutes a tangible reality, a subject which can be identified by its properties and that is generally to be found in every religion – a mysterious power, total separation between a sacred and a profane world, and an ambivalence which renders the sacred an object at once of fascination and of revulsion, of attraction and of terror. In the course of the enterprise, the sacred thus became eclipsed as an adjective and established itself as a noun. Now it serves to denote 'in a rather confused way, the relationship in subject matter between all religions, indeed between all beliefs and between all religious feelings'.[18]

By reconstituting this semantic route Isambert brings out with great acuteness the cultural rationale to which these shifts respond. And the rationale is that of modernity itself, which assimilates the mobile, protean notion – susceptible to different interpretations – by transforming it into a property recognized as a principle of all religion. This transformation, which makes an essence of the intellectual instrument perfected by the Durkheimians, enables one to posit a unique and real subject behind the multiplicity of religious expression in humanity. All spiritual and religious paths are presumed to converge on this same sacred. The perspective corresponds perfectly with the need to legitimize subjective convictions, a feature of pluralist societies where absolute value is placed upon individual choice. Religious discourse, being unable to assume validity through revelation and dogmatic authority, thus seeks its cultural and social rehabilitation by way of the sacred as religious experience. In Isambert's words, 'the right to a faith that holds something to be sacred' becomes the basis for recognizing the existence of the sacred.[19]

In its artificially homogenizing the multiple and plural reality of religions whose convergence it takes for granted, and in its suggesting that the search for contact with transcendence extends far beyond the tracks marked out by institutionalized religions,[20] the notion of the sacred is protective of the image of religion (as an entity) in a cultural atmosphere characterized by the individualization and subjectivization of systems of meaning. A beneficial operation for those who argue for recognition of the irreducibly religious dimension of the human in a secularized world, but at the opposite extreme of the endeavour to construct religion as a subject matter for inquiry which mobilizes sociologists. In fact, as Isambert reminds us, anthropological studies have demonstrated sufficiently that the primary contrast between the sacred and the profane, which provides the pivot for the Durkheimian sociology of religion, is not constant and is far from corresponding to the mode of structure for all religions.[21] By reducing it, as does Mircea Eliade, to its purely formal dimension, it is made to 'merge at the level of significance with any semantic contrast, whatever its substance'.[22]

Hence the Durkheimian concept of the sacred is acceptable only 'if one no longer asks of it to characterize all religious reality and makes use of it only as a particularly potent structural type, whose empirical validity will only be measured later'.[23]

Such prudence is further necessary because the properties specific to all religious matter to which Durkheim gives the term sacred and which he identifies in the 'simplest' forms of primitive religion are none other, says Isambert, than a simplified transposition of Christian attributes of the sacred, indeed of features of contemporary Catholicism made to serve as a reference.

> The first definition of religion by Durkheim was such as to awaken suspicion. Would not a religion defined by obligatory beliefs be far more readily associated with the first Vatican council than with peoples among whom such a notion of obligation would be likely to have little meaning? More explicit still are the considerations on the integrating power of religion following the Catholic model (*Suicide*), the moral crisis stemming from Catholicism's loss of hold (*Moral Education*) and the need to substitute something in place of the sacred character of the basis of morality (*Of the Definition of Moral Phenomena*).[24]

These observations lead Isambert to wonder whether the opposition between the sacred and the profane might not represent a transposition of the specifically Christian opposition between the temporal and the spiritual, given particular emphasis at the time that Durkheim was writing by the opposition between the opponents and supporters of the Church. Similarly, the ethnologically dubious notion of *mana* could well be no more than a transposition of grace. The critique of the notion of the sacred culminates in the exposure of the 'implicit sociology of Catholicism' which is present in Durkheimian theory and which Isambert has no hesitation in setting alongside its more open manifestation in Auguste Comte.

The sum effect of the critique is to leave one with the clear impression that the notion of the sacred has brought more confusion than clarity into the debate on religious modernity. In the minds of those who resorted to it in discussing the symbolic productions of modernity, reference to the sacred was intended to serve either to identify the religious dimension in such productions otherwise than through the analogy with traditional religions, or even to avoid all 'responses to the fundamental questions of existence' being automatically given a religious context. In the first view, the sacred is supposed to wrest the definition of the religious from religion; in the second, to prevent the religious being erected into an all-encompassing category whenever the question of the social production of meaning comes into play. Many writers move easily from one to the other, or manage to combine both. But this is not the problem. The problem lies in the fact that, by the very conditions that have given rise to it, the notion of the sacred is bound to reintroduce surreptitiously the very thing it was supposed to eliminate, namely the preponderance of the Christian model in thinking about religion, and the preponderance of this particular model of religion in analysing modern systems of meaning. It is hard to imagine that one way out of the impasse is clearly to separate the definition of religion as such and the identification of the sacred conceived as the structure of meaning which, in some – and only in some – societies, 'gives to spiritual and temporal powers the reinforcement of sacred power (*omnis potestas a Deo*) and to sacred beings a potency which partakes of the authority of these powers'.[25]

Emotional experience *vis-à-vis* religion

The objection will certainly be raised that the form of sacredness dwelt upon in this critique is essentially that which is embodied in a 'hieratic order, based upon belief in the exceptional nature of the being or beings who provide its source'. And it will be pointed out that there is another approach to sacredness, which stresses the irresistible attraction to humanity of a 'force that is at once overwhelming and lovable', an attraction which, according to Paul Veyne, constitutes the 'essential core of traditional religions' and which can find support in very diverse entities, real or imagined.[26] Hence what is important is less the opposition between the sacred and the profane than the unique specificity of an emotional experience which different religions have applied themselves to orchestrating. Yet a body of research that is very far removed from the phenomenology of religion and that shows no affinity with its declared aim of grasping the essence of religion seems loath to abandon the idea that, beyond the contingent forms it takes, religion is fundamentally a matter of communication with this mysterious 'other' power. So the modern quest for the sacred consists in tracking present manifestations of the experience, which are themselves resurgent and recurring insofar as secularization has lessened the capability of institutionalized religion to contain the experience.

This altered approach to the sacred is given support by the distinction that exists in the classic Durkheimian approach between a sacred order, which fits into a structure of social domination, and a sacred communion of feeling which results from the fusion of conscience within the communal gathering. Durkheim described in enraptured terms this wellspring of emotion, a prodigious reservoir of energy, which all social life draws upon (from however far): 'a ferment . . . a gathering of strength . . . a turmoil . . . an intense passion . . . frenzy . . . transfiguration . . . possession . . . metamorphosis . . . extraordinary powers that excite to the point of frenzy . . . hyperexcitement . . . a psychic exaltation not unconnected with delirium . . .'[27] At the source of all religion, there is this first intense experience of the sacred, an elemental extrasocial (or at least presocial) experience, an essentially collective experience which reproduces the 'dynamogenic influence' upon consciousness and conscience, of which Henri Desroche speaks, through which society creates itself.

With or without reference to the Durkheimian analysis of the primary experience of the sacred, a well-established sociological and psychological tradition has developed out of the notion that religious expressions (beliefs, rites, types of community, etc.) are never other than transmitted (and limited) manifestations of a religious experience which merges with the emotional experience of the sacred. The distinction between expressions and experience belongs to Joachim Wach;[28] but it is also found among other writers: Henri Bergson writes of dynamic (open) religion and static (closed) religion,[29] Roger Bastide of real-life religion and canned religion,[30] and so on.

This duality provides grounds for transposing a psychological analysis of religious experience much developed by William James into sociological terms. For James, the essence of religion is to be sought not in society, nor in intellectual speculation, but in the inner experience of the human being coming into contact with 'the inner order where the enigmas of the natural order find their solution'.[31] This definition of personal religion does not exhaust the reality of the subject matter of religion but it allows James to distinguish the emotional experience, which is at the source of religious feeling, from the manifestations of institutional religion – 'Worship and sacrifice, procedures for working on the dispositions of the deity, theology and ceremony and ecclesiastical organisation' – which are its secondary expression.[32] The sociological transposition of this dynamic in religious experience implies that established religious beliefs and practices are never other than the administered form of a primary experience, which antedates any philosophical or theological formalization and which gives intense expression to the feelings and emotions of the recipient. In the words of Hubert, one of the Durkheimians, 'religion is the administration of the sacred.'[33]

This primary experience – at once collective and individual – constitutes the source of all authentic religiosity and, as such, cannot be reduced to the body of doctrine and the liturgies which comprise its socially accepted expression. Clearly this is not to say that sociologists who make use of the opposition go the whole way with Schleiermacher, for instance, whose ideas in their view have little to do with religion. And Joachim Wach makes a point of denying that he excludes reasoned argument from the domain of religion.[34] But it is an indication of the importance attached, in an entire current of sociology and religious anthropology, to the idea that religion exists on two levels, thus aptly described by Henri Desroche, in his commentary on a little-known text by Émile Durkheim: a primary level, that of emotional contact with the divine principle; and a secondary level, at which the experience is socialized and rationalized, by being differentiated into beliefs and into offices and rites. 'Beliefs, offices and rites have as their function to perpetuate, commemorate, organize, communicate, transmit, propagate, perhaps reawaken – or keep alive – an elemental experience, in itself unbearable, ephemeral, ineffable and circumscribed, in short to render them viable, durable, unforgettable and universal in time and space.'[35]

The distinction between the two levels – that of the immediate experience of the sacred and that of the religious administration of the sacred – comes down to isolating a pure religious core, distinct from the contingent religious forms by which primary religious experience, which is one with the emotional experience of the sacred, is socialized. Does not this, along with the notion of the sacred communion of feeling, provide a means of identifying the nature of religion without its being confused with institutionalized religions? And does it not point to the source of a definition of religion, which would make it possible to identify its diffuse presence in modern societies? It is highly tempting to explore this avenue, for which there is a long research tradition. Such questions are best answered by considering how the approach to religion by way of the emotional experience of the sacred has been applied – and with what theoretical profit – in order to analyse collective manifestations which do not come within the sphere of institutionalized religion but which irresistibly draw an analogy with it.

Between the sacred and religion: the example of sport

Among such manifestations, sport is one whose affinity with religion has been most frequently remarked and dwelt upon. One point of view here seems particularly relevant to our argument.

Sport is frequently presented as an exceptional experience which places the individual or the team practising it in a situation of being outside self, of metamorphosis associated with going beyond the limits of human endurance. The experience readily gives rise to the term trance, is linked with the intensity of orgasm, and suggests itself as a means of access to the inexpressible and the transcendent. In endeavouring to put their experience into words athletes spontaneously resort to language which is akin to that of religious mysticism. Articles in journals specializing in individual high-risk sports – skiing or surfing, free-flying, mountaineering, rafting, canyoning, skin-diving and so on – afford countless instances of this. Time and again they spell out the individual's feeling of powerlessness in the face of natural forces, and the intoxication of transcending one's limits and becoming one with the elements, or of achieving perfect concordance with the forces of nature, such as gravity, water or wind resistance, and so on. Georges Vigarello has made the point that the conception of this kind of confrontation has evolved in the course of time and that the value put on the immediate sensation or pleasure attaching to it (the intoxication of ski or surfboard, for instance) has come to supplant the heroic triumph and ascetic combat of the athlete.[36] One might argue that the spirit (there is a temptation to call it spirituality), which is implicit or explicit in sport, is undergoing transformation, as is spirituality, in line with the growing culture of the individual. But there is still the dialectical tension between the ordinary taste for physical exercise – jogging at one's own pace, for instance, without heroics[37] – and the virtuoso performance, that of athletes in the stadium or cyclists who break away, of endurance swimmers or lone navigators, whose achievements are enhanced by the hardships they undergo, and without which they would be reckoned inhuman.

In the rare instances of self-analysis of such experiences being taken further, the mystical aspect sometimes becomes more tenuous but it rarely disappears.[38] Echoing the terminology used in the field of sport, which itself borrows much from religious terminology, what has been observed of the rituals performed by athletes in highly competitive sports would seem to confirm that they have much in common with the power-placating symbolism practised in religious ritual.[39] The champion is the one who strives hardest metaphorically to ingest this power, and who can do so not only by a self-imposed training schedule, but because of exceptional attributes which are grace-given. The charisma of the champion provides the source of the hold exercised over fans, who identify with him or her, yet are fully aware of the gulf that separates them from a hero or heroine whose feats place them above ordinary mortals. There is a clear parallel to be drawn between what Jean-Marie Brohm calls the mythological structure of sport and the mythological structure which characterizes traditional religions. At all events – and this is intimated by the Weberian allusions above – sport affords a rich terrain in which to demonstrate the value of theories advanced in the sociology of religion outside their normal context.

However, the question of the link between sport and religion is generally raised in connection with mass spectator sports with their dual festive and ritual character; and it is raised in the way that most directly concerns our present purpose, which is to discover whether reference to the emotional experience of the sacred is or is not an obligatory path towards a definition of religion, which avoids the irresistible pull of the model set by traditional religions.

The 'shared sacred' of sport corresponds directly to the capacity for big occasions in competitive sport to rally huge crowds, unite them in their support and bring them to fever pitch, carried beyond themselves in the shared emotions of victory or defeat. Brohm has developed a simple but solidly Marxist analysis which applies equally to traditional religions. In his view, the ceremonial enacted in mass spectator sports is none other than 'the symbolic transference via the mass media of social conflict' in its various forms.[40] The mobilization of crowds at mass sports venues is a venture in ideological manipulation aimed at control. Mass spectator sport is interpreted as being fascist in structure taking over as it does the themes (myth of youth, of the superman, of surpassing oneself, etc.) and practices (parades, banners and so on) of fascism.[41] In advanced industrial societies it functions as a narcissistic regulator of the image these societies have of themselves and as a means of manipulating mass emotions. A unanimity which wipes out social distinctions is created, a symbolic transfiguration of social and historical circumstances comes about; universal values – fraternity, equality, peace, etc. – emerge from the universalization of the spectacle, collective frustration is regulated by being given a lawful, institutionalized and unthreatening opportunity for emotional expression and for the sublimation of all the accumulated aggression induced by the oppressiveness and drabness of daily living. In all these respects, mass spectator sport has taken over the functions assumed by traditional religions. 'Sport', notes Brohm,

> has become the new religion of industrialized crowds . . . Mass spectator sport – thanks to the mass media – has now become the profane substitute for religions with their universal mission. By its universality it has even supplanted all religions inasmuch as its appeal is without distinction, indeed global. Thus the Olympic villages take on a universal vocation that gives them more relevance than Mecca or the Vatican.[42]

Its anti-establishment, post-1960s flavour apart, the interest of this passage is that it takes up in its own way the distinction between the two levels of religion – the primary experience of emotion shared in the collective passion of the moment, and the institutionalization and ritualization of spectator sport. But the level of institutionalization exists only as a function of the primary mass experience, in which the specifically religious dynamic of sport occurs. 'Religious' here acquires its classic Durkheimian meaning – across the emotive intensity which makes the crowd one, society affirms itself. For Brohm, it does so first and foremost as a class society. But the analysis can be developed in a different light.

> Any competitive sport presents itself as an authentic ritual exercise in the course of which a given social group (players and public) assembles, yet at the same time through which, in spite of conflict and division, its unity is contemplated, recognized and celebrated, as well as its identity over and beyond its otherness ... Before being the arenas for a performance, stadiums, gymnasiums, swimming pools, games courts and racing circuits are so many spaces for social commemoration. The competitive game also provides the occasion, the pretext and the mainspring for another game, one of belief in the reality of a society in which every individual can manifest himself or herself at once in the identity and universality of humankind and in the difference and singularity of the human body, in which every individual can be both actor and spectator.[43]

Hence, it would appear that, in modern societies, sport fulfils the social function of self-affirmation which in traditional societies belonged to religion; and that it also fulfils the function of confirming the structure of domination *on account of* the communal experience of the sacred which it can call into being. Can one conclude therefore that sport, by the token applying to traditional religions, *is* a religion? Curiously, most writers, including those who by reducing traditional religions to their social function carry observation of the structural and functional links between the role of these and the role of sport yet further, shy off at the last moment and choose, as does Jean-Marie Brohm, to abstain.

Yet the matter has to be settled. Either religion originates entirely and exclusively in this emotional experience, which (in reality) is the act of adhering to society (and no more than that), and then there are no grounds for declining to describe mass spectator sport as religion in the full sense of the term; or else it proves inadequate as a definition of religion, in which case another criterion must be found and one that explains how traditional religions themselves can be called religions. But that then removes the possibility of there being no more to be said about these religions once one has analysed the alienation associated with the emotional experience of the sacred. And it means starting all over again with the analysis, itself so appealing, of sport as a substitute for traditional religions in contemporary societies.

Clearly the example of sport does not here preoccupy us on its own account. It simply illustrates a reflection which is arguably tenable for all collective experiences (huge rock concerts, in particular) which involve this emotional dimension, frequently characterized as manifesting an irreducible sacred element. The attempt to see the experience of the sacred communion of feeling as the ultimate source of all religion, and so to see it as the centre from which religion within modernity is constructed or reconstructed, is no more satisfactory than was the search for the unifying principle of religion in the 'sacred order'. Whilst the one and the other in theory question the annexation of the sacred by traditional religions (an annexation whose effects can be felt in ordinary or erudite terminology applied to religious matters), both of them get into deeper and deeper water because of an analytical approach which invariably reduces the question of religion (as a social inscription of sacredness) to the model developed by these same traditional religions, and in particular to the Christian model.

The sacred opposed to religion: the emotional culmination of secularization?

It is time to escape from this circle. Yet passage through it is necessary in order to make a correct assessment of the significance of contemporary emotional renewals. The point is frequently made that the development of this trend across the ruins of the major religious traditions, which have been deprived of their social and cultural relevance by the advance of instrumental rationality, is to be attributed to a purported return of religion. Rather too readily, it is suggested that the return of emotion may be equated with a resurgence of the sacred at the centre of modernity; at the same time, it is allowed that the return of the sacred marks a recovery in the place of religion at the centre of secular society. Such a series of implications is, to say the least, problematical. One may even wonder whether recurring manifestations of ecstasy should not be seen – to take the Weberian argument concerning the course followed by religious symbolization from primitive orgy onwards to its extreme[44] – as the symptom of an impoverished religious imagination, manifesting itself in the quest for immediate contact with supernatural powers.

The somewhat provocative assumption of a possible emotional culmination of secularization rests on the classic recognition of the radical rejection which in modernity affects the traditional language of religion (that of the historic religions), on account of the absence of possible and conceivable overlapping in modern societies of the objective order of the world with both the collective universe of meanings and the subjective experience of meaning. More precisely, this coherence can no longer be presented as a human objective, as the continually extended horizon of a collective enterprise. It no longer derives from a revelation granted once and for all. It is this that makes the instances of language deprived of meaning contained in religious tradition so fascinating and so alien to our societies: fascinating, because in a modernity which is unsure of its own identity, they give prominence in their obsolete rationality to the imperious character of the individual and collective need for coherence; alien, inasmuch as they reveal the increasing impossibility of making a culturally plausible response to this quest for meaning where religion is concerned.

By ruling out the intellectualization of the experience implied by its being translated into an articulate language of religion, and by giving value to palpable manifestations of the divine presence (in the face of all the sophistications of theology), contemporary emotional expression tries to get round the structural conflict of the condition of belief within modernity. But it may be asked to what extent such avoidance of conflict is not itself an ultimate expression of the mourning incumbent on modern societies for the coherence imparted by the highly articulate language of traditional religion. To explore this question, one must allow that the emotional experience of the sacred in modernity may well mark not the final triumph of religion over the imperialism of reason but the completion of the process of ridding the modern world of its presence. And thus it has to be allowed that the experience of the sacred may under certain conditions testify to the end of religion, not to its return. Or, to put the matter another way, this implies that sacredness and religion relate to two types of distinct experience which in most cases attract one another, but which may occasion tension and even antagonism.

This is borne out by empirical observation. Most significantly, there is the link that exists between the loss of the language of belief in modern society and the growing importance in new Christian communities (especially in certain currents of Catholic charismatic renewal) of the search for an emotional expression of subjective religious experience, which short-circuits the doctrinal and ritual expressions of faith as regulated by the establishment. The explosion of emotion in the statement of belief is frequently, and not unreasonably, read as a protest against the bureaucratic attempt to direct personal expression in the churches. Such a reaction on the part of the individual is closely in line with the cultural climate of a modernity centred on the individual's right to subjectivity, in the matter of religion too. And analysis of recruitment to charismatic movements very clearly shows their attractiveness to social elements for whom personal accomplishment and self-realization hold most appeal. But one can also shift the perspective by asking whether the search within these communities for non-verbal forms of emotive communication does not also express a protest against the stereotyped nature of approved religious language, something about the diminished quality of (articulate) religious language in modern culture. The place taken in these groups by the gift of tongues raises the question directly. Glossolalia, defined by Samarin as 'a phonologically structured human expression without meaning, which the speaker takes to be a real language but which in fact bears no resemblance to any language living or dead',[45] is not a vehicle for communication but for expression. The content, Samarin emphasizes, is of little importance: glossolalia finds its meaning not in what is said, but in the very fact of speaking and responding, in this form, to an immediate experience of great emotional intensity. 'In the emotive response . . . there is a general sensation of the presence of the divine, profound joy and inward well-being which finds the means of expressing itself.'

The practice of this language beyond language assumes social significance within groups that are deprived of public means of expression. For instance, one may think that in the traditional pentecostalism of North America, the gift of tongues in part corresponded to a highly suggestive staging of being deprived of language (hence of social recognition), as were social groups, such as blacks and poor whites, who were excluded from the benefits of rapid modernization. This interpretation becomes more plausible in that glossolalia, inspired by the experience of the early Christian community itself,[46] reproduced the utopian invocation of a golden age of Christian charity, including a high ingredient of protest. The pattern, with a few modifications, very probably serves to account for the presence in current charismatic movements in France or America of elements that have been brutally desocialized by the recession. Such elements – long-term unemployed, older people without, or with only slender, means – find an environment that gives them both the opportunity for the contact with others they lack and the possibility for all, however culturally deprived, to find a voice. But it fails to account for the fact that the same communities contain very many elements who are perfectly well integrated, reasonably well educated and comfortably off, in fact well representative of advanced consumer society. Clearly, dissatisfaction of some kind may well explain the search for self-fulfilment in a communal religious experience, in particular where there is the gift of tongues.[47]

But one may ask oneself too if the purely emotive direction in their choice is not a direct consequence of their having assimilated the values of modern rationality perhaps so successfully that for them the traditional language of religion, including Christianity, is rendered implausible. Viewed thus, glossolalia reveals itself as the reverse side (or separate phase) of the aphasia that affects the faithful, whose incorporation in cultural modernity is so complete that the symbolism of their religious tradition can no longer be appropriated through language. If that is the case, the development of speaking in tongues would signify not the irresistible upsurge of a sacredness that regenerates the flagging religious utterances in which the sacred is institutionally confined, but the definitive fantastication of religious utterance, and its growing disconnection from belief itself. It would mark the end point of what Michel de Certeau has called objective Christianity:[48] the end of the structural link between the personal experience of belief and the social experience of the community, across the meaningful body of the Church. All that would be left then would be an inarticulate language, whose communicability is essentially expressive and poetic, a meta-language which by definition dodges direct confrontation with the language of modernity, from which the traditional language of religion has ruled itself out.

More generally, it is a question of knowing whether contemporary forms of emotional renewal relate to a torrent of deep emotion, which can no longer be contained in the limits set for religious expression, according to the compromise which governs the relationship between specialized religious institutions and a secular society; or whether, by virtue of the enhanced value put upon manifestations of emotion that escape language, they mark the final exit of a religious utterance that is susceptible to social understanding. A theoretical view of this sort clearly needs to be handled with prudence and tact when it comes to analysing concrete groups. Abruptly to conclude that emotion, caught in the context of the complex reality of manifestations of modern sacredness, is a confirmation either of the renewal of religious experience in modernity or conversely of its final demise, would both be equally absurd. A critical appraisal of the common view that the current spread of emotional experience marks the limits of the process of secularization does not imply that a unilateral pronouncement of its culmination will follow.

However, one thing is clear. The circularity which produces the mutual involvement of the sacred and religion by binding them relentlessly together prevents perception of what is specific to the experience of both the one and the other. It further prevents perception of the rationale of their respective development in a given cultural context.

In being thus confined, one is deprived of any chance at all of casting light on a question which is crucial to analysis of the new religious movements and hence at the centre of any reflection upon religious modernity.

II

As our fathers believed . . .

4

Religion as a Way of Believing

Is there no end to the theoretical snags which frustrate reflection on religious modernity? Given the present state of affairs, one may well wonder what purpose is served by continuing in a direction which is only too likely to end up yet again in the sterile controversy between inclusivists and exclusivists. And one is strongly inclined to take the advice that Henri Desroche gave his students in the 1970s, namely to hold on to the idea that 'religion' is only what society itself claims as such, while employing the conceptual tools of the sociology of religion to examine any social manifestations which appear *by analogy* to call for similar treatment. At the time Desroche was concerned only to warn his students off the pitfalls of the phenomenological approach of 'religion in itself'. But empirical research had long adopted this pragmatism, with visible results. The study of analogically religious phenomena which Desroche proposed extending to Armistice Day parades, workers' May Day marches, revolutionary cults, civil or military ceremony, and so on, offered whoever was engaged in research more than just a practical means of getting round the problems implicit in defining the subject. With the application of sociology to the religion of societies where religion is no longer present, it called for the exercise of imagination. One can see that recent attempts to found a theory on the approach to modern religiosity (whether or not it invokes the notion of the sacred) have regularly come to nothing. If it is the case that these attempts in one way or another suffer from the irresistible attraction exercised on the approach to modern religiosity by the model of traditional religions, the wisest course would appear to be to declare one's hand and study the manifestations of religious modernity across this model. Sooner or later, the modest formula of analogical religion may open up a fresh way of contemplating the problem of religious modernity.

Metaphorical religion, following Jean Séguy

Among others who have chosen this course, perhaps Jean Séguy has made the most original breakthrough by introducing the concept of metaphorical religion. In particular, he has been able to show clearly that the major difficulty for sociologists of religious modernity is not to find a better criterion by which to determine the space occupied by religion, but rather to acknowledge the impossibility of satisfactorily setting limits to a religious field and so equip oneself with the conceptual tools that may help to explain the relocating that is taking place.[1]

Jean Séguy takes as his starting point a detailed reading of Max Weber. While stressing – and, to a certain extent, sharing – Weber's disinclination for a preliminary definition of religion, Séguy attempts to show how the needs of research led Weber to posit an ideal-typical definition of religion so as to distinguish that which within social behaviour was specifically religious. This implicit working definition cuts varyingly across a formal characterization of religious phenomena and a comprehensive approach to phenomena of belief, understood from the point of view of the meanings put upon them by social actors. Weber's constant insistence on the fact that the distinguishing feature of religion is to determine the relations between human beings and supernatural power lies at the convergence of these two approaches. From the conceptual argument he restores, Séguy picks out the ideal-typical outline, 'implicit in Weber's research into religion, or into the greater part of it': 'religion is a form of collective action, accepted by society as "other", and as such meaningful; it relates to "supernatural powers", the subject of individual experience and collective worship; it determines the relations between humans and these powers.'[2]

But at once he observes that this definition fails to contain all Weber's references to religion, when he describes social or political phenomena in which belief plays a part – the instance of a political or scientific vocation in pursuit of an ideal,[3] or of political prophecy made by a demagogue.[4] When Weber speaks thus of the profane in religious terms, it is clear – for Séguy – that he is making *metaphorical* use of religious concepts. This is particularly evident when he deals with conflicts of values in the modern world, conflicts which by the passion they arouse are akin to the battles between the gods of Olympus. This polytheism of values engenders beliefs. It gives rise to acts of devotion and of sacrifice, and to the experience of ecstasy. But this is not to be seen as religion in the theoretical sense given above. 'We describe this religion as analogical', Séguy observes, 'because it does not refer to supernatural powers, but possesses most of the other features of religion in the full sense of the term.'[5] It produces meaning, it opens onto a transcendency which takes one away from the everyday and gives one access to the foundations of moral obligation.

If Séguy's reading of Max Weber stopped there, it would be confined to justifying (as many others have done) the practice of finding a religious analogy in the profane on the basis of a minimal substantive definition of authentic religion ('reference to supernatural powers or beings'). And, by following this path, one can multiply findings indefinitely which point to a similarity between attitudes, observances, practices, forms of socialization and so on of a worldly nature and those that have an expressly religious origin. This is particularly the case in the sphere of politics.[6] The parallel is frequently drawn between party membership and organization, militancy and ceremonial, the presentation of ideals and the insistence on doctrinal purity and the models offered by the traditional religions. Similar parallels may be found in professional institutions and attitudes, in the world of sport and in the arts, given that arts and sciences, eroticism, culture, and the like tend in the modern world to become ersatz or replacement religions.[7]

But Séguy goes further. He reads the process of metaphorization as expressing a principle that is intrinsic to modernity, in which religion is wholly immersed. 'Metaphorization', he remarks, 'is one of the characteristics of modernity at work on itself; it merits attention as does the working of modernity on traditional religions, or the working of these on themselves, at the heart of modernity.'[8]

Far from being an indication of the disintegration of religion in societies where politics, science, art, sexuality and culture have gradually broken free from the control of traditional religions, metaphorization testifies to the fact that their new autonomy has made them available for a new kind of religious function; and it needs to be asked how this function compares with that performed by traditional religions in premodern society. Combined with a reading of secularization as eclipsing religion in modernity, an analogical approach to manifestations of believing that lie beyond the limits of the specialized field of religion has frequently led to these secular religions being treated as substitutes, which retain no more than the outward signs of religion in the full sense of the term. And not infrequently these modern forms of religion have been thought of as residues of a premodern mental universe which bear witness to the cumbersome cultural and psychological forces which this universe still – but transiently – exercises on social actors, even though it is as good as discredited by society. However, Séguy reverses this perspective by making metaphorical religion not a residue of past religion but the formative apparatus of modern religion. The mainspring of his argument is that traditional religions themselves are subject to the effect of metaphorization, through the ever-increasing intellectualization and spiritualization of the beliefs which form their basis.

> If, as Weber appears to indicate and as we assume, religious metaphorization represents one of the characteristic features of modernity, we are bound to ask whether it does not also affect traditional religions. Indeed, is there not a link here with the metaphorizing intellectualization and spiritualization of the content of religion to be found at present in all the major Christian churches? Weber and Troeltsch remarked on the rise of this phenomenon among the intelligentsia of the day in their native land, essentially among Protestants. Over the last thirty years especially, all churches have been affected. With theologians as with believers, many conceptions of heaven or hell or the resurrection, for example, encompass both the supernatural and analogy, when they are not simply seen as analogy. The extent of the situation thus described, its causes and its consequences, both observable and foreseeable, constitute a rich field for study.[9]

Yet, in fact, with one important exception, there are few such studies. The exception is François-André Isambert's semiological study of the changes brought about in the Catholic liturgy for the sick by the 1972 reform. It brings to light in great detail precisely what the reworking of the rite's significance amounts to, a reworking undertaken by the Church itself, with the close involvement of theologians, for the purpose of 'spiritualizing' ancient interpretation.[10] Elsewhere, Régine Azria has interesting things to say about the way in which certain Jewish milieux, which are very much at one with cultural modernity, reinterpret the meaning of practices in order to make it possible to retain them or even reappraise them in present circumstances. These would include a historical and political reinterpretation of Jewish festivals, an ethical reinterpretation of taboos (the biblical prohibition of the consumption of blood is recast as symbolizing a moral requisite, the rejection of murder and of violence), the reinterpretation in terms of hygiene of laws affecting food and circumcision, or of laws to do with sexuality, and an aesthetic reinterpretation of traditional religious symbols.[11]

But beyond identifying spontaneous or institutionalized ways of metaphorizing the substance of ancient religions, Séguy asks a more general question: 'In that it has accelerated the intellectualization and rationalization of the process of acquiring knowledge, hence of cognition itself, does modernity not condemn religion to quasi-necessary metaphorization?'[12]

Does this imply a law governing the development of religion within modernity? Séguy confronts this issue with extreme caution. But however generalized the position he is prepared to adopt, it is the initiative itself which merits attention. And it has three major advantages over all the attempts at a definition of religion mentioned above.

The first is that it effectively precludes ontological definitions of religion by relating definition strictly to the sociological viewpoint required for the purpose of analysis. The sociologist is not concerned to know once and for all what religion is in itself, but to comprehend changes in the sphere of religion, considered by way of its tangible socio-historical manifestations. In this context a definition of religion is required to be no more than a working instrument, an instrument of a practical kind that will help the scholar comprehend socioreligious change, comprehend in fact the modern transformation of religion. Hence attention needs to be drawn to the process of change itself. Definition (if the term can still be used unambiguously) is a dynamic concept, whose aim is not that of fixing the subject matter but of pointing to the lines of transformation around which it reconstructs itself.

The second advantage of the avenue opened up by Séguy is fully to acknowledge what acceptance of socio-historical change implies: that modernity's transformation of the field of religion is in itself new; that historic religions and secular religions cannot – except by denying any reality to the process of change – be purely and simply assimilated; and that the sociocultural significance of the shifts which have occurred should not become obscured either by the prominence given to morphological proximity between the phenomena considered or by the discovery of their having genetic links. Certainly there are a number of parallels between Christian eschatology and secular revolutionary eschatology; and it is possible to demonstrate that the source of radical political utopianism is to be found in the religious utopia of the fulfilment of the world. But there is no basis at all for saying that from a sociological viewpoint it is immaterial whether one awaits the Kingdom of God or the classless society, and that solely what matters is the waiting. Only by taking account of the substance of what one is waiting for, Jean Séguy once remarked, can one 'say what someone waiting for a bus on the day of a strike has in common with someone waiting for the Kingdom of God'.

The third advantage is to grasp the reality of the shift that is taking place in the modern world from traditional religions towards spheres outside conventional religion that have become autonomous and invested with a new kind of religion, and not to associate this shift with the inevitable disappearance of religion in modernity; it represents instead a complete recasting of the substance of religion, and leads to traditional religions themselves being transformed and remodelled.

There is no doubt in my mind that by introducing the notion of metaphorical religion Jean Séguy has provided a clear indication of how the question of the definition of religion should now be posed. My aim here is to extend the search for a dynamic concept of religion in modernity by trying to take the essential argument one stage further. And the reason why Séguy himself appears reluctant to move in this direction is that his objective is an intellectual one, namely not to construct a theory of religious modernity but to delve more closely into the Weberian source text. That being so, it is of course impossible for him to sacrifice the basic substantive premise – 'there is religion when there is reference to supernatural powers' – that he has inherited from Max Weber.

In the process of metaphorization, as Séguy defines it, the loss of this reference occurs, whether because it is simply abandoned or because it is transformed by intellectualization and spiritualization. If one continues to see this loss as the essential and determining moment in the process of transformation one is trying to comprehend, one cannot altogether escape the notion that metaphorical – or, in the case of the major faiths, 'metaphorized' – religion is, to use Marcel Gauchet's phrase in a different context, the religion that marks the exit from religion. Hence Séguy's analysis in part, and implicitly at least, suggests that metaphorical religion marks a transitional phase between a cultural world where to invoke supernatural forces is self-evident or plausible, and a world – the disenchanted world of modern rationalism – where such an appeal has become improbable, if not impossible. This line of argument marks a setback in the development of metaphorization which could result in the religions of modernity being perceived merely as debased forms of religions in the full meaning of the term.

However, by showing that the question of religious modernity is above all one of the *way of believing*, Séguy clearly marks himself off from the classic assumptions of loss. What is original in his approach is that he sets out to conceive of religion in the modern world in terms of its overall reconstitution. It is his insistence on the operation of metaphorization at the heart of traditional religions which leads not to their erosion but to their incorporation in modern culture. At the same time, he suggests that metaphorical religion is not an insipid by-product of authentic religion but a specific mode for articulating belief in the cultural world of modernity, a way of believing which exercises its pull on the historic religions, cast as they are in the premodern world of tradition. The operation of spiritualization and intellectualization whereby they are reshaped from within does not empty them of their religious authenticity; rather it is the means whereby they are able to remain pertinent, and hence survive in modernity, in a form that has been recast. Let us take as an example the last rites, the case studied by François-André Isambert. In the 1972 ritual, the earlier reference to Christ's struggle with the devil at the bedside of the dying person disappears. The gathering of the community round Jesus Christ and round the dying person comes in place of the silence, the doubt and the solitude which assail the sufferer. According to Isambert, in the wake of this shift in meaning the question arises as to whether Jesus still retains an active role as subject, as to semantic function, or whether he becomes purely a *Destinateur* (he to whom one turns embodying destination, a provider of meaning, who stands apart), or simply the figure representing the positive principles he connotes. At the very least, there is a degree of uncertainty, and interpretation can vary between the literal and the allegorical. Within this margin of interpretation, which is where metaphorization comes into its own, some former constructions clearly lose significance, but such reorganization in terms of symbolism is the price paid for the rite to keep its place in modern culture and even to be enriched with a new symbolism. Would one say that the rite has thereby been debased?

Metaphorical erosion of religion as properly understood or a modern restructuring of religious belief? Here it is apparent that Séguy comes up against a dilemma that can be summarized as follows. Either he preserves a – however minimally – substantive definition of religion through belief in the supernatural, which confines religion to a single content type of belief, and of necessity he limits the possibilities of comprehending the modern reconstruction of belief as a transformation (and not a net loss) of religion. Or he abandons this, and he can move forward decisively with the theoretical prospect he has opened up by introducing the concept of metaphorical religion. But in order to do so, it requires that metaphorical religion be clearly presented as not being a lesser form of religion, a fairly debased by-product of religions in the full meaning of the term. It requires that, as a specific form of modern religious belief, it is as fully religious as are traditional religions. Unfortunately, Séguy's attachment to the basic definition provided by Weber would seem to prevent him from realizing as fully as he might the potentialities of the step which he has so carefully prepared.

Towards an analysis of the transformation of belief in contemporary society

The contradiction is in fact Weber's own, and one he resolves by playing with several definitions of religion. And, as it appears to me, the only means of escape is to bring the whole analysis to bear, not on changes in the content of beliefs, but on the structural transformation of belief that these changes in content in part reveal.

Before proceeding further, it is vital to define what one here understands by believing. The term denotes the body of convictions – both individual and collective – which are not susceptible to verification, to experimentation and, more broadly, to the modes of recognition and control that characterize knowledge, but owe their validity to the meaning and coherence they give to the subjective experience of those who hold them. If one here talks of believing rather than belief, it is in order to include not merely beliefs in the accepted sense, but all the resources of observance and language and the involuntary action which such belief in its multiple forms displays: believing is belief in action, as it is experienced. In Michel de Certeau's definition, it is what the speaker, whether individual or collective, makes of the utterance which he claims to believe.[13] Indeed it comprehends the range of practices that mark believing in a climate of monism in which the very notion of belief, implying as it does a distance between the believer and the object of belief, would seem to be meaningless.[14]

Thus understood, believing presents very different levels of structuring. It includes all the states of the body (*états de corps*), which Pierre Bourdieu mentions, inculcated early on and of which one is so unaware that one thinks of them as being inborn:[15] anything which is a product of 'what appears to be self-evident in the experience of living' belongs to the sphere of believing. At the other extreme is the range of formalized, rationalized beliefs of which people are mindful and from which they consciously draw practical implications for their lives. And whether it is a matter of spontaneous evidence or speculative conviction, believing eludes demonstration or experimental verification. At most, from the point of view of the believer, it can be endorsed by a body of signs or signals. But at any time it implies, on the part of the person or persons concerned, either a conscious or an unconscious surrender of self to an order that imposes itself from outside, or a more or less explicit wager, a more or less reasoned choice.

Thus giving centrality to the notion of believing means admitting as a precondition that believing plays a major role in modernity. The statement is by no means self-evident. It has often been said that by shifting the demand for meaning, without which there could be no human society, from the primordial question of *why* to the pragmatic question of *how*, the rationality of science and technology reduced the room for belief in modern societies. Nineteenth-century scientism even formulated the dream of consigning the question of *why* to oblivion. 'Beings in the particular or in general', wrote Büchner, 'are simply a fact of existence that we must accept as such; and since by the laws of nature and of reason and experience, this fact must be considered to have neither end nor beginning in time and space, there naturally can be no question of a predetermined cause, an act of creation or of why.'[16]

But if science and technology have removed most of the mystery from the world, they clearly have not obliterated the human need for *assurance* which is at the source of the search to make the experience of life intelligible and which constantly evokes the question of why. The experience of uncertainty in the life of the individual as in the life of society raises the ultimate threat – of death for the individual and of anomie for society. In the wake of Durkheim, Peter Berger has reaffirmed that the sacred is nothing other than the construct of meanings which humanity objectifies as a power that is radically different from itself and which it projects on reality to escape the anxiety of being engulfed by chaos.[17] Modernity breaks with the sacred in that it invests humanity with the task of rationalizing the world and of subduing the temptation of chaos by means of thought and action. But the fundamental need to dispel the essential uncertainty of the human condition is not diminished simply because the 'sacred cosmizations' (Peter Berger) are brought to naught by the process of rationalization. Nor does it subsist as a residue of a sacred universe become obsolete. It re-emerges from modernity itself in the form of so many fragmented demands for meaning whose urgency reflects a world that is no longer fixed and stable, representative of the natural order, but unpredictable and unprotected, where change and innovation have become the norm. As fast as modernity has deconstructed systems of meaning wherein individuals and society found a pattern of order matching their experience, it has generated social and psychological uncertainty on a huge scale; and in a multitude of ways it has given a new impetus to the question of meaning and the manifold protests against the denial of meaning that corresponds to it.[18] Identifying modern believing involves analysing these different ways of resolving – or at least averting – uncertainty, ways that are refracted in a diversity of beliefs. And within this broader field of vision, which embraces changes both in the substance of belief and in the social and cultural processes that produce these beliefs, the question of the religious productions of modernity has to be perceived anew.

That does not mean that the question of the content of beliefs is taken to be secondary or subsidiary. It has been repeated enough that the weakness in the functional approach to systems of meaning was to attach too little importance to changes in the substance of belief. Believing in the resurrection and believing that human beings live on in the memory of those who have loved them, or in the struggle of those with whom they have shown solidarity, are two ways of giving substance to the desire common to all to transcend their own physical death and confront the death of those round them. Clearly it is not a matter of indifference to pass from one belief to another; but changes in the content of belief are themselves part and parcel of a transformation in the mode of believing, and it is this that has to be explored further.

Let us add weight to the argument by returning to the concept of what Séguy calls metaphorization. As has been said, the crux of the matter lies in the expulsion in whole or in part of references to supernatural powers. The transformation that has been observed to take place is entirely in line with the classic interpretations of modernity as a process of 'stripping away the gods' (Heidegger's *Entgötterung*). The disenchantment of the world responds to the advance of the process of rationalization in which is manifest the capability of human beings, as creatures endowed with reason, to create the world in which they live. The rationalist imperative, which is inseparable from the assertion of the autonomy of individuals in regard to any exteriority or otherness prescribing their beliefs and actions, has gradually deprived reference to supernatural powers of plausibility. Yet such reference showed in its very beginnings the transcendent character and absolute authority of the institution of believing through which this power was deemed to make itself felt. Above and beyond the change in the substance of belief, a sociosymbolic organization has itself toppled. The process of rationalization has established itself by delegitimizing all the figures of transcendency which in traditional societies ensured the stability and coherence of beliefs and practices (ritual, ethics and so on), both individual and collective. One of the dominant characteristics of modernity, at the same time as it has proclaimed the rationality of the individual, has been to undo the traditional order in which the norm governing belief was externally set by means of an all-embracing institution of believing to which society as well as individuals were subject.

Modernity has deconstructed the traditional systems of believing, but has not forsaken belief. Believing finds expression in an individualized, subjective and diffuse form, and resolves into a multiplicity of combinations and orderings of meaning which are elaborated independently of control by institutions of believing, by religious institu-

tions in particular. This independence is, however,
as it is restricted by economic, social and cultural d'
weigh heavily on the symbolic activity of indivi'
their material and social lives. It is nonetheless ⌣
because the inalienable right of individuals to conceive͙
themselves is asserted as a counterpart to progress in the ͪ
mastery exercised over the material world.

What is interesting about the concept of metaphorization is that it
takes particular account of the dual process of homogenization and
dispersion which works on the modern domain of believing. On the
one hand, the imperative of rationality is dominant, chiefly in the negative form of excluding reference to the supernatural; yet, on the other,
the rational homogenization of believing is also what makes possible
the interplay between traditional and secular religion stressed by Séguy:
traditional religions serve as referents to secular religions, which in
turn take their place in a symbolic reinterpretation of their content.
But these secular religions in their turn become points of reference for
traditional religions which reconstitute themselves in different ways
by conforming to the same symbolic system as the former and by euphemizing their reference to supernatural intervention.

The combined processes of rationalization and individualization give
the modern domain of believing the characteristic of *fluidity* that is
proper to it and well illustrated by the reversible interplay of metaphor.

Religion as a way of believing: the example of apocalyptic neo-rural communities

In the fluid, mobile domain of modern belief liberated from the hold
of all-embracing institutions of believing, all symbols are interchange-
able and capable of being combined and transposed. All syncretisms
are possible, all retreads imaginable. Such notions take us straight back
to the problem of the sociological definition of religion. The quest for
this definition, as already suggested, is meaningful only if modernity is
perceived dynamically, as a process of becoming or as a movement, so
that no element in belief can any longer be held to be *a priori* religious,
political or whatever. Hence the definition of religion must be
desubstantialized so as to allow once and for all that a religious way of
believing relates neither to particular articles of belief, nor to specific
social observances, nor even to original representations of the world.
Ideal-typically, a meaningful definition should refer to a particular form
of organization and functioning of believing.

To identify such a way of believing implies underlining one (or more than one) feature to particularize it. Therefore I propose to abandon the traditional markers – the content and function proper to religious belief – and concentrate on the type of legitimation applied to the act of believing, in order to attempt to specify religious believing itself. The assumption I shall make is that there is no religion without the authority of a tradition being invoked (whether explicitly, half-explicitly or implicitly) in support of the act of believing. However, before exploring the implications of this assumption, it is essential to retrace the steps by which it gradually emerged. They developed out of research conducted, with Bertrand Hervieu, some years ago into forms of utopia as envisaged and practised by neo-rural communities.

An early phase of the study dating from 1972 to 1976 had to do with experiments in communal living by young people of educated urban middle-class origin who had set out for the underpopulated regions of southern France – the Cévennes, eastern Pyrenees and southern Alps – to keep goats or bees. What particularly interested us were the social and economic changes taking place in these utopias, with the vast majority of those who stayed on eventually after a few years finding work as monitors or running and assisting with activities in social services.[19] A small minority of them nevertheless managed to stay with the radical alternative they had chosen and which had involved abandoning the prospect of becoming teachers, social workers, industrial psychologists and so on. They invested the life to which they had committed themselves with the sense of a survival operation, mindful of the imminent planetary threats to humanity – pollution, nuclear danger, worsening population imbalance, food and energy crisis, economic recession, brutality on the part of government, war, etc. Some apocalyptic groups, which were the object of further study, drew very practical conclusions from this awesome scenario. They undertook to try out a collective mode of survival on a limited piece of land with the utmost degree of self-sufficiency applied to all aspects of the enterprise, bearing in mind the resources available. The project had an overall economic aim, which was to reduce needs to a point where they could be met independently. Communal living was organized round the precept of eliminating waste in all its forms. It required the group to remain within its territory, to adhere to a degree of control in the use of time and to channel power within the community so as to stem violence.

What led to further study of the experiment – apparently of limited social significance – was the observation that these groups moved rapidly from exhibiting deep environmental pessimism to building a vision of a new world which they took it upon themselves to reveal and anticipate. The link they themselves established between the coming inevitable catastrophe and the possible salvation open to those who like them chose to have recourse to nature justified use of the term 'apocalypticism' where they were concerned.[20] This environmental apocalypse did not in itself have a religious character in spite of its presenting in some of its features – a vision of future happiness, the conception of a new age, the role given to small groups to prepare for and anticipate the world to come – some elective affinities with traditional religious apocalypses, in particular the Joachimist or neo-Joachimist. The dramatization of catastrophe, the flight out of the world and the community's quest for salvation could be analysed in the classic Weberian terms of ideological compensation afforded by pariah-intellectuals in the bitter conflict between their demands for meaning, the realities of the world as ordered, and the possibilities offered them to find their place in it.[21] In this perspective, the interest frequently shown by neo-rural communities in religions, in spiritual and esoteric movements, alchemy and so on, might be interpreted, along with their fascination with alternative medicine or preindustrial agricultural methods, as expressing protest in the form of rehabilitating so-called pre-rational modes of thought, according to modern criteria of knowledge – a way, in fact, for them to take up a distinct position in the face of those possessing legitimate knowledge, hence the means of access to power in society.

The analysis developed by studying these groups over a period, and was focused at the start on the protest element they displayed within modernity.[22] But it needs to be made unambiguously clear that it was not the anti-modern stance of this utopia that raised the question of its religious character, as if the two were linked. As individuals, those who formed the groups were certainly not culturally deprived, however depressed they may have been by the alleged benefits of growth. The creation of a neo-rural utopia served as a constant reminder of the unfulfilled promises of modernity (material well-being, individual liberty, right to happiness and self-fulfilment, etc.), and one could say that there was an inner tension between this anti-modernity, even at its most apocalyptic, and the modern world which gave rise to it. The arguably religious character of the movement developed in our minds as we observed the way in which its rejection of the world as constituted led through its collective experience to a system of believing. It appeared to us that there were three major phases.

The first phase involved the passage from preoccupation with environmental disaster to a pragmatic quest for independent survival, requiring the adoption of a lifestyle equal to the challenge. This meant that nature was no longer the mythical repository of what humanity had lost but a test of the will to survive. To live off land that was poor and long uncultivated called upon the organizational skills and constant application of all concerned. At best, this meant making do with only basic necessities. Indeed the acceptance of austerity in terms of toil and relative penury by those who generally came unprepared for it was the necessary condition of their independence. As they distanced themselves increasingly from the spontaneous character of the late 1960s communes, these apocalyptic groups were forced to develop an internal organization to ensure their survival.

At which point – and this marked the second phase – there developed a code of frugality, itself a justification of the limits necessarily imposed on individual freedom, which gradually replaced the initial, somewhat vague, reference to the laws of nature. Now it became relevant to look beyond the norm of primitive simplicity towards values that ensured the group's survival (a settled way of life, controlled use of resources, action for a common purpose, etc.); and frequently these values became formulated as unwritten (and even written) rules, affecting work-sharing, sexual relationships and internal authority.

Such rules in accordance with nature, and hence good in themselves, did not merely respond to the various internal and external problems encountered by the communities; they lent system to the separateness of individuals who had together opted for a new world, they marked them off concretely and symbolically from the world as it is. In this way, they crystallized a tendency, which is constant in all groups confronting difficult problems of survival, to develop a dichotomizing awareness of reality that grows out of day-to-day living, which is itself both legitimized and given direction. This marked the third phase: an aspiration towards a healthier, simpler, more natural, and hence more human life. This aspiration, which initially responded to awareness of the dangers looming for industrial society, formed itself into a belief in the salvation offered to those who changed their lives by conforming to nature, and such a belief took as an assumption that the separation between those to be saved and those not to be saved was necessary and inevitable.

At the time when this study was carried out and published,[23] our approach to the religious transmutation of the apocalyptic vision of environmental disaster was centred on this dichotomizing experience of reality; and we stressed its pragmatic character – day after day the group was faced with the contrast between the garden it cultivated and the wilderness of brambles surrounding it, the reconditioned house and the ruins, the land that was watered and the land that remained barren. The opposition between inside – the space occupied by the community – and outside – the social as well as the natural surroundings, both equally threatening – was at the origin of the constant struggle to survive. It was also the foundation of a symbolic opposition, which gave meaning to the struggle, between the community and the world, between order and disorder, good and evil, the pure and the impure. The view of reality which developed out of this day-to-day living appeared to us to bring a symbolic dialectic into play, in which the opposition between the sacred and the profane clearly represented the paradigm. All we could do was to refer this process of constructing a sacred cosmos, observed *in vivo*, and the access to a religion it provided for those concerned, to Durkheim:

> Whether simple or complex, all known religious beliefs display a common feature: they presuppose a classification of the real or ideal things that men conceive of into two classes – two opposite genera – that are widely designated by two distinct terms, which the words *profane* and *sacred* translate fairly well. The division of the world into two domains, one containing all that is sacred and the other all that is profane – such is the distinctive trait of religious thought.[24]

The classic Durkheimian reference was further justified by the evidence that this vision of the world, which grew out of daily living, enabled those in the community to establish taboos within the community by giving meaning – the attainment of salvation – to the function of exclusion operating between the group and its social environment. Ritual observance made its appearance – communion and communal reconciliation, purification and decontamination both for the individual and the group, and so on. They served as rites to give symbolic recognition, for each one in the group and for the group as a whole, to the sense of integration and separateness which enabled the austerity of communal survival to be borne as the means of acceding to salvation.

Fairly soon we realized the weaknesses in this approach. On the one hand, it took for granted, without further scrutiny, that the workings of the community that *we* classed as sacred necessarily denoted the presence, implicit at least, of a religious view of the world. On the other, it presupposed rather too readily that the absolute antinomy between nature and modern civilization, which a radically environmental stance and its accompanying problems called for, naturally prompted an affinity with the themes developed by traditional religions.[25] The analysis needed to be taken further. What we had brought to light was a process of developing and shaping and clarifying a way of believing within interest groups confronted with the need to legitimize, *ad intra* and *ad extra*, their separateness from society and their

rejection of the dominant social and economic relations as they operated. In order to preserve and strengthen their plan of action which
was radical yet plausible, because the difficulties in the way of achieving it threatened their existence as a community, those concerned were
driven to investing it with the significance of a means of access to
salvation that required highly organized control over daily living. The
symbolic dialectic brought into play in this regulation of believing conferred an absolute, a sacred, quality on community objectives: it did
not of itself mean that the way of believing within the community had
become religious.

Had it become so, it was not because of having acquired sanctity as
such but because of the invocation of a cloud of witnesses whose presumed existence gave validity to the experience. An initial study might
have led us to this view earlier. It concerned the unusual case history
of a young hermit who after much wandering had settled in the
Cévennes and whose search for meaning had finally led to his seeing
his role as continuing other utopian experiences which he came to
recognize as the matrix in which his longing for another world had
taken shape, long before he was aware of it being so.[26] The highly
individual nature of Ebyathar's – this hermit's – experience held us
back from any attempt to make use of it for what it might reveal in a
general way about the emergence of a religious attitude. Within neo-
apocalyptic communities, reference to witnesses enabled groups, which
were isolated in their struggle to survive, to model themselves on any
forerunners who had faced up to the dangers of destruction brought
upon humanity by human self-sufficiency. Throughout our study, we
noticed the symbolic significance that every community drew from
being able to see itself as forming part of a prophetic tradition. But
initially we restricted our interpretation to concentrating either on internal issues (for instance, on the need felt by the founder to nurture
his charisma with the little group of disciples) or on the groups' efforts
to demarcate themselves from other less radical communities. Certainly the invocation of past witnesses appeared to us to be important;
indeed we took it for our subtitle. Members of these neo-rural communities presented themselves to us as the authentic heirs of a line of
trail-blazing monks who had saved western civilization from barbar-
ian hordes. And their identification with these witnesses could go as
far as introducing monastic rules (chiefly Benedictine) into their own
community rules. But insufficient account was taken of these factors,
so long as the invoking of a core lineage was considered to be of secondary importance, and only later – for the members of the community too – was it seen to confirm the passage from a secular to a religious
apocalyptic.[27]

Paradoxically, the fact that the lineage had a connection with a historic religion (reference to the monastic tradition being especially frequent inside the groups) had obscured the essential. Reference to the monks of the past was not important in its having a religious content (or, in other words, connecting with the traditions of a particular historic religion); it was important in that it rooted the entire enterprise of the group – its imaginative projection into a quite different future as well as the meaning to give to the problems of the present – within a tradition that was authoritative: *as our fathers believed, and because they believed, we too believe* ... On reappraising the premises of an approach which continued to make experience of the sacred coincide with putting a religious construction on day-to-day experience, we were led to consider the appeal to past witnesses no longer as a secondary effect of the groups' religious orientation, but as the instant when such orientation was determined and came about. Thereafter it mattered little that the reference to past witnesses was in the main extraordinarily inconsistent and fanciful. What matters here is not the actual substance of belief but the ingenuity, the imaginative perception of the link which across time establishes the *religious* adhesion of members to the group they form and the convictions that bind them. Seen thus, one would describe any form of believing as religious which sees its commitment to a chain of belief it adopts as all-absorbing.

This statement, of course, is not to be taken to mean that religion is only and always what is said about it here. It represents a working hypothesis which allows *one* sociological approach to religion (among other possible ones) to be formulated; and the one chosen has been determined by the intellectual objective of accounting for the changes affecting religion in modernity. To grasp the significance of this definition, one needs to grasp that the self-legitimizing of the act of believing by reference to the authority of a tradition goes further than merely asserting the continuity of beliefs and practices from one generation to another. For the religious believer, whether individual or group, it is not enough to believe merely 'because it's the right thing to do'. Believers consider themselves, in the expression of Pierre Gisel, the Swiss theologian, 'begotten'.[28] It is not the continuity in itself that matters but the fact of its being the visible expression of a lineage which the believer expressly lays claim to and which confers membership of a spiritual community that gathers past, present and future believers. In certain cases, breaking continuity may even be a way of saving the essential link with the line of belief. This functions as an imaginary reference, legitimizing belief. It functions inseparably as a principle of social identification, *ad intra* (through incorporation into a believing community) and *ad extra* (through differentiation from those who are

not of this lineage). Seen thus, one might say that a religion is an ideological, practical and symbolic system through which consciousness,
both individual and collective, of belonging to a particular chain of
belief is constituted, maintained, developed and controlled.

This definition raises a number of objections and contains a number
of implications. We shall attempt to respond point by point to these
objections and to develop the implications. But the really fundamental
question is whether or not it is useful. At the risk of labouring the
point, it is not required that the last word be said on religion but that
a working concept be found, which, among other possible uses, enables one to grasp over and above analogies made between traditional
and secular religions what justifies treating their situation and their
future within modernity together from a sociological point of view.
Thus viewed, our objective is not only to determine whether the beliefs and practices of this or that political or environmental group may
or may not be termed religious, or whether the emotional investment
of football fans or the fervour unleashed at a rock concert may be so
termed. Rather it is to know whether this or that contemporary expression of Christianity or Judaism or whatever other tradition is regarded by society as to do with religion can, in fact, in the light of this
definition, be characterized as religious.

5

Questions about Tradition

The proposal to apply the term 'religious' to the form of believing whose distinguishing mark is to appeal to the legitimizing authority of a tradition has been tentatively put forward in various discussions and research notes.[1] Understandably, it has often aroused lively comment. Some of the objections raised merit particular attention, the first concerning the paradox implied by defining religion by reference to tradition if one sets out to identify the religious products of modernity, the second concerning the limits of the religious as thus understood. Rather than move straight to the outcome of a debate which owes much to the objections raised, it would seem preferable to describe its different stages, showing how each moved the debate forward and enriched it, showing too what still remains to be achieved.

Tradition opposed to modernity

Until now, the main argument has been devoted to justifying an approach to religion which, for all that its essence remains intangible, may enable one to grasp what is specific in its relation to modernity. Thus it is not surprising that the first question touches on the paradox, if not contradiction, implied by proposing a definition of religion which turns on the concept of tradition, suggesting as it does that religion is wedded to traditional society, which is more often than not identified as being opposed to modernity. This would seem to invalidate the original purpose of examining the religious products of modernity.

The question bears on the reasoning adopted, and hence is a fundamental one. A common notion, to be found even in some scientific studies, is that religion is concerned with the past, doomed to lose all cultural plausibility in the modern world and able only to turn itself to account in instances of cultural regression, which correspond with the sporadic reactions against modernity that mark our crisis-prone society. One way round this frequently accepted notion, which inhibits serious analysis of contemporary religious renewal, might be to sever the notional link between religion and tradition so that the one is no longer identified with the other. However, we would propose rather to rearticulate the core relationship between tradition and religion within modernity. But in order to do so it is necessary to reconsider how the distinction drawn between so-called traditional and modern societies has evolved in the way it has.

Such a rehearsal does not imply questioning the view largely accepted by the social sciences according to which tradition supplies the structure of premodern societies; it simply means that premodern societies are unaware of what Maurice Gauchet has called the imperative of change, which characterizes modernity. In premodern societies, tradition generates continuity, to borrow Georges Balandier's expression.

> It denotes the relationship with the past and the constraint of the past, it imposes conformity resulting from a code of meaning, and hence values which govern individual and collective conduct and are transmitted from generation to generation. It is a heritage that defines and maintains an order, by obliterating the transforming effect of time and by retaining only the initial core phase from which it draws its legitimacy and authority. It ordains in every sense of the word.[2]

In the world of tradition, religion is the code of meaning that establishes and expresses social continuity. By placing the origin of the world outside time and by attributing the order of the world to a necessity beyond society, it erases the chaos represented by reality, at the same time removing reality from the transforming effect of human control. It is the unified matrix of believing which 'imparts all form and meaning to dwelling in the world and ordering its creatures'. In the fully developed form it assumes in societies prior to progress, it presents itself, according to Marcel Gauchet, as the intellectual expression of 'mankind, naked and defenceless in the face of overwhelming nature', and 'at the same time as a means for the mind, by admitting this to be so, to overcome a situation of extreme destitution'.[3]

We shall not here join the debate which has induced anthropolo-

tradition are part and parcel of the dynamics of social relations whereby a society creates itself and creates its own history means that tradition is not simply a repetition of the past in the present. This goes not merely for modern societies in which the demand for change always conflicts with the logic of tradition. In all societies where the past asserts its authority, and in the spheres of societies that are moving into modernity where this authority is still dominant, the distinctive mark of tradition is to actualize the past in the present, to restore to human lives as they are lived the living memory of an essential core which gives it existence in the present. As Louis-Marie Chauvet observes, the concept of tradition cannot be reduced to a ranking of established fundamental references – sacred texts, immovable ritual and so on – set for all time (traditionalist tradition). And he points also to 'the hermeneutic process by which a community of human beings rereads its ritual or statutory practices, its own historical narrative or again the theoretical constructions received from its institutional tradition (traditionalizing tradition)'.[12]

The process of rereading is inseparable from the process of creating a new relationship with the past, in the light of the present, hence with the present too. Even in so-called traditional societies, which are presented as being entirely ruled by the injunctions of tradition and unlikely to breed disorder, Georges Balandier makes the point that 'tradition manipulates change but only indirectly plays on the appearance of stability'. Tradition must also adjust to the possibility of disorder and the peril of opposition to change, and comes into action here only if it can truly convey a 'forcefulness that enables it to adapt and deal with events and exploit alternative possibilities'.[13] This insistence on dissociating tradition from outright conformity or continuity leads Balandier to distinguish three forms of traditionalism:

> Fundamental traditionalism upholds the maintenance of the most deep-rooted values and models of social and cultural observance; it serves a state of permanence and what is considered to be a constituent of human beings and social relations according to the social coding of which it is both product and preserver. Formal traditionalism, incompatible with the previous form, makes use of forms that are upheld but changed in substance; it establishes a continuity of appearances, but serves new designs; it accompanies movement while maintaining a link with the past. Pseudo-traditionalism corresponds to a tradition that has been refashioned; it occurs in periods of accelerated movement and major upheaval; it enables a new construction to be put upon change and the unexpected; it enables them to be tamed by being given a familiar, reassuring aspect. It feeds interpretation, assumes continuity and expresses a dawning disorder. In this sense, it reveals the extent to which the

gists to describe the primitive world as an immobile world or to conceive of the absolute domination of religion in primitive society. We would simply remark that Marcel Gauchet puts the fundamental change initiating the march of humanity at about 3000 BC in Mesopotamia and Egypt; a march, as he calls it, 'from an order that is endured to an order that is increasingly willed'.[4] This dating, in its very lack of precision, is a way of pushing as far back as possible into human history a time when the world of tradition imposed itself in its pure form. Probably the only way to interpret Marcel Gauchet here is to take him as defining a representative extreme, to which stands opposed the extreme of pure modernity, characterized by general acceptance of 'responsibility for an order recognized as proceeding from the individual will, itself held to pre-exist the tie that binds society together': on the one hand, 'a predisposition to the precedence of the world and the law of things'; on the other, 'a predisposition to the precedence of human beings and their creative activity'.[5] On the one hand, heteronomous society, its institution beyond reach and outside its own control; on the other, autonomous society that recognizes itself as at once self-created and creative.[6]

But this conflict of type does not allow for an absolute discontinuity between so-called traditional and modern societies to be situated empirically. Were this so, it is difficult to see how the transformation of cold societies of tradition (themselves far from corresponding to one model) into warm modern societies could be brought about. The problem of putting a date to the start of modernity (the Enlightenment? the Reformation? the twelfth or thirteenth centuries?) further shows that modern society is equally elusive, as immune to being encompassed in a single definition as is traditional society. Neither is self-enclosed, the opposition between them is not absolute. The dynamics of each overlap, the one giving precedence to order, the other to movement. Human life is witness to the gradual predominance of movement over order, and of human autonomy over heteronomy. But the process does not completely resolve itself in the destruction and disappearance of the former world. There is de-structuring and re-structuring, disorganization but also re-development and re-employment of elements deriving from the earlier order in the fluid system of modern society.

Religion, as total expression of the former order in the register of symbolism and ritual, has become caught in the same dialectic of change. In choosing a definition that stresses its being anchored in the world of tradition, it is not thereby excluded from the world of modernity. Its place there is signalled from the outset, but in the reconstructed form of tradition within modernity.

The creative power of tradition

Yet it is clearly only a partial response to the problem raised. To say that religion has to do with tradition, namely with continuity and conformity, in a world dominated by pressure for change effectively denies it any active social or cultural role in modern society. It is thereby effectively consigned to a function of nostalgic or exotic remembrance, apart from fulfilling the function of memory and upholding the survival of tradition in the world of modernity.

This is a serious objection and calls for a dual response: first, to examine more closely the connection between tradition and social change; then, to consider whether the dynamic of tradition which is active and creative in society (always supposing it has been given prominence) still has a role to play in society, perhaps as a force for renewal.

The first point calls for the removal of a common misunderstanding. To say, as does Georges Balandier, that tradition is bound up with a view of society as continuity and conformity does not mean that societies in which it plays a vital role are static and impervious to change. What tradition, and more specifically religion which is its code of meaning, brings about is a world of collective meanings in which day-to-day experience that can play havoc with groups or individuals is related to an immutable, necessary order that pre-exists both individuals and groups. The world which thus constitutes *traditionalism* is characterized, according to Max Weber, by a 'propensity to accept the customary round of everyday life in the belief that it constitutes a norm for action'.[7] This imaginative force for action implies that the past can be read as the exclusive source of the present. To experience the real meaning of being part of a continuing tradition, one can hardly do better than refer to the book in which Josef Erlich describes in minute ethnographic detail the celebration of the Sabbath in a Polish *schtetl*. Every gesture expressed, every moment passed by the Jewish family followed through the course of the feast day is invested with a sense of immemorial continuity in which it is supposed to find its place.[8]

And one concludes at once that a definition such as that given in the *Petit Robert* dictionary, reducing tradition to 'ways of thinking, doing or acting which are inherited from the past', by wrongly reifying the dynamic source, ignores the essential, that is to say, the authority attributed to the past to settle the problems of the present. What defines tradition (while, in fact, it serves present interests) is that it confers transcendent authority on the past. This transcendence shows itself in the impossibility of determining its origin. The origin of tradition for

ever moves back in the sense that it is fed only from itself. It implies, in the words of Joseph Moingt, 'assenting to a past, determination to prolong it in the present and the future, the act of receiving a sacred, intangible trust, humble and respectful resolve to repeat something already said'.[9]

This means that one cannot, as Edward Shils does,[10] make tradition encompass the whole body of *tradita* of a society or group, that is to say, the whole stock of representations, images, theoretical and practical knowledge, behaviour and attitudes which is inherited, received from the past. All that constitute tradition in the proper meaning of the term are the parts of this stock whose value is linked to the continuity between the past and the present of which they are the evidence and which on this account are passed on. The invocation of such continuity may be fairly crude ('it's always been done') or highly formalized, viz. the case of all doctrinal tradition. But in all instances the invocation is at the source of the way tradition is able to establish itself as a norm for individuals and groups. Looked at thus, tradition describes the body of representations, images, theoretical and practical intelligence, behaviour, attitudes and so on that a group or society accepts in the name of the *necessary* continuity between the past and the present.

Thus what comes from the past is only constituted as tradition insofar as anteriority constitutes a title of authority in the present. Whether the past in question is relatively short or very long is only of secondary significance. The degree of ancientness confers an extra value on tradition, but it is not what initially establishes its social authority. What matters most is that the demonstration of continuity is capable of incorporating even the innovations and reinterpretations demanded by the present. To grasp what this implies, one has to bear in mind that any tradition develops through the permanent reprocessing of the data which a group or a society receives from its past. The sifting and the shaping by means of which this heritage becomes a norm for the present and future are theoretically carried out by those in the group or society who are invested with the power to do so and/or dispose of the instruments of physical, ideological and symbolic coercion to have them carried out. The social monopoly of the regulation of tradition is in fact always threatened by the shattering impact (*coup de force*) of the prophet, who claims to redefine the principles by virtue of the personal revelation that has come to him.[11] More generally, there is a constant issue of social conflict, through which the political, ideological and symbolic equilibrium of group or society disintegrate and are reconstituted.

The fact that the social mechanisms for regulating reference to

work of tradition is not separate from the work of history, and how far tradition constitutes a stock of symbols and images, and also ways of appeasing modernity. Tradition may be seen as the text that constitutes a society, a text according to which the present is interpreted and processed.[14]

It would be more correct to use the term 'traditional society' only where fundamental traditionalism applied. Manifestly, in an unalloyed form it is an ideal type, as is the wholly religious society of the past which directly corresponds to it. Ancient societies based on tradition have all in varying proportions combined these three forms of traditionalism whose interaction enables change to mesh with continuity.

Religion as folklore

The problem is to know – and this is the second aspect of the question above – whether the creative dynamic of tradition, which inaugurates change by invoking continuity, still has relevance in a society where change is valued for itself, where the principle of continuity is no longer inviolable and where reference to tradition plays only an ancillary role in society's production and legitimization of norms, values and symbols proposed for acceptance and credence by the individual or group. What is there for religion to do in modern societies except play a subsidiary cultural and symbolic role? Or, to put it more bluntly, is it not bound to be marginalized as having little real significance except as folklore?

In 1973, Michel de Certeau opened a broadcast discussion with Jean-Marie Domenach by asking: 'Has Christianity transformed itself into the folklore of current society?'

'Any discussion which has to do with moral standards in public or private life', he remarked with reference to the media,

> inevitably brings in an ecclesiastical figure and religious discourse. The figure and the discourse are no longer there as witnesses to a truth. They play a theatrical role. They are part of the repertoire of a social *commedia dell'arte*. The situation is quite different from what it was only a matter of years ago, when Christian belief still had solid roots in society. Then a certain type of discourse was upheld or it was actively resisted. It did not simply drift as it now does. Christianity defined particular associations and observances. Now it has become a fragment of culture. Cultural Christianity is no longer connected to the faith of any particular group.[15]

Michel de Certeau's remarks throw light on what the term 'folklore' may here convey. There is a process of dislocation at work which affects traditional religions (the discourse of Christianity, in particular) as a corpus of meaning in very advanced societies. The process is itself linked to the break-up of communities in which the discourse acquired consistency in the form of practices and behaviour; and at its source is the growth of rationalization. By gradually demystifying whole sections of human reality, rationalism inevitably provoked (and still provokes) the dislocation of comprehensive systems of meaning, which in past societies gave sense and coherence to the chaos of experience. The historic religions were subjected to the full force of the change, while primary communities which experienced this meaning and coherence in common as certainties (in the form of elementary beliefs that Pierre Bourdieu refers to as states of the body) simply faded away. The process of secularization implicit in modernity is by now too familiar to be dwelt on further;[16] it needs only to be acknowledged that the marginalization of traditional religions as folklore constitutes one of the outcomes facing religion in modernity. The dominant religions can still supply individuals with a unifying ferment from their own experience, yet they have all but lost the power to inform the organization of social life, with the exception of those voluntary groups which depend on individual membership. The transfer of the potential for meaning vested in the historic religions from society to the individual has meant that in all advanced societies they have become sources of cultural heritage revered for their historical significance and their emblematic function, but to all intents and purposes poorly mobilized for the production of collective meaning.

In modern societies which are no longer governed by reference to tradition, is religion indeed able to *create* meanings that correspond to the new problems that are there to be faced? For some writers the answer is unequivocally no. The German sociologist, Niklas Luhmann, has recently made use of the concept of resonance, describing the interplay between the system and its environment, in order to examine whether religion might not be able independently to contribute to the production of meanings which would enable advanced societies actively to integrate ecological issues into their own functioning. He provides a highly developed analysis of why religion is incapable of fulfilling this role. In his view, no problem relating to the environment and accommodating the technological, economic and ethical demands of modern society can be inferred from a religious code, because, for all the changes it has undergone, it remains fixed in the vision of a transcendental world separate from the real world. At best, religion 'offers a language of protest against deforestation, against air and water pollution, against the nuclear threat or against excessive medicalization', when these scourges have reached a certain point of visibility. But beyond denouncing and admonishing, it is incapable of formulating a truly independent approach to such problems, because it is slave to an outmoded perception of society. In Luhmann's words, in the end religion 'has no religion to offer'.[17]

Luhmann's analysis of the inadequacy of religion in producing meaning that corresponds to the new problems facing modern society is explicitly directed at the official theology of the dominant Christian churches. But in a wider focus it concerns the inexorable disparity between a religiously integrated view of the world and the culture of modernity, a disparity that leads to its marginalization as folklore described by Michel de Certeau. Yet the question remains whether there is any more to say about the situation of religion within modernity, once one has accepted that the tendency for the dominant religions to be marginalized to a point where they are no more than picturesque and parasitic is inescapable.

Historically, modernity's questioning of the world of tradition unified by religion has led not merely to the confinement of institutionalized religion in a specialized social field. For the very reason of its having initiated a conflict between the separate field of institutionalized religion and other social fields, it has opened the way to novel applications of the stock of symbols constituted by traditional religions in the context of aesthetics and culture, of morals and politics too. The tension between religion and politics, a consequence of their distinctiveness, has been instrumental in mobilizing religious symbols for the cause of utopian politics. In the course of several centuries the memory of religion nurtured by societies which acceded to modernity provided the chief imaginative source for visions of the coming order, those of a golden age for instance.[18] The imaginative function of the early Christian community in nineteenth-century utopian socialism,[19] and the significance of messianic themes from Jewish tradition in the shaping of libertarian ideals in central Europe,[20] are merely two examples of the utopian fecundity of the major religious traditions.

The point underlined by Michel de Certeau that religious beliefs and practices no longer – or at any rate decreasingly – identify particular groups perhaps implies the destruction of the creative potential that religion enjoyed within modernity. Bryan Wilson seems also to be of this opinion and draws attention to the absence of a utopian dimension in most of the new religious movements, thus disclaiming their authenticity as religious movements.

The creative strength of a politico-religious utopia stems from its being a source of both imaginative and social energy and from its conveying a multitude of symbols and values that can be given concrete collective form. Without its being rooted in society, the utopian mobilization of unfocused religious references is unlikely. But recent developments show that the social uncoupling of religious beliefs and practices is reversible; given certain circumstances, these may become socially reidentified, thus playing an active role in the production of meaning and in the expression of collective aspiration, with social, political and cultural consequences. The role of religion in the transition to democracy in eastern Europe or the importance of the Islamic reference for young second-generation North African immigrants in France in search of their identity[21] provide two illuminating examples.

The religious productions of modernity: is this concept meaningful?

But, it will be objected, the last two cases (to which we shall return in the final section) are not entirely convincing. Certainly they provide evidence that religion in the modern world is more than just a residual facet of culture; they show that it can retain or reassume a creative potential in society, given that it functions as reawakened or invented memory for actual social groups. But they also suggest that the inability of modernity to respond to the aspirations it gives rise to, and to produce corresponding collective meanings, is what favours the renewal of belief linked to the authority of tradition – thus, the collapse of the promises of socialism and the mirage presented by the promises of integration. Rather, they lead to the conclusion – reinforced by the knowledge that religious expression may well be a very transitional cover for social and political protest which is denied an outlet[22] – that religious activity may, by way of compensation, move into areas that have been left more or less untouched by modern rationalism. This consideration alone cannot justify us talking of the religious productions of modernity any more than can the observation made earlier that traditional beliefs, in part or in whole, may persist in the modern world though in altered form – spiritualized, intellectualized and so on. For the term to be meaningful, it requires more than simply registering limitations in the modern process of rationalization, or even recognizing the constant intermingling of the modern demand for change and the ancestral demand for continuity, even in highly advanced societies. It requires one to be able to declare that the modernity in question, which ideally is defined by the self-affirmation and future of the autonomous individual, *prompts* a need on the part of both individuals and society to refer to the authority of tradition. Failing this, one must reconcile oneself to the fact that the definition of religion as a form of believing whose distinctive quality is to invoke the legitimizing authority of tradition is no more than a renewed demonstration that religion is structurally alien to modernity and that it survives only as a residue of a bygone world. But if one argues, as has been suggested thus far, that modernity and religion are not mutually exclusive (hence that religion retains a creative potential within modernity), one has to accept the paradox that modernity produces what is of essence contrary to it, namely heteronomy, submission to an order endured, received from outside and not willed.

The proposition may cause some surprise but it is not original. The anthropologist Louis Dumont is one among others who have argued it in connection with individualism, itself characteristic of modernity. 'What is the source of non-individualistic factors or elements?' he asks. in *Essais sur l'individualisme*.

> In the first place, they stem from the permanence or survival of premodern and more or less general elements, such as the family. But they owe their source also to the fact that the very development of individualistic values set off a complex dialectic which, in many spheres, and in some instances as early as the late eighteenth century, resulted in combinations where they find themselves with their opposites.[23]

The same dialectic holds for the social and economic sphere. Louis Dumont has referred to the work of Karl Polanyi, which demonstrates that economic liberalism led to the need for protective social measures and finally brought about what may be termed contemporary postliberalism.[24] It holds for the political where, he explains, 'totalitarianism is a dramatic expression of something one constantly comes across anew in the contemporary world, namely that individualism is both all-powerful and perpetually haunted by its opposite.'[25]

We would argue that the dialectic holds too in the case of religion, where affirmation of the autonomy of the individual which undermines the authority of tradition paradoxically rekindles, but in new forms, the need to have recourse to the assurance this authority imparts. Some clarification is needed.

Modernity has not done away with the individual's or society's need to believe. Indeed it has been observed that the uncertainty that flows from the dynamics of change has made the need stronger, as illustrated by the infinite diversity of the demand for meaning, on the part of both individuals and groups, and the imagination-fed solutions arrived at. In a society in which affirmation of the autonomy – the liberty – of the individual is inseparable from the insistence on independence in private life,[26] the question of meaning that comes to the fore in extreme situations – where there is suffering, where there is death – is more than likely to receive a subjective, an individual response. This tendency towards the individualization and atomization of belief has often been stressed, but that it inevitably encounters a limit has been less often remarked on. This is not simply the effect of sociocultural circumstances that externally demarcate the area of what the philosopher Paul Ricoeur has called the available scope for belief (*le disponible croyable*) at any one time. It also marks an internal limitation to the process of producing meaning: in order for meaning to have an effect, there must be at a given point the collective effect of meaning shared; meaning that is individually constructed must be attested by others, it must be given social confirmation.

In premodern society, the need for meaning to receive social confirmation did not arise, except for the bearer of charisma, who was constantly obliged to furnish the confirmation (normally in the form of prodigies, according to Weber) necessary in order to obtain recognition on the part of followers and justify the breach of commonly accepted norms and certainties.[27] But ordinarily such confirmation was implicit in conforming with the code of meaning received from the past and binding on all through a system of stable norms. In more differentiated societies where the emergence of the state had broken this immutable religious order by giving an institutional framework to social order, primary communities – family or locality – for a long time continued to fulfil the function of confirmation in the sphere of meaning, in spite of increasing competition from dominant ideological systems, such as churches, schools or political parties, vying for monopoly in the production of meaning.

In the more advanced modern societies which are subject to the psychological modernity described by Jean Baudrillard, where the individual rules with 'the autonomy of his or her individual conscience, psychology, personal conflicts, private interests, of his or her unconscious even',[28] social confirmation of meaning tends increasingly to be entrusted to a diversified network of affinity groups, where the sharing of meaning is a matter of private initiative. The significance of community expectations and experiments in societies where individualization has been taken to the greatest lengths is often presented as expressing a reactive protest against modernization and occasionally as a disturbing rejection of the universal values of modernity. A return to tribal reflexes is called to mind as a worrying sign of social and cultural regression to be set against the individual's conquest of autonomy and the noble heritage of the Enlightenment.

Such a reading of contemporary community practices as a protest against modernity is to a considerable extent legitimate, with the reservation however that the motivation here comes from individuals, not from any external force. Such practices and the aspirations informing them underline the growing importance of relationships based on affinity in the production of meaning, inasmuch as such meaning is no longer externally imposed, that is as both a corpus of meaning and as a system of norms.

The consequences of high mobility and the remoteness of social relations which characterize modernity are now intensified by the collapse of the dominant ideological systems which claimed to embody meaning for society as a whole, these being undermined by the unending acceleration of social change and their own inability to have a positive impact on it. In highly complex societies where there is no sense of permanence or certainty, the production of collective meaning and the social authentication of individual meaning are a matter for voluntary communities. The community stands in opposition to urban industrial society but comes into its own once again in societies of mass communication where individualism is triumphant, because it nurtures fundamental social relations. The demands of French *lycéens* in 1990 that their schools should be living communities, and the gangs of youths in suburban ghettos, can be taken as representative of two socially differentiated methods of articulating one and the same urge to put an end to atomization by communal action; the corollary of the difference, of course, being that in the one case official recognition follows virtually automatically, while in the other for its full expression it requires recourse to violence. But what is at issue in both instances is the need to stand up to a dearth of collective meanings which precludes individuals giving or attaching coherent meaning to their existence otherwise than by endowing the groups to which they relate with extraordinary symbolic or emotive force.

Gilles Lipovetsky, in *L'Ère du vide*, has remarked upon the scale of what he calls the relational craze. He links the proliferation of situational networks and the multiplication of collectives with miniaturized, hyperspecialized interests to a generalized outbreak of narcissism which feeds the 'desire to get together with people who share the same immediate and clearly demarcated interests'. 'The ultimate form of individualism', he writes,

> does not reside in sovereign asocial independence, but in link-ups and connections with collectives with miniaturized, hyperspecialized interests – groups bringing together widowers, parents with homosexual children, alcoholics, stutterers, lesbian mothers, bulimia sufferers, and so on. Narcissus needs to be found a new place among the integrated

circuits and networks. Microgroups in their solidarity, voluntary movements and support groups, situational networks confirm a trend in narcissism, they do not contradict it . . . Narcissism is not distinguished
just by self-absorbed hedonism, but equally by the need to link up with
individuals who are 'identical', so as to be more effective certainly and
to campaign for new rights, but also for self-liberation, to resolve personal problems by articulating them through contact with others and
shared experience.[29]

And the purpose of such support groups is precisely that they provide
a forum for saying: '*Your* problem is *my* problem; the answer *you* come
up with is *my* answer too.' The more painful or complex the problem,
the more it involves extreme situations, the more vital the exchange.
Sickness, calamity, failure, death – once such scourges are no longer
resigned to as an inevitable part of human life – are necessarily seen as
appalling injustices and reversals to self-realization. In doing away with
the fatalism that distinguished traditional societies, modernism has re-
leased a huge creative potential within individuals and society, while at
the same time rendering individuals vulnerable to the sense of their own
limitations, which may be acute in periods of instability. At such times
resources that offer mutual comfort and support constitute the only
antidote to the often unbearable sense of isolation of having to stand on
one's own. They constitute an elementary form of what we have pointed
to as a form of social recognition of individual meaning.

Moreover, it has been observed that, alongside or in combination
with the tendency for like to associate with like, one of the main-
springs of this recognition is reference to a common lineage, and one
which is the more effective as and when social solidarity weakens. The
appeal to tradition and explicit reference to the continuity and authority of a shared past frequently accounts for the way voluntary groups
are set up and are able to endure; and it affords a source of compensation for the looseness of current social ties. Nor is it necessary for this
sense of continuity to be historically verified. It may be purely imaginary, so long as its recall is strong enough to allow identification to
build and preserve the social bond in question. Loyalty to the traditions of the Republic or of the Church, the proclamation of continued
attachment to ancestral values, the declared intention to return to the
authenticity of a past that is lost or deformed, serve to validate meaning bestowed on the present or on plans for the future.

It is in places where an imagined reference to tradition, which re-
emerges from modernity itself, encounters modern expressions of the
need to believe – linked to the endemic uncertainty of a society facing
constant change – that the religious productions of modernity come

into being. We shall take a closer look at this later on. For the moment, in reply to the question posed, it only needs to be said that the modern domain of religious believing is in no sense a residue in the world of modernity of a world that is obsolete. It has its source in the rationale of modernity, in the very movement by which modernity undermines the traditional foundations of institutionalized belief.

Back to the question of definition

The insistence on the process whereby religious belief is based on appeal to a line of witnesses (for all that the line may be dreamt up) again raises the question of the limits of religion. One of the aims of the task of definition carried out so far has been to maintain a clear distance from inclusive approaches to religion which are inclined to dissolve it into the totality of ultimate meanings. But would not making tradition the fulcrum of religious believing in the end produce the same result by incorporating anything society claims to be a heritage from the past into the sphere of religion?

It would certainly be a misunderstanding to conclude from what has just been argued that whatever has been socially transmitted must be included in the concept of religion. The definition we are proposing is much more precise, given that its three elements are closely adhered to – the expression of believing, the memory of continuity, and the legitimizing reference to an authorized version of such memory, that is to say to a tradition. In modern society, freed from the constraint of continuity which is characteristic of so-called traditional societies, tradition no longer constitutes an order constricting the life of the individual and society. Hence it no longer represents the unique matrix of expressions of believing that result from the uncertainties of living, which themselves are as characteristic of the human condition now as they were when human beings were defenceless and nature was hostile and mysterious. Hence there is no automatic overlapping of the fragmented world of believing and the equally fragmented world of tradition. This point need hardly be dwelt on further. On the other hand, before putting the proposed definition of religion to the test, two further implications must be considered.

The first implication can be expressed as follows: everything in modernity that has to do with tradition is not necessarily an integral part of believing, and therefore does not necessarily fall within the sphere of religion. Thus, for instance, all the know-how and expertise acquired through experience is vindicated because it stands the test of time. This is best illustrated by an example. Makers of string instruments who continue to apply ancestral techniques of treating wood do what they do, not in the name of a belief but of a practice that has been verified, that of the special quality these time-honoured methods bring to the sound of the instrument. Upholding the tradition is not valued in itself, or if it is, only secondarily, as is the special sense of complicity created between members of a guild who possess a secret in common, or else as is the cultural heritage such knowledge represents, and which is worth while preserving along with other equally esoteric knowledge. But what above all counts is the result obtained, in the absence of proof that more modern techniques are capable of producing at least comparable results. There is no occasion here for adding to the vast assortment of so-called implicit religions the case of the instrument-maker who says of himself: 'I've tried other ways, but this way has not been bettered.' Étienne Vatelot, with a world reputation as a string instrument-maker, shows no sign of an inclination to develop string instrument-making into a religious practice. Questioned recently about the mystery of the varnishes used by Stradivari, he had this to say:

> What secret? The varnish used by Stradivari was produced by a Cremona apothecary, proof of which is that all the varnishes used by string instrument-makers in Cremona have the same quality. If you go to Naples, they are quite different, the reason being that the humidity of the air is different; with the result that a violin needed the protection of harder varnishes. In Venice too, you'll find a more or less similar varnish used by all string instrument-makers, but different again from the one used in the other cities.[30]

The advice Vatelot is giving to young string instrument-makers is not to rediscover and copy the lost secret of the Stradivarius, but to perfect new products so that they can be as effective as possible in protecting and enhancing violins. The past does not furnish a model for reproduction, which as such would be unsurpassable. It merely affords proof that it is possible to achieve success with the means available at any given moment, and that is quite a different thing.

On the other hand, once the act of conforming to a recognized lineage becomes a passionately felt obligation and finds concrete expression in observance as a believer, the possibility arises that one is dealing with religion. Thus one would need to look closely at the case of a string instrument-maker who might say: 'For me this method is special because, when I apply it, I take on the gestures and even the spirit that enabled Stradivari or Guarneri or Amati to give life to violins whose perfection has never been equalled.' Confirming or denying the religious nature of whatever traditional practice can only come from a highly refined empirical exploration of each case to establish whether it shows signs of ideal-typically embodying religion. It is very likely that such an approach will only exceptionally produce a clear answer, so in most cases leaving one to conclude that religious features are there in a more or less marked degree. Clearly, an approach which consists in measuring the religious ingredient in terms of its degree of conformity to an ideal type removes us decisively from classifying religion into what is implicit or analogical on the one hand, and what is fully religious on the other, according to the substance of the beliefs conveyed.

The second implication can be put in the following way. Anything in our society which relates to believing does not necessarily relate to tradition, and hence cannot be attributed to what is implicitly or potentially religious. One can believe in progress, in science, in revolution, in a better tomorrow or in impending disaster. In each of these cases (and in that of any other referents), the work of the imagination can merge with the task of projection in extrapolating on the basis of known and established facts or of analysing change that has occurred or is currently occurring. But the evidence of past historical experience serves to justify rational projection of the future, it does not constitute, in principle at least, the invoking of a tradition that is validated by its own continuity.

The scientist who believes in the science he practises certainly recognizes himself as continuing a line. He sees himself as heir to Galileo, Newton, Pasteur, Einstein and so on, the heroic figures of modern science. But, aside from a mythological anomaly which would take him outside the sphere of science, it is not his belonging to this lineage that justifies his conviction that he will obtain a result; rather it is the proven certainty of the efficacy of the experimental and control methods which are those of his discipline and which enable him to innovate and to invent, just as they enabled his predecessors to do in the course of making their own discoveries. It could indeed be shown that belief in the inherent value of scientific method has sometimes been taken to the point of making it the condition of the authenticity of any discourse or action. This scientism which triumphed in the second half of the nineteenth century, in the writing of Ernest Renan and Marcellin Berthelot and others, has acquired in our own time, with someone like Jacques Monod, a new – but no less lyrical – formulation of the dream of scientific method reaching into all aspects of human behaviour and conditions.[31]

The unrestricted validity of the model of scientific knowledge has sometimes been presented as conferring a sacred quality on science, whereby scientism is equated with religion. We have already given our opinion about a too great readiness to establish correspondence between processes of conferring sanctity and processes of constituting a religion. It need only be remarked here that the scientist's recognition of what he owes to his predecessors and the will to preserve the memory of their work, as a legacy that is precious and valuable for his own endeavour, cannot constitute ends in themselves. If they did, and only then, could one speak of science having a religious extension (in which case we should be outside the sphere of science). But the scientific attitude in fact imposes the need to go beyond the kind of fidelity to forerunners that is self-justifying. It implies the need at any moment to break such fidelity should it contradict the rationality which is proper to the scientific process.

According to Gaston Bachelard, scientific thought requires constant conversion which calls into question the very principles of knowledge.[32] The dynamic nature of scientific knowledge, which even so implies belief in the values and potential of knowledge as such, is at bottom radically incompatible with the need to put an exclusive value on tradition, even on intellectual tradition. One knows the extent to which the inertia of the academic attitude in science has in the past worked – and can still work – against this dynamic. One knows also what established interests can, knowingly or unknowingly, be served by the religious anomaly of paying the respect due to the recognized authorities in science. Yet there are no grounds for applying the term 'religious' to the aspect of believing which attaches itself uncompromisingly to the exercise of scientific activity, inasmuch as it invariably looks beyond the present state of knowledge. The modern differentiation of social fields and institutions, each of which functions according to its own set of rules, also produces a differentiation in ways of believing proper to each of the fields, and in particular the ways in which, within such believing, the imaginary link with the past and projection into the future are joined. In our view, religion is only one of the figures in this pluralized world of believing, a figure characterized by the legitimizing exclusiveness of reference to tradition.

6

From Religions to the Religious

Any human activity, whatever it may be, calls for and gives rise to believing. Thus far, the course of our argument suggests that every activity secretes the particular form of believing it needs, just as every activity requires memory and imagination to be mobilized for its own development. From this standpoint, what is specific to religious activity is that it is wholly directed to the production, management and distribution of the particular form of believing which draws its legitimacy from reference to a tradition. But such specialized believing, itself the result of the modern differentiation between institutions, does not mean that every sphere of activity appropriates only one type of believing. It merely implies that a given social activity generates a particular, dominant, mode of believing. It does not however rule out that different modes of believing can coexist and even prosper in any one of the sectors from which they should, by rights, be banned on account of this very institutional specialization.

The instance of the religion of science, referred to above, shows the fluidity of believing, which may transcend the effects of institutional differentiation. Hence the concept of religion we have adopted may be said to present a practical interest to the extent that it constitutes an instrument with which to identify manifestations of religious believing in any social context whatever. To illustrate this statement and to give greater substance to the analytical method it spawns, it is worth pausing to consider an example from the world of sport which we have already touched upon. What we should like to know is whether the approach we have chosen allows us to dispose of the problems raised by describing the mass demonstrations that occur at major sports events as religious.

A second look at sport as a religion

An article by Marc Augé, commenting on a social study of football published in Britain, affords a good opportunity to reflect on the matter, even if the point of view of the author (who initially at any rate concedes that there is an essential link between the experience of the sacred and religion) appears to diverge theoretically from the position we have adopted here.[1] From the outset, Marc Augé distances himself from all analogical interpretations of sport as a religion. For him, 'the relationship between mass sport and religion is in no way metaphorical.' The very fact that the social functions of sport (the alienation or stimulation of mass involvement for example) can be evaluated in contradictory ways according to the situation seems to him significant in this respect. Applying the Durkheimian analysis of the social reality of football developed by Coles,[2] Augé points out that the relationship bears on the attitudes and practices, which are of more significance here than the substance of belief that pertains to them – the gathering of thousands of supporters and the excitement they generate, with the clapping, the cheering and the chanting in chorus, 'create the conditions for a recognizable perception of the sacred which is analogous to that evoked by Durkheim in respect of rites of atonement in Australia'. But Augé does more than simply repeat Coles's argument with the remark that the basis of the religious nature of sport consists in its affording a spectacle. Where Coles sought to identify behind the ritual event of the match something of a social protest symbolically expressed (young fans compensating for the barren prospects of their lives), Augé sets out to suggest a process in the production of meaning, appropriate to a modern society dispensing with its ancient gods.

> Western time is becoming organized – one can even say, structured – around activities which serve to give meaning to human life, inasmuch as they give perceptible social form to the individual expectations they help create. Football is not alone in the matter and an authentic ethnology of the western world would have to establish its place in relation to other institutions . . . In these places [stadiums], large-scale rituals are still performed, rehearsals which are also new beginnings . . . In the ritual of sport, expectation is fulfilled with the celebration itself: at the conclusion of official time, play will be over, but the future will have existed – a fragment of pure time, a Proustian grace for popular consumption. This future, swiftly consigned to what has gone before,

re-emerges as a possibility at regular stages. It is doubtless characteristic of a society and an era that these particles of time suffice to make us happy.[3]

Looking beyond the case of football, these remarks suggest a fresh way of approaching mass ritual occasions, big rock concerts, for instance. Indeed they take us to the heart of the problem. What Augé is describing is one of a number of places – a stadium united as one body, where, he says, a 'secular sacred' (*sacralité laïque*) in which 'day by day the west draws its life-force' is constituted. In his view, the emergence of this sacred quality is reinforced by the erosion of religions of salvation in societies where the 'problem of the ultimate destiny no longer haunts individual consciences'. Does Augé use the term 'secular' for the simple reason that this sacred quality obtains outside traditional religions? If so, one may conclude that this 'secular sacred' is at the source of a secular religion, which presents itself as a functional equivalent of these same traditional religions in a cultural arena where the question of salvation has lost its pertinence. Naturally, the secular religion is no less 'religious', in the eyes of the anthropologist, than the traditional religions it is replacing. The relationship between sport and religion is, strictly speaking, in no way metaphorical.

If one accepted this reading, Augé's remarks might be included among extensive functionalist approaches to modern religion. But in fact his argument reaches further. The particular nature of this mode of producing meaning, which operates in high-level competitive sport, is that it functions *in the moment*, in the immediacy of the gathering in a kind of corporate emotional awareness. In taking sport as representative of the instantaneous production of collective meaning, which in western societies goes along with individualistic atomization and the subjectivization of systems of meaning, Augé is suggesting that the shift which is taking place from traditional religions towards these new forms of the sacred serves to distinguish a transformation that goes beyond changes in the substance of belief and has to do with the very way in which meaning is produced.

In particular, the transformation shows itself in the immediacy of the circumscribed rituals which characterize sporting events. Of their own accord they fulfil the expectations they arouse. This is where, in our view, the major break occurs with the world of religion, a break which Augé does not remark upon, intent as he is to maintain the coupling of sport and religion. What ritual occasions in sport display in their very immediacy is in fact the dissociation, characteristic of modern societies, between sacredness (as collective experience of the presence of a force transcending individual consciousness and hence producing meaning) and religion (as ritualized remembering of a core lineage, in relation to which present experience constructs meaning).

Given this line of argument, one can put forward the notion that the significance of spectator sports in modern society is that they offer in small pieces (and in company with other manifestations – rock concerts, demos, telethons, etc.) access to an experience of the sacred (an immediate, emotional realization of meaning) which *en masse* no longer functions in the religious mode. Certainly, there is nothing metaphorical about the relationship between sport and religion, given that the production of meaning is central to both. But this production does not operate in the same way and the meaning produced is different, both in feature (for instance, in the time relation it occasions) and in substance. The ineffable experience of the surfer or mountaineer, the collective intoxication of football fans in the European Cup (which one knows, since Heysel, can lead to hooliganism), the ordeals of endurance, at times touching on martyrdom, that face competitors in the Tour de France, any such events which can be looked on as modern manifestations of the overwhelming experience of the sacred – *mysterium, fascinans et tremendum* – cannot, merely on account of this experience, be considered as religious manifestations, in the proper sense of the term (or rather in the ideal-typical sense which we have here adopted).

Which is not to say that, across the whole range of sport, religious features are not to be found. There is every justification for treating the celebration of the Olympic Games as a religion in the full meaning of the term: recall of how the games originated with the carrying of the flame kindled at Olympia, and constant invocation of the founding vision and the 'loyalty' it imposes on those who are now entrusted with organizing the games,[4] convey meaning and legitimacy to the rites and celebrations which, as much as the exploits themselves, give solemnity to the event. And it is by reference to the line of heroes that the ideal of the amateur is constructed and reconstructed – over and above the technical, economic and mass-media pressures of competitive sport, an ideal with the merit it attaches to asceticism and abnegation, and with its ethos of collective participation, itself more highly prized than victory ('what matters is not to win but to take part') and so on. The mystique attaching to high mountain-climbing might also be recognized as being in the same category, or to equitation or to sailing, when practised at a high level and free from commercial considerations.

Such appraisals are readily made and their sociological reach is limited. Analysis of extreme situations in which the instantaneous meaning afforded by major sports events assumes a genuinely religious meaning allows a far more subtle appreciation of the way in which sport, in itself not a vehicle of religion, can come to impart religious observance and beliefs. This is well brought out in the fine study made by Grace Davie into the repercussions on the Liverpool fans and on their city of the disaster which cost the lives of ninety-five of their number at Hillsborough at the start of the semi-final against Nottingham Forest on 15 April 1989.[5] An occasion for celebration suddenly turned to horror, with consequences that were felt everywhere. In Liverpool itself, where football occupies a special place in popular culture, religious services commemorating the victims were attended by half a million people from the city and its surroundings. The banner of the football club served as an altar cloth and the song associated with the club, 'You'll never walk alone', was adopted as an anthem.

But it was not so much that the song chanted on the terraces found its way into the church services that was the surest sign of the transmutation (to which the words of the song were peculiarly apposite). The decisive moment in this religious consecration of the grief felt in Liverpool took place on the football ground, not in Sheffield where the match was to be played, but at Anfield, a shrine of Liverpool football. Without anyone summoning them, fans and supporters in their thousands filed for hours across the turf where they had shared in the fever of past matches and which was now carpeted with flowers. The players and their families came there too of their own accord to guide and accompany the crowd. Remembrance of the victims, who had become heroes and martyrs of a community united by the same ordeal, gave a new and decisive dimension to the chanting of the famous anthem, itself borrowed from a well-known 1960s pop group, though originating from a Broadway musical in 1945. The Anfield pilgrims, as they were dubbed by the media, outnumbering the fans who regularly followed their team, were a family of a million people, whose sense of loss produced a bond between them, which was reinforced by their love of the city, mediated by their attachment to the team. It comes as no surprise to read of one magazine describing Anfield as the third cathedral along with the Anglican and Roman Catholic cathedrals. But Grace Davie shows conclusively that what was celebrated was not the cult of some religion or other of football, equivalent to and competing with conventional religions. It represented a sense of belonging, forged by the history lived through, the ordeals confronted, the economic difficulties and the struggles of working people, a spirit peculiar to the people of Liverpool whereby each individual has the sense of belonging to an old family.[6] In turning fervour into tribulation, what Hillsborough revealed was not that there existed in Liverpool a religion of football, but that the highly particular local conditions har-

boured religious potentialities which found expression in major sporting events – a very different thing.

How then does this potentially religious dynamic mesh with the
emotional experience, mentioned by Augé at the start of his article as
being akin to the collective experience described by Durkheim as experience of the sacred? Perhaps we can now give a more definite reply
to the question that was left in abeyance at the end of chapter 3. The
point has more than once been made that the ambiguity of the discussion on secular religions of whatever category lies in the barrier which
constantly divides the experience of the sacred, namely the experience
of encountering a force and a presence that is stronger than self, and
religion, which has to do with the constitution of a chain of belief. The
dimension of sacredness and the dimension of religiosity (taking them
both in this precise sense) clearly can cross. It happens frequently,
which is why they have been so continuously linked with each other.
And the fact that a religion is prompted to present as absolute, insur-
mountable, definitive and exclusive the foundational events to which
it relates the establishment of the line of belief that defines it, willy-
nilly leads it to lay claim to a monopoly of contact with the sacred
(which it makes it its business to define). The idea that is still alive, for
instance among sociologists of religion, according to which sacredness and religion cannot in the end but occupy the same space, is in
fact an ideological fiction, with which the efforts of religious institutions to preserve their monopoly of the production of meaning is by
no means unconnected. But it is one thing to bring to light ways of
mobilizing the sacred variously deployed by traditional religions; and
quite another to make of religion as such the exclusive channel for
experiencing the sacred, and to make of the experience of the sacred,
as such, the source and principle of all religion.

Two ways of thinking

In fact, a perfect coinciding of the two dimensions of sacredness and
religiosity ideally can only be conceived in traditional societies, in which
religion constitutes the exclusive code of meaning. Modern society, by
contrast, pluralizes ways of producing meaning and causes their increasing dissociation. Sacredness still constitutes in modern societies
one of the possible methods of organizing collective meaning in terms
of which human beings make sense of their existence. Essentially it
finds expression in the absolute – sacred – character conferred on objects, symbols or values, which crystallize the feeling of radical dependence experienced, individually and/or collectively, in emotional

contact with an external force. Religion corresponds to another system of organizing meaning, based upon identification with a chain or line of belief.

The overlapping of these two systems of meaning accords with the two types of religious domination which, according to Weber, characterize premodern societies: traditionalist domination, on the one hand, which 'takes as its foundation the sacred character of everyday life' and which gives absolute character to continuity as such; and, on the other, charismatic domination which 'rests on the sacred character or value of what goes beyond the everyday', and which, through the interplay of prophetic disruption and routine, enables change to be acclimatized in the world of tradition.[7] In modern societies, the experience of the sacred may be made to serve a religious ideal of continuity in belief, but the linking of the two dimensions is no longer automatic, nor even necessary. What sport (and other domains) well exemplify is that, in modern society, the form of experience that is known by the term 'sacred' may occur outside any religion. Conversely, one might develop the notion that the autonomous nature of the experience of the sacred has only become possible because traditional religions in the west, in their response to rationalism, gradually dissociated themselves from concepts of sacred cosmization with which religion identified in a world governed by tradition. Hence the Weberian analysis of the religious process of the disenchantment of the world brings together, like different aspects of the same path, the coming of an ethical religion (which is given historical validity first in Jewish prophesying, then in the various Christian views of asceticism, both in and outside the world) and the desacralization of a world conceived of as a field for the exercise of human freedom. And the development of a *historic* perception of a world where human beings personally choose whether or not to respond to the divine offer of a covenant[8] contains within itself the ferment of a radical criticism of any form of hieratic order.

At the same time, the process of rationalization works within religious groups themselves as a factor eliminating – or partially excluding – emotional experience in which a community is made aware of the immediate presence of the divine. Here one calls to mind Weber's remarks concerning the penetration of the legal-rational form of domination into the hierocratic grouping which the Church is (and it may be observed that, in alluding to this third type of domination in the sphere of religion, Weber leaves aside any mention of the relationship with the sacred this implies). Within the Church, pastor and priest conduct their office according to abstract rules. As employees of an institution, they exercise their command in the name of an impersonal norm, and not on behalf of a personal authority.[9] Insofar as it implies the erosion of the emotive dimension of adherence to the person of the one who incarnates the chain of belief, this rationalization of religious power is one element that denotes the erosion, or partial erosion, of the presence of the emotive experience of the sacred in the apparatus of religion. Such erosion, it needs to be said, does not mean that the Church has given up defending its social monopoly for producing and managing the symbolic assets and collective experience to which it gives the name of sacred. But it is precisely because the sacred and religion no longer coincide that defining and determining the sacred, in all societies which have cast off the hold of tradition, has become a prize in the struggle between all institutions (Church and state and its various offshoots) in a sphere of symbolism that is increasingly open and competitive.

Hence the gradual separation between the sacred and religion is a process that started long ago with the emergence of modernity itself. But it is fully developed in the more advanced modern societies in which the two are no longer synonymous. In these societies the emotional experience of a 'we' transcending the individual conscience has not disappeared. But it can intervene in any sphere of human activity (including, of course, the sphere earmarked by society as the sphere of religion). And if one likes, there is no reason why such manifestations should not be thought of as representing the modern experience of a fragmented sacred, provided it is clear that no automatic implication necessarily links the experience with a chain of belief, which should be seen as the source of any religion.

Is the notion of a religious sphere still a helpful one?

Such an approach to religion, as we have seen in connection with sport, provides a means of discovering how, outside the sphere formally assigned to traditional religions, the properly – not metaphorically – religious dimension which any social phenomenon can generate becomes manifest. One may then ask whether, in this new perspective, the notion of religious field still remains pertinent and can still denote a comparable group of phenomena. To be able to answer this, one needs to reconsider the various ways in which sociologists of religion resort to this notion.

In its general acceptance, the notion of religious field has emerged, at the same time as theories of secularization were developed, to denote the outcome of the process whereby modern societies provide religion with its own strictly limited space. According to the paradigm which governs these theories, rationalization has cost religion its claims to govern society as a whole, and it finds itself forced back into a specialized social sphere, with the task of producing and treating symbolic assets,[10] appropriate to religious institutions, which are designated for the purpose. In this specially appointed sphere, religion wears a compact, organized, formalized appearance.

But, as the evidence shows, the generalized tendency to corral religion in no way excludes its presence in areas of social activity outside its control, either because such areas bear traces of having once been under the sway of religion and of having emancipated themselves, or because the non-religious rationale proper to each of these areas sometimes produces the very element that is supposed to be alien to it, a religious element. This fluid quality in religious and non-religious processes criss-crossing the frontiers of institutional fields that have been demarcated by modernity is all-pervasive. Manifestations of believing may occur in political, scientific or artistic fields, but science, politics, economics, aesthetics and so on, in return, work the so-called religious field. Sociological analysis of institutional differentiation lays stress on the trend towards autonomy in the different spheres of social activity, on the specific nature of their mental climate, and on the resulting social and cultural repression of the religious field, to wit religious institutions.

Our present intention is to try to dissociate religion from its institutional, more specialized, aspects and to trace the way it has fragmented across the social spectrum; and this may involve showing how the very fact of this mainstream specialization means that religious expression in social, cultural, even scientific spheres has been occluded or become invisible. The concept of religious field would be ambiguous or misleading if it assumed that fields were so demarcated as to be shut off from each other, frustrating hope of tracing ways in which religion operates across society. Hence, so as not to reduce religious modernity to the space reserved for traditional religions, we shall refer to these as institutionalized or (adopting an Anglo-American usage) conventional religion. In any event, the aim is not to demarcate – or demarcate anew – the place of religion in modernity, but rather to avoid being led into thinking of the role of religion in terms of the hard core of traditional faiths which are supposed to be central to it. Their assumed centrality means that the social sphere of religion is more often than not represented by a series of concentric circles, variously graded, with traditional – that is to say, generally Christian – faiths (for which, in France, read Catholicism) occupying the centre and with a loss of definition as one moves outwards.

The notion of religious field, as developed by Pierre Bourdieu in the context of a general theory of social fields, clearly raises a different type of problem. It forms part of a theoretical system within which – together with other notions, such as *habitus* or capital, with which it is rigidly linked – it serves an overall view of the principle governing relations within society; and discussion of the concept in the meaning given it by Bourdieu has no relevance if divorced from the system. Within the system, the religious field, like any social field, is defined as 'a network, or a configuration, of objective relations between positions'. It is governed by distinctive rules which social actors are in varying degrees adept in applying, 'according to the situation (*situs*) they occupy in the structure of the distribution of species of power (or capital) whose possession commands access to the specific profits that are at stake within the field'.[11] It is one of the 'relatively autonomous social microcosms', which 'are the site of a logic and a necessity that are specific and irreducible to those that regulate other fields', the fields taken together constituting the social cosmos of highly differentiated societies.[12]

Belief – belief in the importance of the enterprise and in the value of the stakes; belief in the validity of (their) dispossession which is instilled in those who are most dispossessed of the aptitudes and skills which determine the relative position of the players competing in each field, etc. – is a dimension of every field. It is requisite in order that social actors should want to be actively involved in the enterprise. But, with the religious field, belief is both a constituent principle – causing it to exist as it does – and a dynamic principle, operating through the struggles that take place, *ad intra et ad extra,* for the control of legitimate belief. The constitution of an autonomous religious field is described as 'the end result of the administration of the benefits of salvation being monopolized by a body of specialists, recognized by society as exclusive possessors of the specific competence required for the production and reproduction of a deliberately organized corpus of secret – hence rare – knowledge'. It implies dispossession of those, the laity (*laïcs*), the non-professionals, who are excluded from such recognition.[13] The opposition between professionals (*clercs*), who possess the monopoly of administering the assets of salvation, and non-professionals which, for Bourdieu, lies at the source of the sacred–profane dichotomy provides the structure of the religious field. It crystallizes conflicting interests which reveal the need felt by socially differentiated groups and classes to legitimize properties attaching to one or another type of conditions of existence.

The problem inherent in this approach is that religion is reduced to a single function, that of consecrating the social order as a structure governing relations between groups and classes.[14] But this critique could only be followed through if it came within a larger critique of society from which it draws coherence. Such a conception of the religious field rules out from the start any chance of allowing religion to have any reality outside the institutional structure where group and class interests are converted into religious interests. The question of religion, as a system of meanings produced by groups of men and women, is totally taken up by the question of the social determination of the division of labour affecting institutionalized religion, of which the Catholic model of relations between professionals and non-professionals provides the permanent reference. The questions raised by Bourdieu's presentation of the religious field are indeed helpful and potent in considering the struggle for control of the legitimate tradition within the Christian faith. They are less readily applicable in the case of monotheistic religions, such as Judaism or Islam, in which the contrast between professional and non-professional is less formalized. But they have little practical value in assessing the religious ingredient in social phenomena that have little surviving connection, or an increasingly distant connection, with traditional religions as strictly understood. And they are of little assistance in analysing trends in secular modernity that show the production and circulation of religious-symbolic assets to be moving relentlessly away from institutional control.

From the sociology of religion to the sociology of the religious: a political example

However, our task is to see whether we cannot develop another method to enable us to trace the dissemination of religion in society that has occurred while traditional faiths themselves are confined to the specialized field of conventional religion. Clearly, this aim would be a limited one if it set out to do no more than make use of the ideal-typical definition of religion we have adopted to identify religious features in the world of sport or politics or the arts and so on. The clarity thus brought into discussion of secular, diffuse or invisible religions would certainly not be served by providing an interminable list of examples as evidence of the current scale of religious fragmentation. The basic question here concerns the factors which in specific historical circumstances cause such features to emerge, to crystallize and perhaps to become organized in the form of a religion. Once it is accepted that the dimension of believing, which is present in all human activity, can assume a religious form and be an essential ingredient in phenomena we can term religions, the really interesting question concerns the transition of virtual into actual religious believing, and so even to an organized religion. Manifestly, it is a question that cannot call for a general reply since each case involves consideration of the social, political or cultural context that allows the legitimizing reference to a chain of belief to be substantially reinvested in areas which have formed independently by breaking away from the hold of tradition. But in the political context at least it has led to much reflection, on a par indeed with the general issues that follow from the religious contamination of believing within the field of politics.

To speak of contamination is immediately to suggest that the development of a religious ingredient to believing in the area of politics is perverse and destructive, a sickness induced in politics with an overall effect that is socially pathological. Certainly the problem is seen in these terms by many political thinkers who, for the most part, have in mind the grotesque political caricature provided by the climax of the communist dream of a total political stake in society. For many of them, this is where the pursuit of a line of thought cuts across a career as militant, so that intellectual and personal elements became inextricably mixed.

In a recent essay, Emmanuel Terray has dwelt cogently on the self-questioning which followed events in eastern Europe in the autumn of 1989 among those who wondered whether for years they had not sacrificed 'their intelligence and energy to defending the indefensible'.[15] And in fact the answers he gives to such questioning spring from an analysis of the religious deviation taken by communism and of the 'process of establishing a clerical order which the workers' communist movement espoused at the end of the nineteenth century and which it never departed from'.[16] Terray does not dwell much on formal and ideological affinities between the Christian (Catholic) religion and facets of the direction taken and practice observed by revolutionary organizations, which frequently go to feed religious sociologies of communism. He merely remarks on the way such affinities might make it easier for young people with a Christian upbringing to engage as militants. At the same time he makes the point powerfully that the religious metamorphosis of communism was inherent neither in its nature nor in its heredity, and that Marx's thinking, in its complexity and its ambiguities, only became transformed into religious doctrine in the course of its implementation. Such considerations place the inquiry into the character of communism as a secular religion in its proper light, as neither being analogical nor metaphorical, nor involving identifying a substance of core belief as religious, but as a historical process which brought about a religious mutation in political believing.

Emmanuel Terray defines this mutation as the consequence of 'a divorce and two omissions'[17] – the divorce from science, and the disregard both of the individual and of politics itself. Divorce from science occurred early on, in the first years of the twentieth century, with the political application of Marxism as a guide and weapon for action taking precedence over an 'attitude of humility, expectation and open-mindedness in respect of new forms of rationality', which properly speaking is the scientific attitude. Marxism became a myth, at once 'a machine for ideas and an expression of the convictions of a group in the language of mobilization'. And the encasing of Marxism as myth entails both the failure to take account of the individual, consideration of whose needs and aspirations are simply postponed until society changes, and of politics, where the same deterministic conception of society finally led to a prohibition being placed on any consideration of its specificity and autonomous development.

Marxism became a doctrine, a closed code of meaning, whose orthodox interpretation was elaborated by a group of experts (*clercs*) and made binding upon militants. These faithful internalized the validity of their political dispossession the more successfully inasmuch as it was subsumed in an overall view of the world which allowed them to number themselves among the righteous in mortal struggle with the unrighteous, consisting of all who stand out against the truth defined from above. The religious deviation of Marxism, in Terray's presentation, is nurtured by an internal perversion of politics that destroys its autonomous self-instituting capability. This perversion is implicit in the process by which politics, with the objective of collective mobilization, makes itself out to be the declared truth of society and of history. The 'already there' of power devoured the 'not yet' of utopia. Human beings who awaited the Kingdom, in Loisy's phrase, encountered only the Church.[18]

The paradox is that the self-destruction of politics is revealed in the statement that everything is political. The claim to be all-inclusive is accompanied by a process whereby reference to a predefined meaning of history gradually destroys society's ability to determine and follow through its policies. In such a context the only possible political struggle involves promoting an equally wide-reaching, equally absolute alternative to the referential myth. Patrick Michel has shown conclusively, in the case of Poland, how the underlying absolutist principle in politics, as it was implemented in Soviet-type regimes, finally came up against the one category, God, it could not incorporate for fear of granting it, negatively even, unacceptable reality.[19] This being so, Catholicism presented itself as a factor both in the removal of the Soviet system and in restoring a sense of autonomy to the individual simply because it was instrumental in the removal of absolute social control.

In a sense the determination to exercise absolute religious control over society which motivates Polish Catholicism, itself shaped by the markedly anti-modern intransigence of Rome, turned out to be the best of battering rams in attacking the Marxist fortress; and one can imagine that the emergence of democratic modernity in an arena thus cleared of politics viewed as religion was not thereby made any easier. The essential point here for our concerns is that the case of Poland, whose recent history is condensed in the confrontation of two integralist systems – one (claiming to be) religious, the other, political – presents an enlarged and remarkably illuminating instance of a political and a religious principle reciprocating one another which an analogical approach constantly attempts to define.

Recognition of this principle has produced much philosophical and anthropological reflection which need not detain us here, beyond causing us to remark that what is at stake is the very question of the political factor when the conviction that it might be extended to include the exercise of coercion is challenged, a conviction itself typically modern since it is linked entirely with the emergence of an omnipresent state.[20] To consider that politics has to do with how human beings live together, the way in which 'human beings make sense of their togetherness',[21] is to see it as a fundamental dimension of the working of the symbolic in society, to which it owes the particular form it takes (in the shape of a system of government). And at the same time the relationship between politics and religion is organized round this symbolic function, in different ways, of course, in terms of the response that each society provides to the essential question of society's basis.

The complexity of the response lies in the whereabouts between two extremes which correspond ideal-typically to two modes of dissolving tension between the political and the religious. With the traditional extreme, the religious response to the question of the basis of society encompasses the political response: the original myth from which the symbolic world of the group derives gives total meaning to the organization of relations in the context of power and their day-to-day working. With the modern extreme, the political response to the question of the basis of society dissolves any possible religious response by interpreting this meaning as the indefinitely open and inevitably multiple result of never-ending collective development. Between these two extremes – where the contrast can only be described as radical if one makes the point that they are ideal-typical, the history – and religious genesis[22] – of political modernity runs its course. The path taken contains the emergence of a society of individuals whose association is no longer represented as inherent, but as a construct that has been collectively willed and brought about. Democracy affords it the space that suits it best, a space described by Claude Lefort as 'indeterminate'.[23]

A major problem posed by the political anthropology of the modern world concerns the increasing tension that has developed in western societies between the process of rationalization which takes in the political element (its other side being represented by the secularization of the world) and the process of individualization linked to it, but which destroys the possibility, from inside, that the meaning collectively arrived at can bind each member of society in respect of the others. What constitutes the foundation of obligation in a society of individuals? In a society which gives precedence to individual autonomy and, within certain limits, to the right of individuals to self-determination, how can a measure of interdependence be established and accepted without which there are no social bonds? In his analysis of *La Révolution des droits de l'homme*, Maurice Gauchet has shown clearly how the question of an 'imperative transcendence of the viewpoint of the whole which cannot be reduced to the sum of individual wills' reemerged, in the deliberations of members of the *Convention* of 1793, on the very issue of the affirmation of rights establishing a society of individuals who themselves are subject to the principle of reciprocity. This principle, he writes, 'defines the restrictions which arise from the rights of others, it does not provide active scope for the respect due to them. This is where the notion asserts itself that a corresponding motive force, so to speak matching the horizontal plane of individuality, can only come from the vertical relationship with an absolute.'[24] As is well known, the argument in favour of recourse to transcendence led the revolutionaries of 1793 into a constitutional dictatorship in which the collective will was held to be the embodiment of the individual wills. The example clearly serves as a useful interpretation of other historical situations, raising the question whether compulsory recourse to transcendence is not the point at which the religious recoding of modern politics inexorably comes into play; and knowing further as one does that a society in which such recoding can no longer occur (hence where politics is reduced to arbitrating conflicts between interest groups) is a society in which social ties, thus society itself, are equally bound to come apart.

The sociological definition of religion we have adopted clearly is of limited scope in regard to the anthropological, philosophical and political issues here raised. But at least it may render a service in preventing reference to the absolute – transcendent – character of this or that value in the social and political order becoming a vector for the religious perversion of politics. The – ever pejorative – consideration of the necessarily religious character of any reference to transcendence corresponds in fact to the same argument which, in a general acceptance of modernity as implying the 'independence of the individual in his or her private life',[25] would exclude the modern affirmation of self and the recognition of mutual dependence between this autonomous self and the other members of society. Both cases illustrate a distortion of the notion of autonomy, whose history in the development of modernity has been well analysed by Alain Renaut and shown by him to be far from inevitable.[26] The reference to transcendent values, meaning that as an individual one's position is relativized regarding that of others, thus affording positive recognition of one's obligations to others as a means of realizing one's own humanity, is not in itself a religious reference. Nor, in our view, does it become so, if recourse to transcendence places at the source of such off-centring of the individual the consideration that a radical otherness – that of God – is the basis for the recognition of others.

It may, on the other hand, become so, without any reference to God at all, when and if political society sees itself as the manifestation here and now of the utopian community, itself implicitly at least a part of the movement by which such transcendent values are taken as indicators. The process of self-destruction in politics occurs when politics sets about introducing the utopia that occupies its imaginative horizon and its spiritual destiny, a destiny it seeks to make concrete in the here and now in a political system which claims to be its visible, total expression. As one knows, the institutional formalization of an egalitarian utopia has invariably led to the authoritarian levelling of society, just as the dream of creating a truly free society has led to condoning the worst forms of enslavement. Every attempt to set up a utopian community as such, remarks Marc Richir, 'is bound to degenerate into establishing its antithesis, an object of totalitarian, terrorist fantasy'.[27] This political distortion presents a (potentially) religious character each time it implies confining the social imagination in the constantly recurring recall of a point of origin which contains within it all possible manifestations of utopia. Utopia is thus robbed of its capacity to revitalize and renew itself, a capacity which stems precisely from the profusion – and incompleteness – of its manifestations. The religious character is fully realized (as a secular religion) when the legitimate interpretation of the core event, the experience of revolution for instance, is appropriated by a community of professionals (the Party, for instance) which controls, by force and/or persuasion, the conditions in which the body of society and its individual members are obliged to relate to the tradition in which utopia is thereafter confined.

Likening the confinement of political utopia within a self-enclosed tradition to a process of glaciation may seem to contradict what has been said in a previous chapter about the potential for innovation

contained in tradition through the constant recomposing imparted to
it by memory. Indeed, it may be remarked that certain ways of appealing to a core lineage so as to reinvigorate the exercise of politics may,
through there being a degree of religious fallout in the political arena,
involve reviving the utopian dynamic. One could point to instances of
the potential utopian dialectical process in politics and religion (not to
be confused with the utopian dialectical process at work in politics or
in certain religions, Christianity for example), in a certain way of invoking the necessary continuity of the revolutionary or republican tradition, through loyalty to the secular, anticlerical principle or the respect
due to the founding fathers of democracy (cases applying to France
and the United States), respect also for the constitution or for socialism or European unification and so on, all this by contrast with the
everyday business of politics. Big commemorative occasions, such as
the festivities that accompanied the centenary of the Statue of Liberty
in New York harbour or, in particular, the ceremonies marking the
bicentenary of the French Revolution, are prime examples of the utopian religious dimension working in politics. Generally speaking, the
function of any civil ritual (frequently ineffectual on account of the
routine character it acquires) is to make use of a special occasion to
lay emphasis on a religious dimension that is normally dormant in
politics,[28] in order to reconstitute collective consciousness of the continuing lineage in which the body politic is rooted and give a new
stimulus to a utopian tension – all too often absorbed by drab routine
– by means of the innovative power of memory.

But one could find yet further instances of the inhibiting of the political imagination on the part of professional theorists occasioned by
providing an *authorized* version of how the core lineage should be
related to. Clearly, the history of communism offers the outstanding
example – the most dramatic one too in terms of human cost – of the
enclosing by dogma of a sterilized tradition, removed from any possibility of discussion by a corps of guardians who assume the exclusive
right to dictate the truth of the moment and the meaning of the future.[29]
Here it is impossible to ignore the analysis developed by Annie Kriegel.
And one is forced to ask oneself whether the religious deviation in
politics does not reveal something of the inescapable totalitarian propensity of religion, a propensity realized – or whose realization is threatened beneath the breaches opened up by prophecy or charisma – in
the constraint imposed by dogma and the policing of conscience, associated with the obligatory conformism contained in any system founded
on the authority of a tradition.

The only way of ensuring that this question does not become purely
polemical is to reformulate it in terms of a religious sociology of poli-

tics which naturally brings new light to bear on the sociology of traditional religions. This is not to make a covert return to the analogical approach, but on the contrary to recognize that the presence of the religious, taken in its full sense, in the political means that politics is susceptible to the same methods of analysis as are applied to the social phenomena chiefly defined by this dimension of religion, to wit established religions. And what major religions abundantly show is that, where this autocratic tendency exists, its aims are developed in two directions: *ad extra*, in a comprehensive search for a way of imposing an all-pervading control over religion; and *ad intra*, in the form of segregating those who participate actively in the chain of belief. Articulation of the external dimension (towards the world) and of the internal dimension (towards the faithful) of this absolutist principle is achieved using various models which, in part at least, command different types of religious adherence. For instance, by applying the typical Troeltschian opposition, one may consider that the Church puts initial emphasis on external control, in order to ensure that its social compromise reaches as far as possible into political and cultural life. On the other hand, the sect, characterized by its indifference to worldly cultural and political pursuits, is less insistent on external than on internal control, through the total commitment it requires of its followers.

Apart from this typical, simplified contrast between Church and sect, the problem is invariably that of discovering the degree to which a religious group is subject to the tension, which can become explosive, between integralism *ad extra*, which in different ways involves conforming with tradition through expansion, and integralism *ad intra*, an intensive application of tradition. However, it should not be overlooked that this dual rationale indicating a contradiction at the heart of all forms of religious integralism does not find a place in theology. It is a *social* rationale and its development is determined by the social, hence also cultural, conflicts that take place within religious conflicts. These conflicts embrace both the interpretation of the core tradition and the designation of the authority properly empowered to supply this interpretation. The question of how the notion of integralism is applied to religious belief, as both an individual and a collective obligation, that is through extending an institutional hold or, conversely, through complete withdrawal, by means of community exemplariness or the promotion of asceticism among believers, this remains as much an issue to be resolved by conflict as a matter for theology. Again this is a dual conflict, having an external aspect (relations between the religious group and its environment) and an internal one (the changing configuration of social positioning within the group).

A sociology of socioreligious protest, with its source in Weber[30] and a field covering religious sects and orders, messianic and millennial preoccupations, revivalism and charismatic movements and the like, has for some time been concerned to throw light on the complex dialectics intrinsic to the social and religious issues in these conflicts. Through these conflicts the dual principle of religious authoritarianism opens up new forms of social compromise which produce multiple readings of the foundational text, thus setting up new representations of the authentic chain of belief. Equally, a sociological study of orthodox religious functioning is needed to shed light on the social rationale of clerical reinforcement to a point where the legitimizing reference to tradition is transformed into a totalitarian apparatus of meaning. A compound of different approaches should lay the basis for a religious sociology of politics that would not be a comparative sociology of organizations (or ideologies, or militant practice, etc.) condemned to a limitless analogical identification of religious deviancy in politics and political deviancy in religion, but a true sociology of the religious in politics. In a wider sense, the extension of such a perspective to those social phenomena where the need for believing may cut across processes of establishing and/or invoking a tradition should enable the sociology of religion to be constituted at last as the sociology of the religious.

III

A break in the chain

7

Religion Deprived of Memory

By placing tradition, that is to say reference to a chain of belief, at the centre of the question of religion, the future of religion is immediately associated with the problem of collective memory. The possibility that a group – or an individual – sees itself as part of a chain or lineage depends, to some extent at least, on mention of the past and memories that are consciously shared with and passed on to others. Yet one of the chief characteristics of modern societies is that they are no longer societies of memory, and as such ordered with a view to reproducing what is inherited. However wary one may be of making a rigid distinction between societies of memory and societies of change, it is perfectly reasonable to point out how the evidence of social, cultural and psychological continuity is eroded through the effect of change. Change, which is a function of modernity itself, has resulted in modern societies being less and less able to nurture the innate capacity of individuals and groups to assimilate or imaginatively to project a lineage of belief.

The empirical sociology of religious phenomena has long insisted on the significance of this characteristic discontinuity in modern societies. With theorists of secularization – especially those influenced by the opposition between community and society in Tönnies's classic formulation – preoccupations are similar, given the consequences of disappearing natural communities, such as families and villages, on religious socialization and, further, on the likelihood of a genuine religious sociability taking shape in modern societies.[1] But theories of secularization, which have tended to view the relations between religion and modernity from the perspective of rationalization, have seldom placed the question of memory at the centre of their analysis. Yet there are grounds for thinking that consideration of the contemporary transmutation of memory, related to commitment to a chain of belief which is specific to believing in the religious sense, may be at least equally fruitful in the analysis of religious modernity. The purpose of this chapter is to explore this assumption in a general way before putting it to the test in the context of French Catholicism.

Memory and religion: a structural connection

In the perspective that we have adopted, all religion implies that collective memory is mobilized. In traditional societies where the domain of religious symbolism is structured entirely by a myth of creation, which accounts for the origin of both the world and the group, collective memory is given: it is totally contained within the structures, organization, language and everyday observances of tradition-based societies. In the case of differentiated societies where established religions prevail and where distinctive communities of faith emerge, collective religious memory is subject to constantly recurring construction, so that the past which has its source in the historical events at its core can be grasped at any moment as being totally meaningful. To the extent that the entire significance of the experience of the present is supposed to be contained, potentially at least, in the foundational events, the past is symbolically constituted as an immutable whole, situated 'outside time', that is outside history. In the Jewish and Christian traditions, the religious wresting of the past from history is given privileged significance by the core events being magnified in time; and this at once opens up the possibility of the utopian anticipation of the end of time. The symbolic integration of time takes on other forms in different traditions (in eastern religions, for instance), but all of them have at their base the essentially *normative* character of religious memory.

This normative dimension to memory is not of itself specific to religious memory. It characterizes any collective memory which forms and endures through the processes of selective forgetting, sifting and retrospectively inventing. Of its essence fluid and evolutionary, collective memory functions as a regulator of individual memory at any one moment. It even takes the place of individual memory whenever it passes beyond the memory of a given group and the actual experience of those for whom it is a reference. This cultural memory which is more extensive than the memory of any particular group incorporates – and constantly reactivates and reconstructs – the currents of thought which have outlasted past experiences and which are newly actualized in the present. In the interpretation given by Halbwachs, this insep_arably creative and normative dynamic function of collective memory is engendered by society itself.[2]

In the case of religious memory, the normativity of collective memory is reinforced by the fact of the group's defining itself, objectively and subjectively, as a *lineage* of belief. And so its formation and repro_ductiveness spring entirely from the efforts of memory feeding this self-definition. At the source of all religious belief, as we have seen, there is belief in the continuity of the lineage of believers. This conti_nuity transcends history. It is affirmed and manifested in the essen_tially religious act of recalling a past which gives meaning to the present and contains the future. The practice of *anamnesis*, of the recalling to memory of the past, is most often observed as a rite. And what charac_terizes a religious rite in relation to all other forms of social ritualization is that the regular repetition of a ritually set pattern of word and ges_ture exists in order to mark the passage of time (as well as the transi_ence of each individual life incorporated in the chain) with the recall of the foundational events that enabled the chain to form and/or affirm its power to persist through whatever vicissitudes have come, and will still come, to threaten it.

The cycle of Jewish feasts clearly provide a paradigm of the specific nature of religious ritual. But the point needs making that the ritual_ized practice of anamnesis is not only a feature of traditional religions; it also gives a religious dimension to secular ritual insofar as this (al_ways potential) dimension is actualized. Thus, the ritual element in politics takes on a specifically religious dimension whenever it assumes the function of reimbuing the routine experience of politics with the presence of the glorious memory of its source.[3] It will be rightly ob_jected that in some religions the element of ritual is slight. This is so with most Protestant sects, where only ritual that conforms strictly with the Scriptures is preserved. Criticism of ritual is taken to an ex_treme by the Quakers who meet on the first day of the week in order to seek Christ within themselves in total silence. But even here, as with religions that are without rites, Baha'i for example, where there is only the reading of or meditation on source texts, a form of anamnesis – but one without ritual – occurs in order to enable the religious group to form. The existence of such a practice, by means of which a group of believers signifies to itself and to the world outside its adherence to a continuing line of descent which gives entire justification to its rela_tionship with the present, is ground enough for considering that one is dealing with religion, not a form of wisdom or of morality, nor a philosophy of life.

The normativity specific to religious memory with regard to every experience of the present is inherent in the structure of the religious group. It acquires substance mostly in the unequal relationship that binds the simple believers – ordinary dependent participants in such remembrance – to the authorized producers of collective memory. Authorized memory develops and is passed on in different ways. It legitimates itself differently in accordance with the type of religious sociality proper to the group in question, and in accordance with the type of domination that prevails. The management of memory – if one takes Troeltsch's categories – differs with a church, a sect or a mystical group. The controlled mobilization of memory by a priesthood who are so ordained by a religious establishment differs from the charismatic mobilization of memory initiated by a prophet. But in all instances it is the recognized ability to expound the true memory of the group that constitutes the core of religious power.

This is not to say that religious memory presents a greater degree of unity and coherence than do other collective forms of memory – family, local, national and so on. Indeed, Halbwachs has insisted on the highly conflictual character of religious memory, combining, as it always does, a plurality of collective memories in a state of tension one with another. In his opinion, the main cause of conflict lies in the opposition between a rational, dogmatic type of memory (which he calls theological memory) and memory of a mystical nature. The two do not order the relationship with the foundational narrative in which the chain of belief is rooted in the same way. According to Halbwachs, whose position appears to be much influenced by Catholicism, the dogma of a religious group is nothing other than the culmination of a deliberate drive to achieve a unified religious memory:

> it [dogma] results from the superimposition and fusion of a series of successive layers and, as it were, so many phases of collective thinking; thus theological thought projects . . . successive views it has formed into the past. It reconstructs the edifice of religious truths on a number of planes, as if its work had been carried out on one single plane.[4]

By continuously homogenizing the various syntheses of memory already effected in the past, theological memory ensures the unity of religious memory in time and its actualization in the present, elements that are indispensable to the subjective realization of the chain of belief. At the same time it protects the chain from the disturbances caused by mystical memory and its pretension to reinstate the foundational event, the point of origin, in the immediate present through direct contact with the divine. One of the advantages of Halbwachs's analy-

sis of religious memory is to give prominence to the process of rationalization that accompanies the unifying effort of authorized memory.
Further, it illuminates the dialectic that develops between the emotive
and symbolic evocation of the chain (secured particularly in the liturgy) and the elaboration of a body of belief, adherence to which is
the formal condition of access to and participation in the chain. The
emotional intensity and symbolic richness in the ritual evocation of
the chain may vary considerably, in the same way as does the degree
of explicitness and formality of shared beliefs in the community of the
faithful in which the chain is actualized. But this dialectic, which one
can see as tradition in the act of becoming itself, constitutes in our
opinion the central dynamic of all religion.

The crumbling memory of modern societies

The question is to know whether this dynamic can still function in a
society in which the acceleration of change obliterates what might remain of 'integrated memory, dictatorial and unconscious of itself, organizing and all-powerful, spontaneously actualizing', for which Pierre
Nora reminds us, 'so-called primitive or archaic societies constituted
the model and took away the secret'.[5] For comprehensive social memory
the crisis came with the emergence and historical development of modernity. The affirmation of the autonomous individual, the advance of
rationalization breaking up the 'sacred canopies', and the process of
institutional differentiation denote the end of societies based on
memory. The fact of being able to differentiate between a family
memory, a religious memory, a national memory, a class memory and
so on is already a token of having left behind the pure world of tradition. The growth of secularization and the loss of total memory in
societies without a history and without a past coincide completely; the
dislocation of the structures of religion's plausibility in the modern
world works in parallel with the advance of rationalization and successive stages in the crumbling of collective memory.

  The differentiation of a specialized religious field, the gradual
pluralization of institutions, communities and systems of religious
thought historically – and exactly – correspond to the differentiation
of total social memory into a plurality of specialized circles of memory.
Industrialization, urbanization, the spread of trade and interchange
mark the waning of the social influence of religion and the piecemeal
destruction of communities, societies and even ideologies based on
memory; Pierre Nora signals their final eclipse under the impact of
globalization in all its forms, together with democratization, the com-

ing of mass societies and media encroachment. The more advanced societies are those in which one no longer finds even a minimal continuum of memory, those currents of thought in which Halbwachs identified the continuation in diluted form of the concrete living memory of multiple groups of humans and which he thought could still be reactivated in certain circumstances. In fact, the disintegration of collective memory in modern societies is the consequence of the conjunction of two trends that are only apparently contradictory.

The first is a tendency towards the expansion and homogenization of memory, resulting from the eclipse of the idiosyncrasies rooted in the collective memory of differentiated concrete groups. For Maurice Halbwachs, this amplification is closely linked to the advent of the bourgeoisie and the modern capitalist economy. The triumph of the bourgeoisie introduced a new fluidity, a liberty, into society, yet implied the destruction of a social framework that assured the transmission of collective memories from one generation to the next. 'Through growth based on every type of input, the bourgeoisie lost the power to establish itself as a hierarchy and set up a system of cadres in which future generations could find a place. The collective memory of the bourgeoisie lost in depth – in length – of memory what it gained in extent.'[6]

According to Halbwachs, the advent of capitalism and technology also signified the gradual alignment of all spheres of social life on the sphere of production, which itself only aroused technical, functionalized and neutral, memories; so that at the end of this homogenizing, functionalizing process, the memory of modern societies took on the aspect of surface memory, dull memory, whose normative, creative capacity seemed to have dissolved.[7] The loss of depth in collective memory which Halbwachs linked to the advance of the modern industrial economy is far more marked in image-fed societies with their developed systems of mass communication. The overabundance of information available at any moment tends to obliterate a meaningful continuity that would make such information intelligible. The image enables any event or any catastrophe wherever it occurs to be instantly available to all and in the process immediately neutralizes whatever preceded it, such is the effect of saturation. The immediacy of communication singles out the occurrence and inhibits its being brought into context.

The complexity of the world shown in the vast incoherent mass of available information is decreasingly amenable to being ordered in the more or less impromptu way that collective memory was able to achieve by finding explanatory links. Such links, it is true, contained much that was illusory or mistaken; they constituted the essence of the pre-conceptions which science in its analysis of reality was bound to cast out; but with all their frailty at least they afforded an immediate and effective basis for developing individual and collective systems of meaning. When this interpretative process collapsed under the onslaught of the scientific method, it was replaced by a rational system which rendered the world more intelligible; thus did the scientific mind gradually triumph over the illusions and reconstructions of legendary memory.

In a wider focus, one must allow that a fundamental provision of modernity lies in the formidable social liberation induced by the advance of critical reasoning, which by its systematic unravelling of official memories, as well as of what was self-evident in the common stock of memory, bearing in mind the tyranny both exercised, called into question the contributory role each played in the pattern of social domination which dictated their preparation. Nevertheless, a consideration of the potential for alienation inherent in the omnipotence of memory in traditional societies need not preclude an examination of the socially and psychologically damaging effects of the fragmentation of memory in the modern world of mass communication. The spontaneously generated interpretative process mentioned above dissolved under the weight of image-fed information only to be replaced by anomic memory, made up of isolated recollection and scraps of information which are increasingly incoherent.

This process of homogenizing collective memory further creates the conditions for a second tendency to develop, that of the limitless fragmentation of individual and group memory. In modern societies each individual belongs to a number of groups. The functional dissociation of the experience he or she undergoes forbids access to a unified memory, which in any case is beyond the power of any single group to construct, restricted as each is by its specialization. The contemporary fragmentation of space, time and institutions entails the fragmentation of memory, which the speed of social and cultural change destroys almost as soon as it is produced. The collective memory of modern societies is composed of bits and pieces. The recurring debate on the growing ignorance of young people concerning history or the scale of their supposed lack of culture (especially where religion is concerned) assumes an altered significance when put in the context of the twin process of the homogenization and fragmentation of collective memory. For the problem is not that of the amount of information stored by the younger generations, which (thanks to television) is probably greater than that of previous generations. What is at issue is whether young people have the ability to organize this mass of information by relating it to a lineage to which they spontaneously see themselves as belonging. The problem of transmission, whether in culture or religion, is not primarily a problem of failure to adjust to the educational methods used to transmit a body of knowledge. It is structurally linked to the collapse of the framework of collective memory which provided every individual with the possibility of a link between what comes before and his or her own actual experience.

A recurring prospect in Maurice Halbwachs's mind was that a society 'which can only live if there exists a sufficient unity of views among the groups and individuals composing it' might be able to reconstitute such unity beyond and in spite of the dissolution of its collective memory. The question of social ties clearly underlies the question of the future of religion in modernity. The question of secularization here takes on a new form, namely that of the possibility, and plausibility, of a group being able, within a context of memory reduced to fragments and made instantaneous, to recognize itself as a link in a chain of belief and entrusted with the task of extending that chain into the future.

Secularization as a crisis of collective memory: the example of French Catholicism

Does this altered, if not altogether new, approach seem to offer a fresh interpretation of what one understands by secularization? Certainly the theoretical attitude that has been dominant in the sociology of religion has hinged very largely on the Weberian reading of the conflict specific to modernity in the west, between substantive rationality, which is that of religion, and formal rationality founded on science and technology. Even if the conflict is a conflict of type (the actual practice of science combining both substantive and formal rationality) and even if the overwhelming preponderance of formal rationality in modern societies itself produces insufficiencies of meaning that arouse new religious expectations,[8] it remains the case that the modern era is indeed, as Weber said, an era that has become 'indifferent to Gods and prophets'.[9] The question of the definitive dominance of formal rationality, which crystallizes essentially material interests and extinguishes the presence of ideal interests in society, interests proper to religion, clearly is of richer theoretical significance than the narrowly rationalist view which mechanically links the end of religion to the development of scientific and technological modernity. It means that the inescapable decline of religious institutions in modern societies

does not necessarily carry with it the social eviction of re
But in fact the complex architecture of theories of secul
scant resistance to the kind of simplification which th
veys conducted into religious phenomena in modern

It is easy to think of diffuse religion as having no more
sient social significance when faced with the cultural exclusion of conventional religion in terms of the decline in belief and practice. Such
reflections recall the old notion of the incompatibility between the ir-
rationality of religion and the rationality of a society governed by science and technology. It is reflected in a number of studies which set
out to account for the collapse of institutionalized religious practice in
western countries as a whole. And one can only accept what the figures reveal of the two-pronged advance of secularization: the cultural
reversal of religious belief as an effect of rationalization, and the dwindling sphere of religion in society as a result of the differentiation and
specialization of modern institutions. Overall, the analysis is conclusive.[10] Yet there is evidence to support a more complex view.

The case of French Catholicism may serve us here. It is common
knowledge that the French, of whom a vast majority continue to profess themselves Catholic, go less and less often to mass.[11] The figure
for regular churchgoers among the under-fifties has fallen below 10
per cent and for the age bracket eighteen to twenty-four is no more
than 2.5 per cent.[12] Yet the assumption that the rational outlook which
increasingly they share draws them away from religious belief and
observance is too easy to make. The drop in observance does not necessarily mean loss of belief[13] (even if belief has tended more and more
to diverge from the Church's official teaching).[14]

Again, the decline in belief and observance within the Catholic
Church is only in part due to the growing sway of the rationalism
accorded to science and technology; it has to be taken along with the
proliferation of beliefs and practices that have been marginalized by
the control exercised by the Church in the matter of believing. And the
mere fact of subscribing to the culture of science and technology does
not of itself imply the removal of the more discordantly irrational forms
of belief – belief in God or in supernatural powers or in miracles, on
all of which points the available evidence is interesting. While religious observance has continued to fall, for instance, there has been a
steady rise in the resort to horoscopes and popular astrology since the
1960s – scarcely witness to the triumph of modern rationality.[15] Furthermore, Guy Michelat and Daniel Boy have shown that belief in the
paranormal and the parascientific is not restricted to those in the rear-
guard of modernity but, in fact, tends to increase with the level of
culture.[16]

It seems that the advance of scientific rationality produces in its wake the growth of beliefs and practices that react against the official orthodoxy of modernity. And the social and cultural reversal of the Church's influence, though in part a consequence of its exhaustively asserting this orthodoxy, provides scope for a multitude of heterodoxies to develop in opposition. Moreover, it is the case that the new religious movements which have been developing inside, at the margin of, or quite outside the sphere of the Church – New Age-type charismatic movements – recruit their followers among those whose educational attainment tends to be above average – those with engineering or computer-technology skills, teachers, medical or paramedical personnel are all well represented, those, in other words, who are scarcely strangers to the culture of science and technology. Similar conclusions hold for the Lubavich community in France, among whom the high number of those with good technical qualifications has frequently been noted.[17]

Hence, rather than attribute the fall in conventional religious observance to loss of belief, and loss of belief to the growth of rationalism instilled by science and technology, one should look at the complex redistribution taking place in the sphere of believing and try to throw light on the social changes that have helped bring this about. As has been noted, the advent at the close of the twentieth century of what Jean Baudrillard calls psychological modernity seals the collapse of the world of tradition by calling into question any authority that claims to direct conscience and behaviour, in the name of individual autonomy and the inalienable rights of subjectivity. The crisis in the authority of the priesthood – a corollary of the distance each of the faithful feels entitled to set between a norm imposed from outside and the authenticity of personal experience – is clearly linked with the general deregulation of belief and observance which is the consequence of psychological modernity. Yet the crisis is merely one factor in a breakdown that reaches beyond the priesthood to what gave substance to religious authority – the whole realm of religious practice and parochial culture in France.

The breakdown is in the imaginative grasp of continuity, which provided the symbolic casing of this civilization and which gave meaning to the material apparatus for exercising control over space and time and to the authority of the clergy, both characteristic of the parish. For centuries the parish represented *the* society of memory; its incorporation of every inhabitant in parish territory into at least a potential community linked to a chain stretching from past to future occurred naturally; and the expression of this was the central position of the church in the village, with the cemetery surrounding the building where the community gathered; this sustained so powerful an image, in fact, that early surveys into religious practice (conducted first by Gabriel Le Bras, then by Canon Boulard)[18] reckoned those who were outside the gathering – Protestants, Jews or declared atheists – as being unattached.

It is of little matter that the reality of the life of the parish never corresponded to the way it was thus depicted; its representation lent strength to a vision of religious society sustained by three different sources: (a) a vision of the family incarnating an ideal of local stability and continuity that nurtured the observance of religion in the community; (b) a vision of rural society, centring on the image of an ordered world, reconciling earth and heaven, the natural and the supernatural; and (c) a vision of the consolation, which a good life – a life of observance – secured, of the bliss promised for the next world in return for the travails of the present one. Despite the impact of successive political, industrial and social revolutions, the underlying structure of imagined continuity, which allowed and embodied the religious mobilization of collective memory, remained more or less in place until the First World War. Yves Lambert's study of Limerzel in Brittany shows irremediable fault lines appearing in the inter-war period,[19] but it was the wave of reconstruction and economic modernization in the 1950s that put an end to the ideal parish which, beyond acting as a register of observance, served to sustain the Catholic identity of the French by enabling them to identify themselves as members of a lineage.

The collapse of the traditional family, wholly dedicated to biological reproduction and the transmission of a biological, material and symbolic inheritance from generation to generation, probably counts as the central factor in the disintegration of the imagined continuity that lies at the heart of the modern crisis of religion. The collapse predates the first half of the twentieth century. Population and historical studies amply show the process under way in the eighteenth century, given materiality in the radical legal reforms of the French Revolution. The two tendencies that characterize the family in modernity are clearly present in the nineteenth century: a fall-back to the limited family and increasing involvement on the part of government, through the development of compulsory schooling and of institutionalized medical care.[20] The crucial moment in contemporary French history is around 1965 with the downturn in the statistics of births and marriages which had risen markedly in the period 1945–50. Beginning in 1965, there is a fall in the fertility rate (the average family numbering two rather than three children) and in the marriage rate (between 1972 and 1985 the number of marriages fell by one-third), and there is an increase in the number of divorces, the rate in relation to marriages rising from 10 per cent before 1965 to 30 per cent in

1989. Added to this, the number of unmarried couples is put at 2 million, and the proportion of children born outside wedlock rose from 11 per cent in 1960 to 16 per cent in 1983 and to 24 per cent in 1987.

These statistics go hand in hand with legalized qualitative changes, such as greater flexibility in marriage laws and the easing of restrictions on contraception and abortion. Individual well-being and fulfilment take precedence; the family is expected to minister to an individual's contingent emotional needs and forgo consideration of its own continuity. This is not to say that the family has less importance; there is plenty of evidence of the focal role the family plays in France.[21] But family stability and continuity are no longer the priority, indeed they may even constitute obstacles to the emotional and expressive function the family affords.

This instability in family structure, according to Louis Roussel's typology, gives preponderance to the 'emotional' family or to the family as a club over the family in its historical dimension. The emotional family is characterized by the primacy accorded to intensely affective relationships; its extreme vulnerability to emotional disenchantment produces a high divorce rate. The 'club' family gives prime consideration to the autonomy of its individual members; it is based on a realistic assessment of the assets and constraints of life in common. The family as history is based on an interweaving of emotional solidarity and a pact of continuity consciously made by its members.[22]

It is pretty obvious that the same typology will serve to identify current forms of religious sociability. But the important point concerns the loss of social evidence of continuity given substance by the experience of the family, reprocessed and assuming symbolic form in religious experience of a parochial type. The acceleration of labour mobility has completed this transformation, with families being relocated on a massive scale. Birth, education and training, employment, recreation, retirement and death, all occur in different places. The loss of local identification intensifies the loss of lineage identification; and the dual movement has finally undermined two of the mainstays of the parochial imagination, which in a country such as France were privileged vehicles of the religious mobilization of collective memory – the ideal of continuous transmission and the ideal of rootedness in a locality.

Seen thus, there is a close link between the end of the world of religious observance represented by the parish civilization, and the objective and subjective crisis of the rural world which has worsened dramatically in recent years in France. As one might have expected, much interpretation in the inter-war period attributed the loss of reli-

gion in the modern world to the loss of the fundamental values of the
soil due to industrialization and urbanization. It owed much indeed to
the intransigent anti-modernist stance within a certain current of French
Catholicism in the second half of the nineteenth century and found an
echo in the nascent sociology of Catholicism. For Gabriel Le Bras, the
transplanting to cities linked with the movement from the land was
the decisive factor in detachment from religion. 'I am convinced', he
was wont to remark, 'that out of a hundred villagers who settle in
Paris, roughly ninety will cease to be churchgoers by the time they step
out of the Gare Montparnasse.' A large part of the clergy, even the
urban clergy, were of the same view: the city was a place of moral –
hence religious – perdition.

Apart from the ideological issue which yet again pitted one France
against the other, the sociological intuition recognizing how the
Church's destiny in France appeared to have been for ever linked to
the countryside rang profoundly true.[23] The loss of the peasant ideal
and the break-up of the parish civilization thus seem doubly linked:
first, because the crisis in the village cuts across the loss of the peasantry, due to the interlocking of peasant and religious memory; sec-
ondly, because both phenomena have to do with the crumbling of the
evidence of continuity in a society undergoing change.

There have been several studies of the way in which the rural
rootedness of French Catholicism produced a connection between the
process of modernization (and the flight from the land it implied) and
the loss of control over French society by the ecclesiastical establishment during the nineteenth and twentieth centuries. Their findings are
well known and need not concern us here. On the other hand, the
second aspect calls for closer attention. As against recent developments
which have resulted in the world of agriculture occupying a very minor place in the French economy and society,[24] the image of the peasant farmer and the symbolism attaching to it is given prominence in
the collective imagination. And the parish civilization, its cogency long
impaired by a process of modernization which emptied the villages
and turned peasant farmers into workers on the land, in fact continued to exist as an imaginative reference for the pastoral condition with
the support of a myth, the myth of the peasant society, a society of
memory *par excellence*.

At the centre of the myth was the image of the peasant who nurtures
society, who bears witness to a special, intimate relationship with nature, who is the vessel of ancestral knowledge, who testifies to values
implanted in a tradition beyond the reach of memory, and who fosters
relationships within stable communities which are fundamental to
human society. This mythology of the peasantry has had exceptional

political fortune in France.[25] But its vision also permeated common representations of a parochial civilization that perceived itself as the transcendent expression of the peasant civilization which gave it substance. The elective affinity of a Catholicism (whose realization was thought of as the parish unfolding to the extremities of the earth) and the rural world was made explicit in the vision of the Kingdom of God to be established on earth developed by Action Catholique working in a rural environment.[26] And it continued till quite recently to pervade discourse on the parochial community.

However, in recent years agriculture has had to face a series of crises[27] which have destroyed the image of the peasant as the repository of memory of a bygone Christian world, and with it have gone the myth of a peasant society and the utopia of a possible restitution of a Christendom at once stable and rooted in the soil. The conflicts born of the dairy quotas, the debate over the insistent economic need to cut the number of producers and the highly symbolic decision to let cultivable land go fallow sum up the state of affairs. For the first time ever, peasant farmers find they are forbidden to produce. More than this, their success in production, which can be metaphorized as a land flowing with milk and honey, is publicly presented as a source of economic and social ills and borne as if a curse had fallen upon them: in the words of one of the farmers' leaders at the time of the mass demonstration in September 1991, 'our mistake is that we have been too successful.'

At the same time, the environment has been made to pay for the consequences of agricultural methods where the only concern is profitability. From being a protector of nature, the peasant farmer finds himself singled out as its polluter, and takes even less kindly to the suggestion that he becomes a waged market gardener. What is more, overproduction and pollution cost society dear: he who fed his fellow men is made to suffer the reproach of living on benefit, at the state's, hence taxpayers', expense. Faced with such contradictions, present-day farmers would sooner abandon the myth that their professional organizations press hard still to sustain. At a time when farming activity (with off-soil production) severs the very specific link with the earth and the natural environment which distinguished it, to invoke a memory of the earth that reaches back beyond time increasingly takes on the appearance of a pitiful incantation.

For a French farmer to set fire to a truck from Britain carrying live lambs is in this light far more than a disagreeable news item. Beyond the sense of individual despair it conveyed, what struck everyone was the indifference to living creatures reduced to the abstract condition of merchandise. It was a symbolic end to the vision of 'l'ordre éternel des

champs' which still fed the political and the religious imagination of
the French. The symbolic death of peasant society, the final stage in
the 'end of the peasant farmer',[28] somehow completes the process of
disintegration of the parish civilization pitted against the modernization of the countryside. The dual process has broken the resilience in
the mobilizing of collective memory by religion. An essential part of
the force of continuity in the French and Catholic imagination is de-
molished and there is a concomitant weakening of the individual's or
group's capacity to relate spontaneously to the authority of a tradition
which compelled recognition through the normative potency of the
enhanced, even idealized, remembrance of lineage.

To lay stress on the part played by family upheaval and the transformation of agriculture in undermining the structure of collective memory
which was the foundation of the parish civilization in France does not
exhaust analysis of the volatile nature of memory in societies undergoing change or of the effects of the crisis of memory in the sphere of
religion. The case of parochially based Catholicism lends itself well to
recognizing how the diminution of memory involves the erosion of the
imaginative grasp of continuity, which is the basis for the objective
and subjective identification of the chain of belief. But a more general
approach is needed to discover how modern societies become cultures
of the ephemeral,[29] how collective memory disintegrates and so how
religious believing dissolves. And the processes involved here affect
not merely institutionalized, traditional religions but the religious dimension that is present, in one form or another, in all forms of social
behaviour. In all domains the conviction of believing, founded on reference to a tradition which is there to be preserved and passed on, is
disintegrating. The gradual dissolution of features that were properly
speaking religious in the values and norms of the Republican school
system among teachers as well as among pupils and their parents is
largely confirmed by specialists in the field. The force of conviction in
the syndicalist strain of French unionism, which was translated by the
religious attachment instilled in its members to themes and forms of
struggle enhanced by the mythicized memory of a 'militant' lineage,
has ebbed in the union movement itself. New forms of organization
threaten to take over, spontaneously formed committees set up with a
specific aim and dissolved when that aim is achieved, seemingly without concern to see their struggle in the context of a cause stretching
back in time. Short-termism informs every field of social action.

There is a need for a clearer understanding of the social factor at
work in advanced capitalist society which obliterates memory.[30] Pierre
Nora and others have stressed the crucial effect of information tech-

nology on the way that the world is now perceived and represented. Attention should also be given to economic changes that have favoured pragmatic individualism at the expense of long-lasting forms of co-operation and social solidarity which cultivated a collective memory. In the 1960s, individualism flourished with the new emphasis that advanced societies gave to gratification. The term 'consumer society' came into vogue. The implication was not that a society of all-round abundance had emerged but, rather, that the problem of regulating consumption had taken over from the accumulation of production as such. In other words, the regulation of the productive (and of its corresponding labour) system was now mainly directed and adjusted to the consumer market. In order to function properly the economy no longer required consumer satisfaction to be limited, it was now looked on as an instrumental part of the economic equation.

The 1960s' promulgation of the individual's right to happiness and self-fulfilment reflected the new economic currency of immediate gratification. Virtually, one had to be young, at ease with oneself, sexually liberated and fit. With the recession of the mid-1970s, the landscape altered. The insistence on individual well-being as a right came up against a sense of precariousness and insecurity, which has remained firmly lodged and affects attitudes to work and to entitlement. But the very sense of insecurity has spawned its own counter-version of immediate satisfaction: what matters is to get by. It functions as the reverse, negative side of the optimistic, immediate claim to satisfaction of the golden 1960s: what matters is to go for kicks. A triumphant each for himself or herself takes different forms according to the times. But the individualistic pressure for immediacy, which accords perfectly well with the coming of mass societies and the increased role of the state – that all categories call for – has finally achieved the expulsion of memory from society, so completing a process which began with modernization.

Clearly, this has had direct consequences on religion, and particularly on institutionalized religion, in respect of the substance of belief and forms of observance. Such changes follow from the necessary compromise between a particular religious tradition trying to remain culturally plausible in the present and the contemporary culture of the individual which benefits from the loss of the precepts of memory. In the context of French Catholicism, one might again direct attention to Yves Lambert's study of religious life over a century in Limerzel in Brittany and the conclusive analysis he develops of changes in the way salvation is represented.[31] More generally, studies made of religious beliefs and of the substance of the new religiosity of Christian persuasion in the developed world all stress the place given to themes of self-realization and personal achievement in this world.

These themes correspond to the subjectivization of the relationship each individual believer is supposed to maintain with a tradition which is identified with voluntarily. The same subjectivity applies in the matter of devotion where practice is *à la carte* in accordance with personal needs; and in its more extreme forms, where authorized memory no longer plays a role at all, there is a pick-and-mix attitude to belief. Such internal modernization, reflecting the obligatory relaxation of the omnipotence of the heteronomous authority of tradition (of authorized memory) in modernity, at the same time allows religious representations – for example, that of salvation – to be rationally adjusted so as to conform with individual hopes of achieving well-being in this world.

The way in which the notion of healing is constantly reworked in new religious movements of Christian persuasion provides the best illustration of this process. In traditional Christianity themes of healing are regularly associated with problems of salvation, salvation being metaphorically signified (and virtually anticipated) in healing. In new religious movements of Christian persuasion (especially in charismatic movements which show the influence of psychology and human relationship theories) the perspective is usually reversed: the theme of salvation no longer refers to the (culturally devalued) expectation of a full life in another world; it functions as a symbolic marker enhancing the hope of being healed in all aspects of self-realization. In this individualistic reinterpretation of the link between salvation and healing, it is the vision of salvation that becomes a metaphor for healing, a means of expressing the extent of personal regeneration – physical, psychic and moral – implied here and now by the fact of being healed (in a way that is beyond the power of modern medicine, highly specialized and technicized as it is). This transferred meaning has produced at least a partial rehabilitation of Christian belief within a culture which prioritizes the immediate interest of the individual. At the same time it is evidence of the attrition of the link – established by tradition and essential to the constitution of the Christian chain of belief – between the subjective aspiration towards regeneration and the story of salvation in which this aspiration is supposed to assume its full religious meaning.

Is it simply a case of reconstruction, whereby a new pattern of religion comes into being within a modernity that undermines every attempt to imagine continuity? Or is it, more radically, a definitive disintegration of religion? Françoise Champion, who has studied an assortment of mystico-esoteric groups in France who take syncretism in belief furthest, opts decisively for the second view. For her, the current spate of new movements, New Age in particular, testifies to a growing submission of spiritual interests to the contemporary culture of the individual and shows religion making an improbable exit towards, in her words, 'the simply magical, the psychological, or the search for a new humanism'.[32] The absolute imperative for each individual to find his or her own way is the surest sign of how subjectivism is encroaching on the territory of religion, but the speed with which this occurs depends on the unloading of memory, a development common to societies in which immediatism in consumption or communication prevails. Faced with this scenario, one might venture to say that the gouging of religion from modern society has reached its culmination through the process of rationalization certainly, but no less effectively through the amnesia induced, in the more technologically advanced societies, by the obliteration of all recall that is not immediate or functional.

8

The Chain Reinvented

Must one end there, with the consideration that the set of phenomena that are commonly held to indicate secularization has to do in the last instance with the draining of memory and the consequent threat to the survival of religion? Of course, actuality never conforms to the neatness of the ideal-typical, which fails to take into account the several forms of compensation that develop in reaction to the symbolic vacuum resulting from the loss in depth and in unity of collective memory in modern societies. And the reaction is the sharper because the gouging of memory, as experienced, is contradicted by the subjective sense of duration felt by individuals who are now in the main longer-lived. It is a contradiction that must be resolved by invoking substitute memories, multiple, fragmentary, diffuse and disassociated as they are, but which promise that something of collective identification, on which the production and reproduction of social bonds depends, can be saved.

Accelerated change, which is at the root of the characteristic instantaneousness of both individual and collective experience, paradoxically gives rise to appeals to memory. They underpin the need to recover the past in the imagination without which collective identity, just as individual identity, is unable to operate. If one can describe societies of the past as societies of memory it is precisely because in them memory was compact and present in every part of life; they had no need to call it up. The uncertainties brought about by the removal of this presence together with the impact of accelerated change cause the demand for meaning on the part of society to proliferate in all directions. Reference to the past no longer supplies a system of meanings which afford

explanation for the imperfections of the world and the incoherence
experience, nor does it provide a scenario for the future.

This uncertainty shows itself in a particularly acute form in the search
for identity to which modern society is ill-suited to respond, lacking as
it does the essential resource for identity of a memory held in common. If human society cannot be imagined without a minimal collective sharing of the effort to produce meaning, the effort itself assumes
that there exists between its members a minimal imaginative grasp of
continuity without which the thought of a common future is impossible. The ever-increasing dislocation of this imaginative grasp at the
same time forces society continually to reconstruct itself in new forms
so as to ensure continuity for both the group and the individual. But
without there being an organized and integrated social memory such
reconstruction takes place in an entirely fragmentary way. Pierre Nora
and his research colleagues, whose aim is to throw light on 'realms of
memory' in French society, have shown this to be the case by identifying, in the political arena, the particular points at which such
(re)constitutions of memory crystallize, points which at the same time
are indicators of the loss of a unifying collective memory. And the
expanding field of their research well illustrates the degree to which
this imaginative search for partial continuity has escalated.

One could take it further with the analysis of such phenomena as
the current French passion for genealogy or for historical novels (especially those centred on family sagas) or the success of French Heritage
days, when a large number of historic homes are thrown open to the
public. To this one might add the taste for antiques or for traditional
crafts. For an analysis of a device whereby a past is reinvented so as to
recreate the true memory of this or that group and serves to re-establish an identity which modernity has placed under threat, major pag-
eants in which the local population participates, for example those
enacted at Le Lude in the Sarthe, at Saint-Fargeau in the Yonne, and in
particular at Le Puy-du-Fou in the Vendée, afford rich material.[1] The
last instance is of particular interest because the spectacle serves a double
purpose: for the locality initially, in which a sense of community remains strong, and then for a wider public, including visitors from
abroad, for whom a sense of the past is rekindled by seeing a local
population re-enacting episodes from the past from which it sprang.

One might also try to account for the frequently emotional response
awoken in the French, whenever the question of the survival of the
peasant society is raised. Broadly speaking, the passion commonly felt
for everything concerned with the celebration of roots may be seen as
the converse of the intensely felt sense of the loss of collective memory.
But it would be wrong to think of France, where the reach of the

nation's memory is indeed long, as being being especially affected; in the United States, with its emphasis on newness and on unlimited possibility, the same need to avert the loss of memory is very marked[2] – with the qualification, noted by Johnston, that generally it is the American nation, personified literally, which occupies the central place in celebrations, rather than a heroic figure taken from history.[3] And the growing number of these attempts on whatever scale in western countries to remobilize and recreate memory, different as they are in the resources they command and in the direction they are given, constitutes the reverse side of the discontinuity of experience which impairs the systems by which identities are formed and transmitted.

Thus modernity's imaginative projection of continuity presents itself as an interlacing of shattered memories, memories that have also been worked upon and invented and constantly reshaped in response to the demands of a present which is increasingly subject to the pressures of change. If one is able to grasp something of the massive process of secularization from modernity's disorganization of collective memory, one should also be able to grasp something of religious modernity by examining the ways in which this body of fragmented memory is constituted and reconstituted and cross-related. The question which arises then has to do with the sort of religious innovativeness which may emerge in modernity in the wake of attempts to reinvent the chain.

Utopia: a major manifestation of religious innovation in modernity

The very mention of religious innovation, linked to the question of memory, immediately calls to mind the notion of utopia as it has flourished in history – a past reinterpreted and magnified into a golden age feeds the image of a future which it is predicted will be different from a present that is decisively rejected.[4] Such an approach to socioreligious change has been well exploited in the major study Henri Desroche devoted to the identification, analysis and inventory of contraband religions which have provided a receptacle for imagination in modern societies.[5]

> In the entire gallery of religious imagination where the utopian and messianic influence is uppermost, there is virtually no instance where hope in the future is not matched by an earnest of a return to the past. It is a well-known fact that those who prophesy the apocalypse draw inspiration from the patriarchs. In virtually every case, imagination calls

upon memory for help. And the correlation is not limited to phenomena that one might – gratuitously – consider to be marginal. Religious
innovation as it is seen in the dominant religions is no exception. They
all look to what has gone before to stand surety for their hereafter.
They look back to – an 'Old Testament', a 'chain of Witnesses', a lineage of precursors, a patriarch or a legion of forebears.[6]

In the view of Henri Desroche, the link between religion and utopia
is first a genealogical one, for which history provides a multiplicity of
ramifications. What he tracks down through time, in the form of utopia, is the posterity of a Judaeo-Christian messianic inspiration which
has profoundly shaped the course of modernity by preserving a constant awareness of expectation. The seven constellations into which
Henri Desroche groups his traditional utopian populations are the
following: medieval dissidence between the eleventh and fifteenth centuries; left-wing reform in the sixteenth century; revolutionary shoots
in eighteenth-century Britain; the millennial flowering in eighteenth-
and nineteenth-century America; new post-revolutionary forms of
Christianity in the nineteenth century; the religious resistance in Rus-
sia between the seventeenth and nineteenth centuries; and cultural proliferation in the underdeveloped world in the nineteenth and twentieth
centuries. These constellations are the milestones and witnesses of the
alternative route taken by religion in modernity, which he describes as
that of hope.[7] Hence the posterity of Jewish and Christian eschatology
is indeed vast and its deployment is coextensive with that of modernity, in which it remains indirectly present.

If Desroche, in the extract quoted above, stresses that total reconstruction of the relationship with the past in view of change itself seen
as total is likely to occur *even* 'in the major conventional religions', it
is precisely because he finds this motivating force in religion at work
way beyond the field of institutionalized religion, along with revolutionary movements, utopian forms of socialism,[8] experiments in communal living and co-operative projects. Furthermore, the current in
academic sociology dominant at the time sought to hold this somewhat exuberant ecumenicalism against him, and frequently turned a
blind eye to what is central to Desroche's argument and to its relevance for a sociology of religious modernity, that is, the intuition of a
religious dynamic of society functioning through and beyond every
measurable advance in the process of secularization.

The unifying factor where this dynamic is at work is the ploy of 'a
tradition of less depth having recourse to a tradition of greater depth
even when the latter has been constructed or reconstructed for the
needs of the cause'.[9] Utopia serves to create in a renewed way an alter-

native imagined continuity: a continuity reaching back further than the one that suits the social conventions of the present, a continuity which reaches more nearly the foundation that feeds the consciousness of the chain, a continuity with a past that is blessed and beneficent, and which stands in opposition to the misfortunes, the dangers and the uncertainties of the present. The utopia dreamt of or put into effect subverts the imaginative projection of continuity within a given society by extending and enriching it; in this sense, it affords an opportunity to come to terms with what is new in the present. The utopian dynamic to a certain extent accords with the reality of the active dimension in tradition which we considered in an earlier chapter.

The remark has been made that any tradition in its relationship to a past, given actuality in the present, always incorporates an imaginative strain. The memory it invokes is always, in part at least, a reinvention. This reinvention is most often effected through successive readjustments of memory, readjustments that are often minute or invisible, above all readjustments that are almost invariably denied on the score of the absolute and necessary permanence of tradition. What is specific to utopia as compared with the ongoing exertion of memory on itself is that it makes of the complete and total break with the old order the condition of access to a new one, which is glimpsed by means of a memory that has been replenished at a source for which greater authenticity is claimed. Utopia contains the proposition to install, in place of an official memory that has become corrupted or misappropriated, a new order of memory (hence a new imaginative order), on the basis of which it is possible to redefine the way that society operates in terms of its economic, political, symbolic and other functions.

The possibility of so radical an aspiration emerging in a given society depends on the degree of dislocation – of destabilization, at least – of the frames of collective memory induced by economic, social and political change. It requires the slackening of the tradition (of authorized memory) to have reached a sufficient degree for it to be possible to invent an alternative memory. Hence logically it is the periods of significant change, marked by the ousting of the compact presence of the past in the present, which have seen a major flourishing of utopias, fed in various degrees from the reservoir of memory that is constituted by religious traditions, more particularly those with a Jewish and Christian messianic and millennial basis. But in order for the utopian dynamic to develop social consequences that extend beyond the voluntary groups[10] for whose social or cultural dissidence it provides justification, it must materialize as a social movement. It must be (or become) the language of collective aspiration nurtured by social forces which are themselves capable of intervening in the central conflicts where a

society's orientation is decided, whatever the outcome of these conflicts.

The history of utopias in Europe, from the fourteenth to the eighteenth century, is inseparable from that of urban and/or rural revolutionary movements, whether violent or peaceful, articulating the major
conflict which set the peasantry against the encroachments of the feu-
dal system and land monopoly: Lollards in fourteenth-century England; Hussites, Calixtites and Taborites in fifteenth-century Bohemia
(where national and cultural demands intensified the socio-economic
and political aspect of the conflict); the epic tragedy of the peasants
who followed Thomas Münzer in sixteenth-century Germany; Level-
lers, Ranters, Diggers or Quakers in seventeenth-century England, and
so on. In all these cases, the explosive force of the movement lay at the
junction of a social upsurge which corresponded to a major economic
upheaval and an egalitarian radicalism that found its justification in
the promises of the Bible and the example set by the early Christian
community. The English Revolution, better than any other example,
illustrates how the 'backward' working of memory carried out by these
new religious groups which challenged both the dominant sociopoliti-
cal and ecclesiastical order was the ferment of a process in the reshaping of values essential for the emergence of political modernity.[11]

If the picture Desroche presents of Christian and post-Christian
utopian posterity in the modern world is of considerable interest in
understanding the fluctuating pattern of relations between memory
and religion in modernity, it is not merely because it reveals the links
between the western ideal of historical fulfilment and its Judaeo-
Christian base. It is also because the internal dynamics of utopia in
the terms analysed by Desroche offers an understanding of the complex process whereby in modernity utopia is a formula both for
secularizing memory *and* for its religious recharging. The secularization
of memory, the first stage in the dual movement, is fairly easily
identifiable if one considers, for example, the large number of cases
where the messianic promise of the Kingdom has been transposed by
means of a utopian transformation here and now of social and political relations. In this perspective, utopia is witness to the fact that
politics is finally delivered – or on the way to being delivered – from
its religious accoutrement, to borrow the term used by Engels with
reference to the French Revolution, the first in his opinion to fight its
battles 'in disregard of religion and in an exclusively political form',[12]
unlike the peasant wars for instance, in which the social struggle was
still confused with the religious struggle to establish the Kingdom on
earth.

The converse dynamic comes less readily to mind. To place it one has to confront the fateful destiny of utopia, doomed for ever to go in search of its realization. Henri Desroche has made the point that utopia as practised is caught in a strange dilemma: either it miscarries (because it is powerless to change the dominant order which it opposes and/or because it is exposed to often ferocious repression on the part of those in whose interest it is to see the order preserved); or it succeeds, and fails just as surely, either because it loses its momentum by achieving cultural integration within a society and/or a religion which it has been instrumental in reforming,[13] or because it acquires rigidity by becoming institutionalized as a new authorized memory, programmed to preserve and reproduce the new social interests it consecrates. The religious recharging of collective imagination may then intervene both as a consequence of the process of routinization or glaciation of utopia and as a protest against this process.

The absorption of utopia into religion occurs whenever a group or a movement, with variable social consequences depending on the place it occupies or comes to occupy in social relationships, monopolizes the ideal of expected change and erects it as a norm for the present. In the process of the normative acceptance of utopia the invocation of the foundational narrative in which the group has become established frequently takes over from the evocation of a radically different future. More exactly, the assumption is made that the future's meaning is already enshrined in the narrative, whose presence must be permanently restored to the life of the group. The process is taken to an extreme when a group of religious experts (*clercs*) assumes the monopoly of defining the legitimate memory of the foundation and its implications for the present. But apart from extreme instances involving the dogmatic fossilization of utopia, the religious return to the origin is normally accompanied by the utopian experiment acclimatizing to everyday life and acquiring an enduring mould. Fidelity to the initial inspiration then nurtures the message it sought to dispel – the dissipation of the dream of change by the commonplace. This tendency becomes more marked inasmuch as the group identifies with a founder whose explicit message it can invoke (especially if it can refer to texts left by the founder) or whose intuition it can explore and/or whose conduct it can propose as an exemplar. Nevertheless, apart from the case of the group's developing complete sectarian indifference (in the Troeltschian sense of the term) towards the world and the culture of its time, and so far as possible withholding contact with a present it rejects, the religious stabilization of utopia constitutes a possible means of its being incorporated into a culture it has helped transform.

The history of the religious orders[14] and utopian communities[15] of the nineteenth century and, more recently, of the anti-establishment movements of the 1960s and 1970s[16] or the present environmentalist movement[17] afford many instances of utopian radicalism being absorbed into forms of collective experimentation. At the same time as falling short of their aims, they have constituted or constitute, by means of (re)mobilizing memory through believing, magnets of religious innovation and social and cultural innovation. This type of approach might well enrich an analysis of some contemporary religious movements – certain currents in Islam, for instance – whose exteriority in regard to modernity is too readily inferred from the rejection of the world they proclaim.

At the same time it has to be seen that the absorption of utopia into religion in the form of dogmatic glaciation or of innovative routinization secretes its own antibodies, paradoxically by allowing the possibility of an alternative reading of the foundational stories retriggering the utopian dynamic of protest from within religion itself. From the radical movements of the Reformation to the efflorescence of leftism there is no shortage of examples to illustrate this resurgence of utopia, even when and to the extent that it loses strength by becoming institutionalized in a new religion. Such resurgence presents a religious character (or religious features) whenever it takes the form of radicalizing demands based on devotion to an inspirational source for which the religion it is opposed to claims to provide the only legitimate reading. In this dialectics of religious conflict, utopia constitutes the third term, as essential as it is destined for annihilation.

For the purposes of our argument, an understanding of the complex dynamics of utopia and religion is necessary only in that it may make it easier to reply to a question raised earlier as to the possibility of such a process being able to function in the present event-laden phase of modernity. The theme of the end of utopia recurs constantly in political studies since the mid-1970s. The inclination to dispense with utopia, characteristic of more advanced societies, is explained variously in terms of the saturation and listlessness induced by the primacy given to consumerism, the social lethargy consequent on the recession affecting the west in the wake of the first oil shock, and disillusionment linked with the eclipse of the historical vision, whether liberal or Marxist, which nurtured utopia within modernity, or again to the anaesthesia resulting from the violence of worldwide disturbance to political equilibrium.

More cogently, evidence is produced of interaction between the lessening plausibility of grand dreams of a different society and an assertive individualism which gives priority to particular interests and aspirations. One way of taking up these different approaches to the depreciation of utopia in modern societies might be to stress the link between the (relative) inertia of the collective imagination – in itself an obstacle to the projection of a different future – and the (equally relative) amnesia induced by the dormancy of memory in the supermodern universe of superabundant communication and the corresponding transience of events. The collapse of the total, all-powerful memory of traditional societies was the indispensable condition of the freeing of imagination which for modern societies opened up the vision of constructing history. But it is doubtful whether the creative capacity of collective imagination can survive a total atomization of memory which would make reference to the past dependent on the whims of individuals.

The prospect that the utopian capacity in modern societies may founder irretrievably is closer still if the ultimate possibility of the individual being able to relate to the past dissolves, as has been suggested, under the impact of an omnipresent actuality which devours any sense of duration by allowing every event to be swallowed up by an event that is more topical. But while recognizing that the possibility exists one should guard against accepting the logic of a scenario embracing disaster and the extinction of utopia. For the structural crisis is not becalmed in the same way in every society or region or social group or economic category. What is more, the heightening of social and/or cultural contradictions within any given society may unleash an explosive torrent which can lead both to effective social and cultural change and renewal of the utopian potential thanks to which religious innovation may emerge.

In an entirely different setting, it is possible to see something of this reciprocal activation of social and religious movement (in the context here of traditional religion) through the utopian medium in the growth of base communities in Latin America[18] or in denominational feminist movements in the United States.[19] It remains the case that in western societies as a whole, the utopian dynamic for religious innovation today is barely capable of countering the collapse of memory whose effect, both in the sphere of traditional religion and in society as a whole (especially in the political arena), is the loss of plausibility in collective reference to a chain of belief. More precisely, the innovative resources of religion now find expression through a different articulation of this reference, which is itself inseparable from the formation of individual and collective identities.

The religious reinforcement of elective fraternities

One means of articulation arises out of an elective fraternity to which its members ascribe a more or less distant genealogy. What is specific here resides in the fact that the relationship to the chain of belief is constructed – one might say, deduced – from the quality of the emotive relationship pertaining between members of a similar group. It is not recognition of common ancestry that determines the relationship between brothers, but the experience of brotherhood justifying the invention of common ancestry. An elective fraternity corresponds to a certain community of values and references which has developed through shared interests, experience and hardships. Elective fraternity is a relationship that is both willed and ideal in the sense that it is presumed to bring into being what ties of blood are so often incapable of ensuring between members of a family – real solidarity, transparency of thought and communication, and common values and memories.

The primacy given to an individual's personal commitment in relation to the group is witness to the modernity of this type of voluntary association, and opposition between the natural and the chosen family has always gone along with the assertion of the rights of the individual conscience against the omnipotence of attachments linked to birth. What gives such elective fraternities a new significance in our societies is that they multiply in inverse proportion to the collapse of primary communities in the face of which they established themselves in the past. It would be tedious to reiterate points already made in chapter 5 in connection with the link that exists between the proliferation of affinity groups and the massive assertion of individualism in the more advanced societies.

Indeed it is now commonplace to make a connection between the growth of collectives, networks and associations which group individuals confronting similar situations or who have micro-interests in common, and the attraction exercised on the collectivity as a whole by the abstract world of complex large-scale organizations, in which each individual is entirely and exclusively defined in terms of the function he or she fulfils. The spread of voluntary groups offers a form of compensation for the anonymity and isolation resulting from the atomization and high degree of specialization that mark social relations. And compensation is the better assured in that an individual's emotive investment in the group is more intense with the result that interrelationships have greater emotional content and are frequently seen by those involved as being akin to family ties. The emotional community within which each member is attached to the person of a charismatic founder constitutes, in this perspective, the consummate form of elective fraternity.[20]

It has been shown elsewhere that this form of grouping, which Weber associates with traditional societies where charisma constitutes the sole force for change, was also likely to develop in a modernity which puts value on individual experience and provokes the demand for communal interaction.[21] It is here too that the elective fraternity of members with one another is likely to be most explicit, the founder being designated as father, or elder brother, of a genuine family in heart and mind. The development of new religious movements and charismatic communities, just as of gangs and clans in big cities, testifies in different but equally striking ways to the resurgence of these very old forms of sociality at grass-roots level and in response to the destruction, or absence, of family or social or local or denominational ties.

The constant presence by default of the family model, as soon as a voluntary group accedes to the position of elective fraternity, is in itself of considerable interest. The fact of identifying with the family of one's choice is these days not so much a protest against the oppressive obligatory tutelage exercised by the natural family as a way of acknowledging the void in the family's socializing function at the very time when the family has lost its traditional economic and political function and is supposed to provide for no more than the immediate emotional needs of a relationship.

This profound change in the natural family which has become the repository of the individual's independence and privacy has had an equally profound effect on the relationship between elective fraternities which individuals join by choice and the family sphere which is determined by biological and legal ties incumbent on individuals. For a long time the family constituted the point of reference – both repellent and inviting – for voluntary groups, which were still disposed to beget the omnipresent system of the biological family: in monastic orders, where entry is in principle by vocation and by publicly signifying that one renounces one's natural family, the abbot remains as his title indicates the father of the monks. In our societies, it is the natural family which the elective fraternity tends to take as a reference by 'euphemizing' the relations based on authority and seeing the functions of exchange and communication it is called upon to carry out for its members in an excessively positive light. Clearly this shift redounds on the continuity of the family structure, inasmuch as the nature of the actual and legal ties that underlie it often conflict with the priority accorded to emotive and subjective elements, when it comes to legitimating the relations of dependence that unite its members. Even so, it is this ideal family, free of any contradiction between the individual's freedom of commitment and the stability of ties that have their basis both in nature and in law, which is the exemplar for most elective fraternities.

The possibility of an elective fraternity transforming itself into a religious group, or at least presenting religious features, occurs when the group finds it needs to acquire a representation of itself that can incorporate the idea of its own continuity beyond the immediate context of its members' interrelating. This happens when the group takes on permanence and, seeking to legitimate its existence beyond the inevitable routinization of the emotional experiences that led to the sense of forming a single heart, needs to call upon a common spirit that transcends its individual members.

The transformation implies a profound change in the elective fraternity. It is uniquely founded on the act of the choice by one of another and it depends on the strength of the emotional ties that unite the individual members. This emotional strength is put to the test at every moment, and hence is incompatible with any religious bond, as we have defined the term, since it does not imply that the relationship is itself represented or situated with regard to a more extensive genealogy. Reflecting on the emergence of Christianity in the form of a religion from the first community of Jesus' disciples, Hegel brings out unambiguously that the elective fraternity has no part in religion:

> A circle of love, a circle of hearts which mutually renounce their rights over any particularity, and are united only by a common faith and a common hope, whose enjoyment and joy alone constitute such unanimity of love, this circle is a miniature Kingdom of God; but their love is not religion, because union, human love, does not at the same time contain the representation of this union.[22]

The elective fraternity may even clash with religion, each time it places the communion of the hearts and minds of its members above fidelity to the chain of belief. Clearly this goes some way to explaining the reservations of religious institutions when confronted with the appearance of such groups in their midst. Nor does the fraternity have to harbour utopian designs, and bear an interpretation different from that offered by tradition, for the conflict to come out into the open. This has frequently been the case at the birth of religious orders and has usually given rise to two forms of ruling: direct exclusion, and an institutionally regulated compromise, negotiated with the ecclesiastical authority and inscribed in the order's constitution.

Nor does the elective fraternity have to present itself as an intensely emotional community of disciples which places the charismatic authority of its founder or leader over other forms of authority and especially that of the orthodoxy of the institution in question. But the power struggle which occurs in this case is only one – though the most extreme – of the possible forms of tension resulting from the propensity of any elective fraternity to be self-sufficing, to find in itself every reason to justify its existence, hence to do without any exogenous reference, not excluding the institution which brought its members together in the first place. The rejection shown by all revolutionary organizations in the 1970s of the experiments in communal living developed by their most devoted militants, who sought direct experience of the new values aspired to in the political sphere, or the ambivalent attitude of the Church in respect of the small communities of ardent followers who, in spite of irreproachable orthodoxy, were always suspected of withdrawing into themselves, illustrates the fact that emotional intensification of commitment within an elective fraternity, by lending emotional immediacy to the profit the members draw from belonging to the community, may constitute an unlikely form of exiting from religion.[23]

But the paradox increases, for the emotional intensity of what is experienced is also capable of arousing what is in theory its opposite – and in most cases a fatal – effect, the feeling that the union of hearts transcends immediate individual experience, that it pre-exists their gathering and will survive their breaking up. The more powerfully the union is felt, the more unacceptable the notion that it is as transient as the gathering itself. Rejection of the volatile nature of emotional states is a decisive factor in the religious institutionalization (or reinstitutionalization) of the elective fraternity; it opens the way to the imaginary (re)constitution of the cloud of witnesses, the starting point for a possible (re)formalization of the authentic chain of belief in which the authorized memory is guaranteed. One should point out that this development occurs not only with highly charged elective fraternities, but can occur also when fraternities are constituted in the looser form of affinity networks, so long as such networks act as a powerful emotive force on those who belong to them.

It would be as well at this point to provide an example of a process till now characterized as ideal-typical, hence abstract. The story surrounding the cult-following of Jim Morrison, the fabled lead singer of The Doors, who died at twenty-seven, affords a striking instance of an affinity network turning itself into a religion. It began with a far-flung elective fraternity comprising those who identified with the songs and provocative stance of one of the figureheads of the American protest movement against the materialism of the 1960s and the Vietnam war. With his personal charm and angelic countenance, his notorious excesses, his self-destructiveness and his undeniable poetic gift, Morrison became one of the heroes of a generation in revolt, and his rock concerts unleashed a special fervour. For his fans he stood apart from the group he led, personifying a brother figure, at once fearless, rebellious and untameable, heedless of discipline or rules or accepted standards.[24] His sudden death from a heart attack in Paris in 1971 was received with incredulity, since he had managed to survive drug and alcohol abuse and countless misadventures. His death was the more unacceptable because his existence provided the only link between all those who related personally to him.

Morrison spread no message and developed no clear critique of society.[25] All he did was execrate it while using the vehicle of poetry to invoke the dream of another life. The bond between those who followed his revolt was strictly emotional, and hence unlikely to last. An initial means of preserving it was therefore to deny the death of the hero. 'Ten years later', writes one of his biographers, 'there are people who question whether he really died . . . What did he die of? Over the last years countless theories have been produced, some of them owing their existence to quirkish forms of self-deception. Many people have said perfectly properly that it was quite unlike Jim Morrison to go and die in his bath of a heart attack.'[26]

However, faced with the clear evidence of his absence, the elective fraternity which had identified with him sought stability in terms of religion. In the twenty odd years that have followed his death, his memory has been secured by massive sales of his recordings and the texts of his songs, variously compiled. Circles of his followers in North America, Europe and elsewhere gather to read his texts or come to chant and recite them at his grave in Père Lachaise, which is now a place of pilgrimage throughout the year, with many travelling from a great distance in order to commune there. At times it has been something of a nightmare for those responsible for security in the Père Lachaise cemetery, with the graveside offering a mixture of cults – esoteric and spiritualist, but often involving music and alcohol and drugs too. Such practices have helped bring about the constitution and spread of an oral memory of the singer which has now been passed on to a second generation of followers, born after Morrison's death. Needless to say, it lacks coherence because of the variety of interpretations it gives rise to and the lack of agreement as to the form it should take, this being compounded by the several biographies, each purporting to provide the 'true' account of the phenomenon.

The appearance in 1992 of the film, *The Doors*, added a further element to this confusion by raising the hitherto neglected question of the role played by the other members of Morrison's group in The Doors' distinctive style; hence there is a new problem to nag those who claim to be the true custodians of Morrison's memory: is it to Morrison that fidelity is due, or to The Doors? The issue is of little more than anecdotal interest to those outside the world of rock, yet for the sociologist of religion the manner of its being resolved is of as much concern as certain theological issues which, on the face of it, may be deemed more 'serious'.[27]

Analysis of the dialectics of exiting from religion and resocializing religion, characteristic of elective fraternities, is of particular interest when it moves into the sphere of conventional religions, where the burgeoning of elective fraternities in various forms is clearly not new. In fact, this has always represented one of the expedients by which, openly or imperceptibly, tradition comes to terms with change. It has operated both inside and outside institutions invariably accompanying the modern assertion of pluralism in religion. At the present time, it serves both to express and, in part at least, to resolve the increased tension, within conventional religion itself, between the modern culture of the individual, with its insistence on the rights of subjectivity and on self-realization, and traditional rules affecting belief and observance.

The group of elective brothers and sisters is a forum where authentic personal initiative can find expression and recognition, without reference to an institutionally regulated orthodoxy. The sense of belonging is bound up with attachment to those within the group who share the same interests and emotions. In such conditions, reference to a chain of belief may turn out to be secondary or even unnecessary, dissolving in the magnification of the community to the extent that, for some individuals, the group's withdrawal may imply the abandoning of any reference to religious tradition which membership of the group was initially supposed to mediatize. But frequently a contrary attitude introduces itself into the dynamics of exiting from religion and this implies steering clear of the hazards of communal excess by maintaining a high visibility of endorsing the lineage; which, after all, affords emblems of continuance, in the absence of a body of meaning which no tradition operating in modernity can claim to incarnate.

Discussions with younger members of religious orders have provided me with evidence of there being coexistence between the forces of the immediacy afforded by the community and an appeal to lineage. The more that presentation of commitment to the consecrated life yields to the influence of the immediate and highly emotive links between the individual concerned and his or her brothers or sisters in the order or community, the more a concomitant insistence is placed on the need to signify publicly (by a vestment, for instance) membership of a religious family.[28]

The same line of argument might go some way to explaining certain contradictions in charismatic Catholic groups that puzzle observers. We can take as an example the propensity shown by some, whose overall religious style is very much in keeping with the modern culture of the individual, to develop a cult of sainthood that one would normally associate with a popular premodern form of religiosity. Such a tendency is most frequently explained in terms of a strong desire on the part of these groups to give the ecclesiastical institution an earnest of their Catholic loyalty, which charismatic practices are always held to cast doubt upon. This interpretation is shown to be largely correct when one analyses transactions which have enabled charismatic currents – a contentious enough issue when they first emerged – to be acclimatized into the institutional framework of Catholicism.[29] But it fails to explain why this insistence on Catholic identification attaches in particular to a type of reference which, from the establishment's point of view, no longer occupies a central place in the definition of Catholic identity.

The French episcopate does not give prime importance to the conditions imposed upon charismatic communities for them to obtain full recognition as Catholics loyal to the present pope, nor require them to show their special devotion to the Curé d'Ars; St Louis-Marie Grignion-de-Montfort, or the Blessed Marguerite-Marie Alacoque, who initiated the cult of the Sacred Heart. At most, evidence of such devotion might be considered as a further positive element in the body of evidence testifying to such loyalty.

Before considering the eventuality of these groups thereby manifesting a desire to return to an earlier (pre-Vatican Council) state of Catholicism (an eventuality that is far from being confirmed by those in Renouveau Charismatique), it would be well to examine how reference to the personalized figure of major past witnesses, the saints, can serve, conveniently and immediately (in that they are capable of representation), the process of constituting the imagined genealogy accompanying the group's emotional stabilization and its validation as permanent. Clearly this does not exclude such stabilization serving, in a further degree, the group being enrolled in a larger denominational family (here the Catholic Church), even its being incorporated in this or that branch within the family. No more does it exclude emblematic reference to this or that saint being able to function in such a group, with less immediate ideological implications than those possibly attributed, within Catholic institutions.[30] In extending the argument beyond the limited case of charismatic Catholic communities, it needs to be stressed here that the ongoing deregulation of authorized memory, which favours the burgeoning of elective fraternities, at the same time favours the pluralization – hence incompatibility – of forms in which these same fraternities can bring about, should the need arise, their own religious consolidation.

The rise of ethnic religions

Consideration of the processes of *emblematization* of religious tokens within affinity groups and networks leads us on directly to take account of another dimension of the religious reconstruction of memory in modernity, one that comes into play in the current ethnic revival. The particular attraction that operates between what is ethnic and what is religious springs from the fact that the one and the other establish a social bond on the basis of an assumed genealogy, on the one hand, a naturalized genealogy (because related to soil and to blood), and a symbolized genealogy (because constituted through belief in and reference to a myth and a source), on the other. It is common knowledge that these two genealogical systems overlap closely and reinforce one another in a great many cases. Long observation has shown the process (of the affirmation of identity) activated when it assumes both an ethnic and a religious dimension; the Jewish or Armenian[31] examples are here ideal-typical.

One could also point to the various studies underlining the decisive role played by religion in preserving the ethnic identity of immigrants to the United States.[32] In recent years, the question of the ethnic mobilization of religious symbols arises immediately and dramatically wherever genuine wars of religion reinforce community, social and national confrontation. Limiting oneself to Europe, one only needs call to mind the case of Northern Ireland or that of the fractured societies of central Europe and the Balkans. In the last instance, the various ways of making religious and confessional references an instrument for constructing ethnic and national identity repay particular attention; such instrumentality would clearly function differently depending on how these references have affected the history of the groups mobilizing them and on the actual hold they maintain over their lives.[33]

But cases such as these involving the reacquisition of ethnic and religious memory do not only concern the troubled societies of the Europe that was under Soviet domination. The parallel occurrence of ethnic and religious revival in western democratic societies affords a no less interesting opportunity to make sense of the two phenomena. And one might start by acknowledging that they offer the same sort of emotive response to the demand for meaning and personal recognition which the abstract nature of modern societies with their meritocratic form of government makes ever more urgent; the religious and the ethnic strain compete or combine in re-establishing a sense of 'we' and of 'our' which modernity has at once fractured and created a nostalgia for.

In the course of conversations with Dominique Schnapper, I have become aware of the rewards of combining the methods of the sociology of both religion and ethnicity so as to focus on contemporary neo-community revival. Dominique Schnapper has not limited her approach to discovering functional analogies between ethnic and religious renewal. She has outlined the possibility of convergence to a point where they overlap, except where (as in the Jewish or Armenian context) this has been brought about by history. At the outset of such converging, there occurs the change in conventional religion under the influence of modernization,[34] which enfeebles the transcendental reference 'to the advantage of an initially moral humanitarian conception': 'The personal God, creator of heaven and earth, makes way for man as exemplar. Christ becomes a moral ideal, common to all religions. The so-called vertical – the transcendental – dimension loses force in favour of horizontal morality, the ideal of fraternity between human beings.'[35]

The gradual loss of reference to a personal God,[36] the increasing metaphorization (or symbolization) of the objects of religious belief, are the two chief dimensions in the transformation of religion into a system of ethics which, taken to its extreme, can allow one to confuse it with a morality of human rights. One might consider that the ethical standardization of historical religious traditions goes some way towards accomplishing the universalist design these traditions convey, thus making them less accessible to the appropriation of identity than they once might have been. According to the argument advanced by Dominique Schnapper, the reverse is the case. Transformed into a reservoir of signs and values which no longer correspond to clear-cut forms of belonging and behaviour that comply with rules made by religious institutions, religion (in the meaning of traditional religion) has become a raw material of symbol, and eminently malleable, which can be reprocessed in different ways as required by those who extract it. Thus religion can be incorporated into other symbolic constructions, especially ones which come into play in the development of ethnic identity. If one allows that 'the ethnic factor in the same way as the religious is based on a composite of symbols and values', the coming together of both factors can be seen as a form of overlapping, even of superimposing, of ethico-symbolic entities that are less and less distinct. In Dominique Schnapper's opinion, Islam or Judaism, 'where values that are indissolubly historical and religious merge and are reinforced', could paradoxically provide models for such ethno-religious or politico-moral overlapping.

The chief value of Schnapper's analysis is to point to the improbable connection between the rise of the ethno-religious factor, which is ordinarily taken to be a feature of societies where the process of modernity is little advanced and where institutional differentiation has barely appeared, and a modernity which dissolves religious traditions within a fragmented mass of symbols and values. The process by which these symbols and values are reappropriated for identity is helped on by the decline of the socializing and organizational capability that was proper to religious tradition.

As mentioned earlier, Michel de Certeau has drawn attention, in the context of Christianity in more advanced societies, to the cultural availability of religious signs, which in modernity are no longer associated with specific practices or attitudes or forms of social life. Not that all connection is severed between Christian belief and institutional membership, the observance of ritual, family lifestyle, sexual behaviour or political choice. 'But', he remarks,

> the links are obscure, frequently dramatic, increasingly ambivalent, and slowly uncoupling. The component pieces in the system are adrift. Each one is imperceptibly taking on a different meaning, in one case remaining an expression of faith, in another a catchphrase for conservatism or an instrument in political strategy. . . . The ecclesialogical constellation disintegrates as its elements move out of orbit. The centre no longer 'holds' because there is no longer a firm link between the act of believing and objective signs. Each sign follows its own path, wanders off, submits to different employment, as if the words in a sentence were scattered across the page and produced different combinations of meaning.[37]

In this context, the symbolic heritage of the historic religions is not only made available to individuals who put together a set of meanings that enables them to make sense of their existence. It is also there to be recycled collectively in widely different ways, with the mobilization of denominational symbols for the purposes of identity being given pride of place. The Polish case is here particularly revealing, since the process developed to the point of producing, at the time of active struggle against the Sovietized regime, non-believing followers, individuals actively engaged in the political opposition whose Catholic practice stood both for 'bearing witness against the fundamental hypocrisy of the official secular model'[38] and as evidence of the political, moral and cultural permanence of a Poland that rejected its subjection to the Soviet system. It is clear here that that 'non-belief' extends to matters of substance which in observance would be of primary importance (the existence of a personal God, the Redemption, the real presence in the Eucharist, and so on), but, with the dislocation, observance itself becomes observance of another belief which has to do with the reality

and continuity of the community and which alone ensures its representation as 'we' and 'our'.

It would, however, be quite wrong to think that this scenario is only
likely to develop when the community concerned is put under threat
by exceptional social and political circumstances. In fact, the weakening both of social and political links and of the confessional link, which
is a feature of western democratic societies with their culture of the
individual, produces the apparently reverse phenomenon of ethno-
denominational identification, and this connects with what has been
described above. Confirming Schnapper's demonstration of the ethico-
symbolic imbrication of ethnics and religion in modernity, Eva
Hamberg's account of the situation in Sweden is of particular interest.
She points to the sparsity of church attendance among Swedes and the
evaporation of Christian belief such as the Lutheran Church defines
it.[39] At the same time, she insists that 90 per cent of Swedes declare
themselves to be members of the Church of Sweden – and expressly so
since such a declaration has implications for taxation,[40] and by so doing identify with a historic community and culture whose symbols and
values they accept and whose distinctiveness they lay claim to. For the
Swedes, whom she describes as 'belongers but not believers',[41] Lutheranism fulfils the function, she says, of a civil religion.

For Susan Sundback, observing an identical scenario in Finland, it
would be more accurate to speak of a people's religion,[42] a somewhat
ambiguous description since such a religion, accessible to all social
classes, is not itself defined by opposition to an officially promoted
form of Lutheranism representing the dominant class. The notion of
ethno-religion here aptly describes the system of signs in the service of
religious references – which retain their confessional character, thereby
making reference to a civil religion questionable, in that the function
of these references is to preserve a sense of community which is in
danger of being trivialized by the material and moral uniformity of the
welfare state.

Such manifestations of ethno-religious compensation for the loss of
collective identity are variously present in all western countries. Economic uncertainty or social and political crisis may make them assume more acute, perhaps more threatening, forms; and because
religious institutions, which profess to be the sole legitimate guarantee
of the authentic reference to tradition, have little or no influence over
this appropriation of their role, this threat may appear the more real.
There is nothing new here. The deregulation of access to the symbolic
heritage of historical tradition followed as a matter of course from
institutional differentiation, as we have already said.

Recourse has always been had to this stock of symbols as much by

artists in search of inspiration as by politicians in justifying t
cise of power. The exploitation of traditional religious syml
der to confer identity has the same motivation but acquires disquic...
undertones in the context of multicultural societies where the resurgence of community identities may pose a direct threat to democracy.
The mobilization of symbols of France's Christian identity, from Joan
of Arc to the Gothic cathedrals, by the leader of the French Front
National might be regarded as quaint and fairly harmless were it not
that such references (frequently associated with the childhood of those
addressed and accompanied by images of past glory belied by the uncertainties of the present) can still arouse strong emotive echoes in
sections of society which are culturally deprived or hit by economic
recession. Jean-Marie Le Pen has a clear appreciation of the political
capital to be made by manipulating these emblems; and, with the vigorous support of integrist Catholic groups,[43] in his speeches he constantly couples the threat to national identity with the threat to Christian
civilization.

The growing visibility of a Muslim community, for whom the reaffirmation of religion provides at least partial evidence of the failure of
integrationist policies and which is readily equated by public opinion
with the rise of fundamentalist extremism, draws a response from a
potential audience which is far in excess of the Front National's hard-
core sympathizers. When Jean-Marie Le Pen has a mass celebrated by
a Catholic integrist priest before sending in a 'commando' to wreck an
Islamic cultural centre near Nevers, he is enacting, with the help of
media orchestration, the potential reality of ethno-religious confrontation in a context where the code defining the respective fields of
religion and politics, and their interrelationship, no longer operates.

It might be thought that the absorption of the religious by the ethnic
factor represents in modern societies another version of the exiting
from religion, which with all the manipulation it has been subject to
may have lost all autonomous social reality. But the problem is more
complex. It is noticeable that while the ethnic factor puts the religious
factor to use by assimilating its symbols and values, it takes on a religious function each time it allows this or that social group (possibly
by way of replacement for reference to a chain of belief which traditional religions have weakened by recognizing their common ethical
heritage) the possibility of finding a place within a history which transcends it so as to give meaning to its existence. Thus the convergence
of the ethnic and the religious is a dual movement, operating both
through the ethico-symbolic homogenization of traditional religious
(confessional) identities and through the neo-religious recharging of
ethnic identities. It is a dual movement which involves both a process

of disintegration and one of reintegration through reference to the continuity of a line of belief. This reintegration itself implies renewed forms of mobilizing and inventing a common memory, from symbolic material taken from the traditional stock of historical religions, but equally from the resources offered by profane history and culture, which are themselves reprocessed in accordance with the social and political interests they serve.

To return to the case of Poland, which again serves well as a model here, Patrick Michel points out revealingly that the equation linking Polish and Catholic is of relatively recent origin and came into its own only by way of the political exploitation of Catholic references that occurred in the context of Sovietization. At the same time, he shows how Catholic practice, by instilling an awareness (through images, ritual and pilgrimages) of Poland's rootedness in a past which enables a future to be conceived, laid the foundation, where there were no other symbolic resources available, for a religion of patriotism, giving the word 'religion' its full sense.[44]

Thus the ethno-religious element (re)constitutes itself and develops in modern societies to a point at which the contracting membership of traditional religions intersects with the various attempts to invent or reinvent an imaginative hold on continuity, whereby a group or a society discovers new reasons for belief in its own permanence, over and beyond the perils that threaten its existence (as in the case of the Balkan states or Northern Ireland) or over and beyond the atomization that constitutes a multiple threat to its own cohesion (which is more a feature in the west). Insofar as it has become possible to 'believe without belonging' (to borrow Grace Davie's admirable formula for characterizing the post-religious attitude in Britain,[45] and which looks set to become the prevailing attitude), it has also become possible to 'belong without believing', or more precisely while believing only in the continuity of the group for which the signs preserved from the traditional religion now serve as emblems – a shift in the nature of religion which fails to protect society from some form of return to religious wars, rather the reverse.

Conclusion: Post-traditional Society and the Future of Religious Institutions

Thus far, the emphasis has been on change and fragmentation. Fluidity and mobility are the keywords in modern religion, which finds itself in a world that is pluralistic through and through;[1] and the metaphor used *ad nauseam* to describe the pattern which religion has assumed in this context is that of a symbolic market, a metaphor originally and tentatively proposed in a classic article by Berger and Luckmann.[2] What was simply put forward suggestively as a means of invigorating the sociological imagination has been turned into an all-embracing assumption, with attempts being made to regulate the trading of symbols, which no system of meaning can any longer claim to control on its own, with the help of concepts taken from economic theory.[3]

The effect is to produce a model which is mechanistic and convenient, and which ascribes to religious institutions unequivocal strategies of symbolic marketing. This is taken to somewhat absurd lengths in the attempt by Lawrence Iannaccone, the Californian religious economist, to apply theories of rational choice to the analysis of personal piety, on the basis of the notion that individuals assess the benefits of choice in religion just as they do with any other choice they make.[4] For Berger and Luckmann, the metaphor of the symbolic market was in no sense meant to imply that the production and consumption of religious signs relate literally to highly problematic laws governing the production and consumption of goods and services. Their notion, as developed by Peter Berger, is that in modern society religious adherence has become purely a concern of the individual who incurs no sanction should he or she keep it at a distance, decide to change, or resolve to do without it altogether.[5]

This 'availability' of individual believers for a long while pushed up competitiveness between the dominant purveyors of meaning (established religions, political ideologies, scientist fantasies in a world wholly rational, and so on), whose diversity has been a feature of the course taken by modernity. The current radicalization of modernity, which probably played itself out in the collapse of the last polarization of meaning systems represented by the east–west divide,[6] is demonstrated by a general uncertainty regarding all references, itself an expression of the mistrust felt for the dominant traditions and their claim to permanence and stability. Some see this process as the social consummation of what Nietzsche long ago forecast as the era of nihilism, in which all values lose their value, since they obtain no further than does the power of assertion that proclaims them.

Without touching on the properly philosophical side of the debate, one need only observe that, sociologically speaking, our late twentieth-century generation, the first post-traditional generation, is the first one to find itself in a situation of structural uncertainty symptomized by the mobility, reversibility and transferability of all markers. The situation is one that does not even allow of a compensating recourse to belief in the continuity of a world whose complexity fails to draw out a modern version of belief in progress and a positive future for humanity, beyond crisis and cataclysm. The final collapse of the world of tradition has to be confronted without the eschatological predictions on offer from either traditional or so-called secular religions.

The break between the rule of tradition and that of modernity has occurred at the (clearly ideal) point at which evidence of continuity has become transformed into a vision of change represented as progress. The present transformation of modernity is taking place at the (equally ideal) point at which the dynamic representation of continuity whereby tradition could be given a utopian reconstruction has itself disintegrated. Does this mean that we are entering the phase that is sometimes called postmodernity? In the sense which Alain Touraine gives to the term, postmodernity is characterized by the 'complete dissociation of instrumental rationality which has now become a strategy in mobile markets and communities locked in their distinctness'. It corresponds to 'the dissociation of economic strategies and of the construction of a form of society, culture and personality', in a world in which the conditions for economic growth, political liberty and individual happiness no longer appear analogous and interdependent.[7] The process of dissociation is a logical development of modernity itself; and Alain Touraine scrutinizes the different variants – hyper-modernism in Daniel Bell, anti-modernism in Baudrillard or Lipovetsky, cultural environmentalism in opposition to the universalism of the modernist ideology or other attempts to refute the claims of modernity to represent the fictitious unity of a world ruled entirely by the market – variants of a post-historicism that in several ways acknowledges the elimination of the individual rationally engaged in creating a society.

Postmodernisms assume charge of this essential reshaping of the relationship between human beings and society which is a consequence of humanity being immersed in a world of signs and language that lacks historical depth, in which 'everything fragments, from individual personality to life in society.' Touraine's purpose is to look beyond the success of the postmodernist critique in a search for a new definition of modernity which recognizes the relative autonomy of society and actors and sets a distance between itself and both neo-liberalism 'which describes a society reduced to being a market with no actors' and a postmodernism 'which calls to mind actors without a system, enclosed in their imagination and their memories'.[8]

Thus he is led to address the notion of postmodernity itself, aside from the many and frequently ambiguous meanings attributed to it. These ambiguities are of little concern to us here and we would recommend concentrating on the notion of high modernity used by Anthony Giddens to denote the omnipresence of risk (hence of uncertainty) peculiar to modern societies. Giddens sees the massive exposure to risk as the result of globalization which places the everyday life of each individual at the mercy of upheavals affecting society on a planetary scale.[9] Deprived of the security of stable communities which supplied evidence of a code of meaning that was fixed once and for all, deprived too of the great universalist visions imparted by modernist ideologies, individuals are adrift in a universe without fixed bearings. Their world is no longer one they can construct together. Self-fulfilment is now the chief aim, the subjective unification of fragmented experience that corresponds to different sectors of activity and different social relations. Given such a context, the deliberate choice of invoking the authority of a tradition, by becoming incorporated into a continuing lineage, constitutes one possible, post-traditional way of constructing self-identity among others, all of which call upon an individual's affectivity and are fed on his or her search for community, and his or her memories and longings.

Post-traditional religion and the institution of the religious

The very dissemination of ways in which individuals attempt to reconstruct meaning for themselves, through reflecting on the diversity of experience they have undergone in a kind of perpetual present, is at the source of the explosion of the religious in the context of high modernity. Any such experiences, emotional, aesthetic, intellectual or of whatever sort, can act as a fulcrum for the subjective reconstruction of meaning, by providing a hold for the imaginative (re)constitution of a chain of belief. The act of acquiring religious coherence may be absolute and afford an organizing principle for an individual's entire life; it may be partial and combine with other forms of imposing meaning on subjective experience. However that may be, the religious reference to a chain of belief affords the means of symbolically resolving the loss of meaning that follows from heightened tension between the unrestrained globalization of social phenomena and the extreme fragmentation of individual experience.

The rise of the religious does not necessarily give rise to religion. For that to be the case, it would require reference to tradition to be capable of generating social links. In other words, it would require assembly of the minimum conditions for a collective validation of meaning necessary for a community of believers to be able to establish itself, in the dual form of a tangible social group – whose organization may range from very informal to very formal – and an imaginary lineage, both past and future. Inasmuch as there no longer is any broad spontaneous evidence of temporal and spatial continuity experienced within the family, at work, in a neighbourhood or a denominational gathering, such a pattern has to come from commitment on the part of individuals who acknowledge their membership of a genuine spiritual community.

This helps in understanding why the sect, entry to which is invariably through conversion, that is to say personal choice, constitutes a form of religious association presenting, ideal-typically, more affinity with current features of cultural modernity than do church-type groups, which nevertheless apply themselves, according to classic Troeltschian typology and unlike sects, to seeking a compromise with cultural modernity. It has often been observed that the forms of religious renewal which occur within the major churches favour the acclimatization of sect-type features (personal commitment, emotional intensity, egalitarianism, closed community and so on) within church-type systems. In standard approaches to analysing routinization within religious institutions, the sectarian dynamics of renewal is often linked to the radicalism of beginnings, a radicalism destined in the medium term to become subdued, to be 'ecclesiasticized'.[10]

If this perspective presents some interest, it nevertheless skirts the essential – namely, the eminently modernizing function of the sectarian argument itself and its renewed applicability to cultural pluralism.[11] Thus, just as it dissolves, as does its opposite, all religious systems built on the heteronomous authority of a tradition, modernity, like its counterpart, gives rise to the possibility of post-traditional religion. Such a religion, instead of making individual obligation ensue from its assumed generation within a tradition, defers recognition of a tradition's power of generation to the effectiveness of individual commitment.

In modernity, being religious is not so much knowing oneself begotten as willing oneself so to be. This fundamental reworking of the relationship with tradition which characterizes modern religious believing opens up theoretically limitless possibilities for inventing, patching together and playing with systems of meaning that are capable of 'establishing tradition'. But only theoretically, for history and sociocultural determination impose limits on what can be believed, conceived of and imagined and, further to these limits, context itself is restrictive. This is well illustrated in the studies made by Roland Campiche of the case of Switzerland.[12] Yet in spite of there being effective limits to a self-assembling construction of belief, the transformation in the relationship to tradition does not simply mean that no particular tradition can any longer claim a monopoly of meaning. It affects, at its very source, the institution of the religious, by way of the institution of believing. What is called into question today – and probably irreversibly – is the possibility of an authoritative system being able to impose itself in society, of its being in a position, while vouching for the truth of this or that body of belief, to exercise exclusive control over its proclamation (by selected representatives) as well as over what is proclaimed (by sifting, standardizing and grading the authorized content) of such a body of belief.[13]

Beyond secularization, de-institutionalization

This last proposition, as I see it, implies that the discussion on secularization – to what extent are modern societies secularized societies? Is secularization irreversible? – is now superseded. The real debate, and the real issue for a sociology of the major religions, relates to the consequences for the traditional institutions of religion of the radical de-institutionalization of the religious. For the problem they face is not primarily the management of their fairly discordant relationship with a secular environment which tends to marginalize their influence, still less that of knowing whether their loss of influence is the result of eagerness or reluctance to make concessions to modern culture. There is indeed something desperate in the contradictory self-criticism shown by Christian institutions, Catholic and liberal Protestant alike, in the face of the mounting indifference surrounding them, and in their reproaching themselves both with 'carrying their compromise with worldly attitudes too far' and with 'being unable to talk the language of today'. The real problem that concerns the future – perhaps the survival – of traditional religious institutions has to do with their ability, as an essential part of their function and a mark of their credibility in the world of high modernity, to give serious attention to the flexible nature of believing as it affects them, and which must oblige them to come to terms with the dynamics of the propagating and reprocessing of religious signs, itself a negation of the traditional mode of administering authorized memory.

How can religious institutions, with their prime purpose of preserving and transmitting a tradition, reform their own system of authority – essential for the continuity of a line of belief – when the tradition is thought of, even by believers, not as a sacred trust, but as an ethico-cultural heritage, a fund of memory and a reservoir of signs at the disposal of individuals? All religious institutions, whatever the theological notions of the religious authority they deploy, are faced with this question. Their problem, in every single case, is not primarily the cultural risk to the symbolic heritage in their possession: the point has already been made that in an uncertain world this constituted a singularly potent attraction. The problem is the possibility open to them of dispensing the true memory that can be used as a weapon against believers for whom the subjective truth of their own line of belief is primary.

This shift in the repository of the truth of belief from the institution to the believer does not only concern those who assemble their beliefs ('I'm religious in my own way'), or those who allow the possibility, if not the probability, of their believing ('I believe in something, but I'm not quite sure what'), both of whom surveys show to be on the increase, particularly in the younger generations, where relativism counts for more.[14] The trend towards a metaphor-fed subjectivizing of the contents of belief and the separation of belief and practice, the crisis facing the notion of religious obligation, the shift in the importance of observance in relation to the institutional norm defining the terms of authorized recall and so on, are merely the most readily available and assessable symptoms of the disintegration of all religious systems of belief. But the same current affects certain neo-integralist movements – Catholic or Protestant charismatic movements in the first place – which are not necessarily to be counted as part of the demodernizing strain disturbing the dominant churches in spite of the assertiveness of their certainties in belief. Manifestly such movements start from the premise, in clear contradiction of modern thought, that the world in which they live has a wholly religious meaning and this gives it fundamental unity. But this religious meaning in their view can only be recognized subjectively, through the personal experience of the one who can read the signs providentially placed in his or her path.

> Everyone round me has a religious meaning, everything that happens to me, every event has religious significance. But the meaning is for me. It is up to each person to discover it in the course of his or her own experience. It is up to me to discern the sense of what is granted me in my everyday life, through the inspiration the Spirit gives me, and with the help of my community, with whom I share my experiences.

This extract of a conversation with a young management expert, who holds a doctorate in computer science and is a member of a charismatic prayer group, well illustrates this subjective fundamentalism, expressed through a construct of signs, whose unified representation of the fragmented world in which the individual in question lives is open to him or to her alone; a world whose ground rules, albeit profane, he or she can accept since in any event they are secondary in comparison with the 'real meaning of things' for which he or she holds the key. The separation – which might be described as schizophrenic if taken to its extreme – between the real world, with its own laws, and the subjective world of constructed meaning – 'realer than the real world' – constitutes a paradoxical means of recognizing the autonomy of the world, at the same time as it offers a possibility of religious integralism ('the whole of religion in the whole of life') becoming adapted to the modern culture of the individual ('the whole of my religion in the whole of my life'). It goes some way towards explaining the mystery, as it is sometimes seen, of the very large number of individuals with high scientific and technological qualifications who belong to renewal movements which promise their followers a complete rehabilitation in religion of their personal existence.

But these believers for whom everything is a sign perhaps pose as many problems to religious institutions as do those who profess a 'take it or leave it' form of belief. In both cases the institution's capability to control, or at least regulate, meaning, in this instance a product of the individual and of the community, is in some degree at least called into question.[15] In both cases, such questioning is a function of the assertion of the primacy of the individual and of his or her experience over institutionally controlled conformity with the norms of belief implicit in the lineage. In both cases, religious experience is compatible with full and entire participation in this or that branch of secular culture; either because its scope is strictly limited to what is private and intimate, or because its domain is that of 'another reading', a purely spiritual and subjective reading, of the reality of the world.

The point needs to be made once again that Christianity – unlike Judaism or Islam, both of which attach more emphasis to the fulfilment of observances as a criterion of religious belief[16] – has itself facilitated the destabilizing of the essential structure of the religious, constituted by reference to an authorized memory, by giving the believer's personal faith, 'in spirit and in truth', pride of place. The modern de-institutionalization of the religious which reaches its culmination in the cultural world of high modernity is, in part at least, an offshoot of the Christian subjectivization of religious experience.

But pointing to this vulnerability in the Christian religion, itself a source of support for a theology advocating the coming of Christianity without religion, in no way implies that the other traditional religions can avoid a fundamental reworking of the relationship with tradition which is the peculiar feature of religious modernity. In the Jewish context, the development of movements embodying a return to tradition conforms, somewhat paradoxically but surely, to the general mood of destabilizing the institution of the religious, which displays innovative ways of redirecting a tradition that has been turned into a toolbox of symbols. This is well illustrated in Herbert Danzger's study of the Ba'alei T'shuva in the United States, in which young people of Jewish extraction began in the 1970s to make a total commitment not to a reformed or conservative doctrine of Judaism but to the most anti-modern orthodoxy.[17] Danzger shows how broad the divide is between these returnees and earlier instances of return to Jewish observance. Judaism in North America has long witnessed cases of young Jews, who generally for very personal reasons of wishing to assume their identity, return to the tradition of their forebears. The Talmud Torah and the congregational schools had, with them in mind and after negotiating a settlement with American educational authorities, already set up a system of remedial classes designed to meet the needs of those who had, and expressly felt, a lack of background in Jewish culture. In the 1970s these classes were swamped by new candidates, most often from a counter-culture, who were looking to an integral form of Judaism, removed from the slightest compromise with the secular world, to provide them with an alternative means of decrying the American way of life, from a stance which they had in most cases previously developed through the experience of different sorts of alternative community. Danzger shows clearly how for the first elements among them, sizeable enough in the 1950s, the principal aim was to revive the memory of their origins and re-establish contact with their past, and thus by way of 'backward' reidentification be able to reconstruct their Jewish identity within American society in the wake of the Shoah. Jewish institutions offered them teaching programmes, summer camps, beginners' *minyans* and placements within practising families, a close contact with their culture and religion which they had missed in their own upbringing.

The second wave have quite different aims. Jewish orthodoxy attracts them because it affords an opportunity to break away from the secular world, to change one's life. Danzger gives prominence to the affinity that exists between these new converts to orthodoxy and a culture of self secreted by the modernity they reject (unfortunately he does not develop analysis beyond recognizing the problem this causes the Jewish establishment). Judaism is seen by them as a community of publicly declared affinities (special food, special clothes and so on), in which the charisma of the *rebbe* and insistence on ritual serve to strengthen emotional ties within the community. Religious radicalism which prompts them to seek the strictest conformity with Jewish laws has the unexpected effect of setting off a shock wave in currents of orthodoxy that one would least expect of compromise with the outside world; because the significance put upon observance by these neophytes places the system of institutionalized observance in an ambiguous position on sensitive questions such as the weight given to personal experience or the place of women within the community. More fundamentally, the question that arises from Danzger's observations (confirmed by other studies of the return to tradition in other contexts) concerns the institution of traditional Jewish life itself, when tradition ceases to represent the evidence of a way of life passed down from generation to generation and becomes an object of subjective preference on the part of individuals who choose to relate to it.

The institutional production of a chain of memory

One question that is bound to arise is that of knowing whether the impact of the crisis affecting religious institutions upon traditional religions does not apply especially to those in which the authority of tradition is expressly formalized under the guidance of a *magisterium* recognized as having the exclusive power to regulate religious observance. This would further justify sociologists of Protestantism in again pointing to the difference with churches which grew out of the Reformation and which do not conform to the 'ritual institutional model', identified by Jean-Paul Willaime as being one of the three ideal-typical models for regulation in religious institutions.[18]

In the case of this last model, best exemplified by Catholicism, the institution itself is the repository of truth. With its hierarchical structure directly threatened by the recognition that the growing number of new communities it is harbouring closely matches the tendency for belief to become individualized, it has reacted energetically by reaffirming the centrality of the doctrinal authority of Rome. Thus it is committed to normalizing the references offered not just to the faithful but to all humanity. This is borne out by the recent publication of a universal catechism whose aim is both to reassert the articles of belief in a unified form and to impose restrictions on conduct admissible in every area of life, for believers and for the whole of humanity as well. In an uncertain world, whose socially and psychologically destructive features it never tires of dwelling upon, the Catholic Church strives to offer recourse to a stable system of clear references.

But there is a contradiction in that its offer of meaning is only credible, in a world where the subjectivity of the individual predominates, inasmuch as it avoids being a recital of duties incumbent on the faithful. The Church is obliged to compensate for the loss of authority sustained by its message by giving it a prophetic character; and the distance between the message and the values of those to whom it is addressed is presumed to testify to its truth. But the prophetic charge given the normative discourse fails to operate outside the decreasing circle of believers for whom in any event it has always been the norm. Hence the breach (which is very clear over the question of contraception and the use of condoms as a safeguard against Aids, though rather less so over abortion) leaves priests with no alternative but to reiterate the interdiction and/or reflect rather sadly – as did the chairman of the conference of French bishops recently – on what could be done to 'narrow the gulf between the Church and civil society'.[19]

Clearly, the Reformed Church with its long experience of internal pluralism and a religious mentality which affirms the believer's autonomy outside the authority of the Bible, is able to be more flexible. But one must be careful not to see a too systematic contrast with the Catholic model of doctrinal normalization. It may be true that Protestantism establishes the continuity of the lineage (the apostolic succession, in theological language) in a way that is appropriate to the message rather than through conformity in observance, but the problem of legitimate interpretation, and hence of the authority constituted to convey the true memory of the message, is nonetheless present. It is in fact more acute to the extent that the Protestant churches have fewer means for imposing the true memory. As Jean-Paul Willaime remarks, 'the affirmation of the *sola scriptura* and of the universal priesthood of believers may easily result in a religious group only bringing together people who practise a given reading of Bible texts and who only recognize religious power in the person or group promoting a specific understanding of the Christian tradition'.[20]

The threat of sectarian fragmentation is constantly alive in the Reformed Church inasmuch as the ideological institutional model which prevails makes religious truth a matter of interpretation, leading to constant criticism of the formulation used in the presentation of articles of faith. The need to face this historically recurring threat has led Protestant churches themselves to develop an inclination to institutionalize ideological power, which can serve to construct and reconstruct authorized memory within the religious group. The Protestant desacralization of the institution has weakened authorized memory, but alongside 'schisms which have come about because of a reading judged to be more truthful to a biblical context', Protestantism has continued to create tradition for itself – a more mobile, more fluid tradition perhaps, but tradition nonetheless, which constitutes it as an exclusive religion, hence makes it answerable for the destabilizing of all authorized memory that is a feature of high modernity.

The problem which confronts the major religions because of the crisis in the institution of the religious, itself a product of high modernity, occurs outside their various differences about how the relationship with the truth is to be managed. It has to do with the possibility that the capital of memory each one constitutes may continue to create tradition, in other words that it may take on lasting representation as a chain of belief, transcending the different communities in which the chain has been and is made actual. The cultural demise of the comprehensive memory which historically provided the dominant religions with their legitimacy is a consequence of the tendency to uniformity and fragmentation in modern societies. It nurtures a dual process of reconciling the different ethical traditions, on the one hand by extracting a number of universal values, on the other through the spread of community-based small memories which absorb the need for identity, itself suppressed by the modern culture of uniformity masquerading as universality.

Thus all religious institutions mobilize their resources in the endeavour to seek out the possible symbolic benefits of the contradiction in which they are inevitably placed. They resort to an ecumenicalism of values so as to bring out the closeness of all believers within a culture that shows no response to institutionalized religious discourse and at the same time the divergence of communities which enables them to meet the demands for identity that match present uncertainties. It is a high-risk endeavour, in that a too great insistence on one dimension of the strategy immediately alienates those among their faithful who identify mainly or entirely with the other. The problem for all religious denominations is to have to give equal attention to the expectations of the faithful who seek authority in a message rather than an institution, and to those of other faithful who choose to belong to a community rather than submit to a body of beliefs and values. The best means of lessening the risk (in particular, the risk of sectarian splintering which such a situation encourages) is to exercise as little control as possible over signs and thus intervene as little as possible in the attempts by the different tendencies to reach a compromise.

Two registers seem particularly to favour the policy of conflict-avoidance which religious institutions have opted for in order to tackle the danger both of implosion and of outside competition to which they are subject because of the generalized fragmentation of the religious – emotional mobilization on the one hand, cultural rationalization on the other. Emotional mobilization provides a means of transcending conflict by recreating an individual and collective consciousness of emotional belonging, cultural rationalization of playing down conflict by giving it the appearance of a worthwhile expression of diversity in culture and feeling; in fact, the religious establishment, which is itself grappling with cultural modernity, is well able to accept this. In each case, the institution arms itself against the possibility of those it considers its constituents exiting from religion – employing the expression of belief without obligatory reference to tradition in the register of emotion, and the reference to tradition, without its necessarily implying believing, in the case of cultural rationalization. At the meeting point of these two dimensions it seeks to reconstruct the effect of lineage for which there is no longer a natural place in the continuity of generations.

To see this complex strategy in action, it is instructive to turn to the various operations which religious institutions are obliged to engage in so as to maintain their visibility in a cultural and symbolic climate, where their message is under threat of dilution from anodyne generalized ethical systems[21] and from attempts to rebuild identity over which they have no control. If one simply takes recent instances from France, one might again point to the Église Réformée de France and its attempts to recover its own memory in order to head off the danger of its own disappearance in view of the compromise it has made with modernity.[22]

These attempts well exemplify a strategy of marrying the emotivity of belonging with a reasoned appeal to ethico-cultural heritage. From the commemoration of the tricentenary of the revocation of the Edict of Nantes to the setting up of museums of Protestantism,[23] the urge to restore the Protestant grasp of continuity, the lifeline of its survival as a religion, has coalesced with the emotional remembrance of a minority, living its faith under the permanent threat of destruction, and with the celebration of Protestantism's historic contribution to the modern ideals of the Republic.

Judaism in France has adopted a similar strategy. The mass festival called by the Chief Rabbi and the Consistory at the Le Bourget exhibition centre outside Paris in 1991 was both a celebration of the unity of Judaism – cemented by the experience of genocide and recalled in commemorating the Shoah – and a buoyant testimony to its cultural diversity. It had the dual aim (a) of exorcizing the aggravated antagonism between models of Jewish identity extant in the community, and (b) of facing up to the threat posed to this same community by the steadily growing number of mixed marriages.

As a further instance of institutional top-down attempts to revive consciousness of a chain of belief there is the initiative taken by the Roman Church in launching worldwide pilgrimages of young people to places of special significance in Christian history, such as Rome, Santiago de Compostela and Czestochowa. Again the double strategy is clear – emotional remembrance and historico-cultural reconstruction of the failing memory of the continuity of belief. The masses of young pilgrims (500,000 in Spain, 2,000,000 in Poland), prepared for the final gathering by the long journey across Europe by bus, by train, in some cases even on foot, were invigorated by the sheer impact of their numbers, by the elation of taking part in an event that was being given worldwide media coverage and by the scale of the final celebration with the pope himself as principal actor.

The purpose behind such mobilization of feeling, involving as it did discovery of visible traces of the history of Christianity in Europe,[24] was to induce all who participated resolutely to take on – and be seen to take on – a Catholic identity, an identity given respectability by rapid immersion in religious instruction during the ten days that the pilgrimage lasted with its solemn confirmation by the papal presence. Yet one cannot say with complete conviction that the effect of this consciously organized (re)assembling of the chain of belief on those taking part fully corresponded with the aims of its promoters. It would seem that the essential element in the whole experience was its cultural (and ethical) affirmation of youth, given universality because of its cosmopolitan character, and not the assertion of religious and denominational identity.[25] Beyond the contrast in the position and perception of the young pilgrims *vis-à-vis* those who took charge of the pilgrimage (as it became clear from the different surveys conducted after the event), the abiding impression is that from an institutional point of view the attempt to instil and control voluntary identification with tradition is an extremely hazardous operation.

What clearly emerges here is the ambivalent character of religion in modernity, in which the traditional religions can only hold their own by tentatively exploiting the symbolic resources at their disposal in order to reconstruct a continuing line of belief for which the common experience of individual believers provides no support. How do these policies that are based on tradition meld with the production of the religious in modernity, which it has been the purpose of this book to analyse? What new patterns of belief play a role in this encounter? Together with what types of religious sociality, implying what modes of symbolic and ideological regulation? What new interlinking of religion with politics and with culture is likely to come about? There is a vast field of investigation for a comparative sociology of traditional religions, which might open onto a more general sociology of the problems of transmission in modern societies. Certainly, these concluding remarks give little idea of the potential of such a project. But it was never our purpose actually to set our course in that direction. Our purpose has been to try to prepare the ground for an initiative which is capable of drawing the sociology of religion away from its abiding propensity – beyond every reappraisal of the theories of secularization – to conceive the relation of the religious to the modern through the spectrum of an inevitably damaging transformation of the historic religions. Such an approach would enable transformation to be conceived as inseparable from the problem of religious modernity itself. The aim is ambitious, probably too ambitious. But it waits on a more credible one being found.

Notes

1 Sociology in Opposition to Religion? Preliminary Considerations

1 See Poulat (1987) and Béguin, Tardits et al. (1987).
2 Le Bras (1956: 6).
3 Desroche (1968: ch. 1); Desroche, Séguy (1970); Poulat (1986, 1990).
4 Le Bras (1956: 6).
5 Ibid.
6 Ibid., p. 7.
7 François-André Isambert gives a penetrating analysis of this essentialist deviation in phenomenology in his comments on Roger Caillois's interpretation of festivals (1966: 291–308), which he returns to in Desroche, Séguy (1970: 217–57); see also Isambert (1982: 125ff).
8 Bourdieu (1987: 155–61).
9 Ibid., p. 160.
10 Boudon (1988: 73–6).
11 Burnouf, *La Science des religions* (Paris, 3rd edn, 1870), quoted in Desroche, Séguy (1970: 175).
12 Touraine (1974: 26).
13 Durkheim (1982: preface to 2nd edn).
14 Bourdieu (1968: introduction).
15 See Bertrand Russell's graphic summary in *Science and Religion* (1999).
16 Bellah: 'Christianity and Symbolic Realism', *Journal for the Scientific Study of Religions*, 9 (1970), p. 93, included in Bellah (1970); also see Bellah: 'Comments on the Limits of Symbolic Realism', *Journal for the Scientific Study of Religions*, 13 (1974), pp. 487–9.
17 Robbins, Anthony, Curtis, 'The Limits of Symbolic Realism', *Journal for*

the Scientific Study of Religions, 12 (1973), pp. 259–71; 'Reply to Bellah', ibid., 13 (1974), pp. 491–5; and Anthony, Robbins, 'From Symbolic Realism to Structuralism', ibid., 14 (1975), pp. 403–13.
18 Durkheim (1984: 119).
19 Vidich, Lyman (1985).
20 Le Bras (1956: 15).

2   The Fragmentation of Religion in Modern Societies

1 Le Bras (1956: 10–11).
2 Gauchet (1985: introduction, p. 11).
3 Marx (1977: 63).
4 On the debate surrounding the question of the future of religion in Marxist theory and research, see Bertrand (1979).
5 See Cathy Rousselet: *Secte et église: essai sur la religion non institution-nalisée en Union soviétique*, thesis at the Institut des Études Politiques de Paris, supervised by Hélène Carrère d'Encausse, June 1990.
6 Pickering (1984: 421–99).
7 Three different interpretations of Durkheim's thought on religion, and in particular his conception of new religion, are contained in three articles which appeared together in a special number of the *Archives de Sciences Sociales des Religions*, devoted to Durkheim: *Relire Durkheim*, 69 (1990). See Jean-Claude Filloux: 'Personne et sacré', pp. 41–53; José A. Prades: 'La Religion de l'humanité. Notes sur l'anthropocentrisme durkheimien', pp. 55–68; and W. J. Pickering: 'The Eternality of the Sacred: Durkheim's Error', pp. 91–108. On the basis of these three articles and of three earlier studies by their authors, François-André Isambert has brought together three views on Durkheim's conception of the religion of mankind (1992: 443–62).
8 See Isambert (1990: 129–46).
9 See Alexander (1990: 161–71).
10 Séguy (1990: 127–38).
11 Weber (1978: 399).
12 Witness the following statement on the part of an anthropologist of religion to the effect that religion has had its day: 'The evolutionary future of religion is extinction. Belief in supernatural beings and supernatural forces that affect nature without obeying nature's laws will erode and become only an interesting historical memory. . . . Belief in supernatural powers is doomed to die out, all over the world, as a result of the increasing adequacy and diffusion of scientific knowledge' (Anthony F. C. Wallace, *Religion: An Anthropological View*, New York: Random House, 1966, p. 265).
13 See Balandier (1985).
14 de Certeau, Domenach (1974).
15 See the illuminating analysis of the Swiss context provided by Campiche, Bovay et al. (1992: chs I and II).

16 Nora (1996a: introduction, in particular; and 1996b).
17 Nesti (1985).
18 See Séguy (1986: 175–85).
19 Poulat (1986: 400).
20 For example, the volume in question – *État des sciences sociales en France* (Poulat: 1986) – places the sociology of religion not in the sociology section but in that reserved for religious sciences.
21 Ibid., p. 399.
22 See McGuire (1992: Ch I, III–X).
23 Tylor (1871).
24 Robertson (1970: 36ff).
25 See Champion (1989: 155–69) and 'La Nébuleuse mystique-ésotérique. Orientations psycho-religieuses des courants mystiques et ésotériques contemporains', in Champion, Hervieu-Léger (1990).
26 Ibid., p. 52.
27 Luckmann (1967).
28 Luckmann (1990).
29 An assessment of Durkheim's far-reaching influence on the sociology of religion in North America is to be found in Talcott Parsons: 'Durkheim on Religion Revisited', in Glock, Hammond (1973).
30 In his introduction to Max Weber's *The Sociology of Religion*, Talcott Parsons describes the process of rationalization as the business of systematizing the 'pattern or program for life as a whole, which is given meaning by an existential conception of the universe, and within it the human condition in which action is to be carried out' (Parsons, 1969).
31 See, for example, T. F. O'Dea:

> Religion, by its reference to a beyond and its belief concerning man's relationship to that beyond, provides a supraempirical view of a larger total reality. In the context of this reality, the disappointments and frustrations inflicted on mankind by uncertainty and impossibility, and by the institutionalised order of human society, may be seen as meaningful in some ultimate sense, and this makes acceptance and adjustment to them possible. (O'Dea, 1966: 2)

32 Yinger (1957).
33 Tillich (1955), in which this quotation from Reinhold Niebuhr occurs.
34 Luckmann (1967: 48–9).
35 See Wilson (1982: 41–2).
36 For Bryan Wilson's analysis of the NRMs and, more generally, of the situation of religion in modernity, see Wilson (1976: 268–80; 1979: 315–32; 1981; 1990) and Barker (1982).
37 See also Lambert (1991).
38 The notions of sacred cosmos and of cosmization are taken up by Peter Berger (1967). Religion is 'the human enterprise by which a sacred cosmos is established' (p. 25). Cosmization, upon which religion rests, enables humankind to project itself as far as possible outside itself, by

creating in imagination a universe of objective meanings and hence in the most complete and effective way imposing its own meanings on reality.

39 Bellah (1970; 1975); Bellah, Hammond (1980). On the debate concerning civil religion in the United States, see Gail Gehrig: *American Civil Religion: An Assessment* (Storrs, Conn.: Society for the Scientific Study of Religion, Monograph Series, no. 3, 1979).
40 Coleman (1970: 76).
41 Bellah (1957).
42 For a detailed account of the theoretical issues and the debate surrounding the problem, see O'Toole (1984).
43 Lambert (1991).
44 Campiche, Bovay et al. (1992: 33–6).

3   The Elusive Sacred

1   See, for example, Desrosiers (1986); Hammond (1985); Rivière, Piette (1990).
2   Hervieu-Léger (1986: 225–6).
3   In the overall perspective, these terminological differences count for little: 'sacred cosmos' and 'invisible religion' are given equivalence by Luckmann.
4   See Zylberberg (1985) for an incisive approach to this question.
5   Bell (1977: 420–49).
6   Wilson (1979: 315–32).
7   Richard Fenn (1978) argues lucidly that religion and the sacred are symbolic constructs which are historically defined in terms of the social struggle for the legitimation of authority and power structures.
8   Voyé (1991: 45–56).
9   Phillip Hammond (1985) affords a good instance of the contradiction in that his aim is to reassess classical theories of secularization on this basis; see also Hunter, Ainlay (1986: 143–58).
10 Rivière, Piette (1990).
11 Ibid., p. 203.
12 Ibid., pp. 219–20.
13 Nonetheless there are interesting reflections on the issue, involving mimetic, metonymic, analogical and metaphoric religiosity (ibid., pp. 228–9).
14 See Rivière's introduction, ibid., p. 7.
15 Piette (1993). The modifications here made to the earlier definition are substantial yet fall short of constituting a new model: the three elements forming the basis of the definition – the representation of transcendency, the production of the sacred and the specific mythico-ritual whole – remain the same.
16 Isambert (1982: section 3).
17 Ibid., p. 215.
18 Ibid., p. 250.

19 Ibid., p. 255.
20 In this connection, see the observations on art as a means of access to the sacred in C. Bourniquel and J. C. Meili, *Les Créateurs du sacré* (Paris: Éditions du Cerf, 1966).
21 Isambert has further developed the critique of the cross-cultural application of anthropological concepts (1979: introduction); see also his critique of religious phenomenology in Desroche, Séguy (1970: 217–40).
22 Isambert (1982: 267).
23 Ibid., p. 266.
24 Ibid., pp. 266–7.
25 Ibid., p. 270.
26 Veyne (1976: 586).
27 Durkheim (1995: 216–28).
28 Wach (1955: 21ff).
29 Bergson (1977).
30 Bastide (1967: 133–4).
31 Deconchy (1959: 51–70).
32 James (1985: 32).
33 Introduction to the *Manuel d'histoire des religions* by Chantepie de la Saussaye (Paris, 1904).
34 Wach (1955: 21).
35 Desroche (1969b: 79–88).
36 Vigarello, 'D'une nature . . . l'autre. Les paradoxes du nouveau retour', in Pociello (1981: 239ff).
37 See Yonnet (1982).
38 See contribution from Gabriel Cousin – 'Du stade à la création' – to the symposium *Sport et société* (Saint-Étienne, *CIEREC*, June 1981).
39 See Reid Cole, 'Rituals among track athletes', in McNamara (1974: 36ff).
40 Brohm (1976: 243).
41 Ibid., pp. 249ff.
42 Ibid., p. 260.
43 Michel Bernard, 'Le Spectacle sportif. Les paradoxes du spectacle sportif ou les ambiguités de la compétition theâtralisée', in Pociello (1981: 355).
44 See Champion, Hervieu-Léger (1990: 217–48).
45 Samarin (1972: introduction).
46 Acts 2: 1–4, 42–6. See Synan (1971).
47 This would appear to be an instance of emotionalism on the part of heirs in the sense in which Jean Séguy speaks of 'millenarianism of heirs': see Séguy (1983 and 1975).
48 de Certeau, Domenach (1974: 13).

4 Religion as a Way of Believing

1 Séguy (1989).
2 Ibid., p. 177.
3 Weber (1991: 77ff).

4   Weber (1978 and 1952).
5   Séguy (1989: 178).
6   See Mothé (1973) or Bourdet (1976).
7   Séguy (1989: 178).
8   Ibid., pp. 178–9.
9   Ibid., p. 180.
10 See 'Nous pouvons donc recommander notre frère. Essai d'analyse sémiologique d'un passage du rituel des malades', *Bulletin d'Information du Centre Thomas More*, 14 June 1976; also Isambert (1975), and 'Réforme liturgique et analyse sociologique', *La Maison-Dieu*, 128 (1976), included in Isambert (1979).
11 Azria (1991: 53–70).
12 Séguy (1989: 181).
13 de Certeau (1983).
14 Jean Pouillon, 'Remarques sur le verbe croire' in Izard, Smith (1979: 43–51). Instancing the '*margaï*', the spirits which hold so important a place in the individual lives of the Hadjeraï', Pouillon stresses that the Hadjeraï 'believe they exist, just as they believe that they themselves exist, and that animals, objects and atmospheric phenomena exist. Or rather their existence is not a matter of belief but a fact of life; there is no more need to believe in the *margaï* than in the fact that a stone, once thrown, will fall to earth' (ibid., pp. 49–50).
15 Bourdieu (1990: 68ff).
16 Karl-Friedrich Büchner, *Der Mensch und seine Stellung in der Natur* (1870), trans. as *L'Homme selon la science* (1878), p. 194; cited by Jacques Natanson, *La Mort de Dieu. Essai sur l'athéisme moderne* (Paris: PUF, 1975).
17 Berger (1967).
18 Including myth, which Claude Lévi-Strauss defines, in *La Pensée sauvage* (Paris: Plon, 1962; transl. J. and D. Weightman, *The Savage Mind*, London: Weidenfeld and Nicolson, 1966), as 'a vigorous protest against the denial of meaning', p. 22.
19 Hervieu-Léger (1979a and 1979b: 45–63).
20 Hervieu-Léger (1983).
21 Weber (1978: 503–8).
22 For a detailed account, see Hervieu-Léger (1982a).
23 Cf. nn. 20 and 22.
24 Durkheim (1995: 34).
25 Some of these points were tellingly made by Michael Löwy in the account he gave of the book in *Archives de Sciences Sociales des Religions*, 56–2 (1983), p. 390.
26 See Hervieu-Léger (1980: 23–57).
27 Hervieu-Léger (1983: 183ff).
28 'Believing is to know oneself begotten'. See Gisel (1990).

5 Questions about Tradition

1 In particular, *Relimod* (Religion and Modernity) *Documents*, 1 (1988); 'Tradition, Innovation and Modernity', *Social Compass*, 36–1 (1989), pp. 71–81.
2 Balandier (1988: 36–7).
3 Gauchet (1985: v–vi).
4 Ibid., p. xi.
5 Ibid., p. xiii.
6 On this conflict of type, which makes religion and heteronomous society coincide, see Castoriadis (1986: 364–84).
7 Weber (1991: 296).
8 Erlich (1978).
9 Moingt (1990).
10 Shils (1981).
11 Here 'prophet' is understood in the sense that Max Weber gives to the term, namely 'a purely individual bearer of charisma, who by virtue of his mission proclaims a religious doctrine or a divine commandment' (Weber, 1978: 439ff).
12 Chauvet (1989).
13 Balandier (1988: 37–8).
14 Ibid. Balandier in fact broaches the theme in an earlier work (1984: ch. vii).
15 de Certeau, Domenach (1974: 9–10).
16 For a presentation of the theme with a bibliography, see Hervieu-Léger (1986); see also Tschannen (1992).
17 Luhmann (1989: 159).
18 We resort here to Jean Séguy's ideal-typical definition of utopia: 'An appeal to the past, which is frequently magnified into a golden age, in comparison with the present which is rejected and in anticipation of a radically different future' (1971: see 328–54).
19 Desroche (1965).
20 Löwy (1988).
21 Kepel (1987).
22 The frailty of the politically instrumentalized reinvestment of religion is one of the hypotheses advanced by Patrick Michel with regard to eastern Europe (1992: 183–201).
23 Dumont (1983: 28).
24 Ibid., p. 29.
25 Ibid., p. 28.
26 See Benjamin Constant: 'Our own freedom must comprise the peaceful enjoyment of private independence' (1980: 501).
27 Weber (1978: 242).
28 Baudrillard (1988).
29 Lipovetsky (1983: 16–17).

30 *Le Monde*, 28 March 1991, p. 28: Les Mystères Stradivarius.
31 See Jacques Monod, *Le Hasard et la nécessité* (Paris: Éd. du Seuil, 1970), pp. 190ff).
32 See Gaston Bachelard, *La Philosophie du non* (Paris, PUF, 1940), p. 7.

6   From Religions to the Religious

1   Augé (1982).
2   Coles (1975).
3   Augé (1982: 66–7).
4   One instance of the legitimizing role of reference to the deeper purposes of Pierre de Coubertin, who was instrumental in reviving the Olympic Games: on the occasion of the 1992 Winter Olympics at Albertville, there was some discussion about the opportunity thus provided for different cultural manifestations – concerts, exhibitions and so on – to accompany the various events in the ski resorts of the Savoy Alps, and it was decided that these were entirely in keeping with the games, whose prime function in the view of Pierre de Coubertin was to foster better understanding between peoples.
5   Davie (1993a and 1993b).
6   Grace Davie shows that this sense of belonging is further evident in the religious membership of Liverpool's population, which has features that set it apart from that of other big cities in Britain.
7   Weber (1991: 297).
8   Berger (1967: ch. 5, p. 116).
9   'This also holds for the supreme head of the Church. The present concept of [papal] "infallibility" is a jurisdictional concept. Its inner meaning differs from that which preceded it, even up to the time of Innocent III' (Weber, 1991: 295).
10 On the manner in which the several theories of secularization have shaped the two main components of the paradigm, rationalization and institutional differentiation, see Tschannen (1992).
11 Bourdieu, Wacquant (1992: 97).
12 Ibid., p. 97.
13 Bourdieu (1971: 304).
14 Ibid., p. 315.
15 Terray (1992: 26).
16 Ibid.
17 Ibid.
18 L'Abbé Alfred Loisy (1857–1940), a leader of the modernist tendency, was excommunicated in 1908 and appointed Professeur d'Histoire des Religions at the Collège de France in 1909. The reference is to his book, *L'Évangile et l'église* (Paris: Picard, 1902), which launched the modernist crisis in France.
19 Michel (1988).
20 See Clastres (1974) and Abensour (1987).

21 Richir (1991: 39).
22 Gauchet (1985).
23 Lefort (1986).
24 Gauchet (1989: 248ff).
25 See p. 000, n. 26.
26 Renaut (1989).
27 Richir (1991: 138).
28 Clearly the function is enhanced when the religious dimension in politics is fostered through the ritual of a conventional religion, as is the case in Britain.
29 Kriegel (1968).
30 Linked in France with the names of Jean Séguy and Henri Desroche.

7 Religion Deprived of Memory

1 See Wilson (1969; 1982) and Martin (1978).
2 See the three classic studies of religious memory by Maurice Halbwachs (1952; 1968; 1971); also Namer (1987).
3 Thus social, political, legal or other forms of ritual are not even inherently religious, for all that they may give the appearance of being so. The political ritual of an election or a party congress may, in exceptional cases, display religious features, whereas in the case of a May Day demonstration, the religious dimension may well take precedence over the political.
4 Halbwachs (1952: 201ff).
5 Nora (1984:I, xviii).
6 Halbwachs (1952: 247–8).
7 Ibid., pp. 265–72.
8 See Séguy (1990: 127–38).
9 Weber, 'Science as a Vocation' (1991: 152–3).
10 Among recent summaries, see *La religione degli Europei* (Turin: Fondazione Giovanni Agnelli, 1992); and Roof, Carroll, Roozen (1993).
11 Recent surveys reveal a drop of seven or eight points below the figure of 82 per cent which remained stable for years. Even so the gap between this figure (for religious membership) and that for religious observance is significant enough.
12 Survey conducted in December 1989 by the consumer organization CRÉDOC (Centre de Recherches, d'Études et de Documentation sur la Consommation).
13 A joint survey conducted in 1986 by IFOP (Institut Français d'Opinion Publique) and the Catholic newspaper *La Vie* revealed that the existence of God was considered as certain by 31 per cent of those participating, probable by 35 per cent, improbable by 14 per cent, and rejected by 12 per cent, with 8 per cent not responding. To the question: 'For you, is Jesus Christ the Son of God?' 64 per cent replied in the affirmative, 17 per cent in the negative, with 19 per cent holding no opinion. These

findings were little different from those resulting from a similar survey in 1958.

14 A further survey conducted in France in 1986 showed that 20 per cent of the sample believed in reincarnation; furthermore, 51 per cent declared their belief in the resurrection of Christ, 37 per cent in the Trinity, 41 per cent in the real presence in the Eucharist, 43 per cent in the Immaculate Conception, 35 per cent in original sin and 24 per cent in the devil. For a fuller analysis of this survey, see Michelat et al. (1991).

15 In 1979–80, 63 per cent of French newspapers and periodicals carried a horoscope, twice the percentage recorded twenty years earlier. The variation between the national and regional press was pronounced (39 per cent as against 72 per cent). Women's magazines nearly always contained a horoscope (92 per cent). Exceptions to the trend included the Catholic press, political party organs and scientific and technical publications. On what he terms a multitude of heterodoxies, see Jacques Maître (1988a and b).

16 Boy, Michelat (1986: 175–204).

17 According to Laurence Podselver's ongoing thesis on the Lubavich community in France.

18 Le Chanoine Fernand Boulard is known for his celebrated atlas of religious practice in mid-nineteenth-century France and for a monumental body of work tracing this pattern region by region into the mid-twentieth century. His findings, based chiefly on diocesan records and surveys, were assembled and published after his death (in 1978) as *Matériaux pour l'histoire religieuse du peuple français* (Paris: Presses de la Fondation Nationale des Sciences Politiques, Éditions de l'École des Hautes Études en Sciences Sociales, vol. I (1982), vol. II (1987), vol. III (1992)).

19 Lambert (1991).

20 See Roussel (1989).

21 See Marie-Claude La Godelinais, Yannick Lemel, 'L'Évolution du mode de vie. Bouleversements et permanences sur fond de croissance', *Données sociales* (Paris: INSEE, 1990), pp. 182ff.

22 Roussel (1989: ch. iv).

23 See Émile Poulat:

>   In a society where the soil was the basis of the economy and the source of nobility, Christianity took on a rural aspect which outlasted the passage of the centuries and the profound changes in the means of production . . . This constituted a major influence on ecclesiastical organization and had a profound impact on the Catholic mentality, both in its popular, traditional and syncretic forms and as represented in liturgy, teaching, spirituality and even canon law. (1960: 1168–79)

24 The farming population now represents some 7 per cent of the workforce in France (1.6 million), a loss of four million jobs over forty years. Only 15 per cent of the farming population are under fifteen, whilst those over

fifty-five number 32 per cent. More than 500,000 mainly small farmers (representing roughly one million farms or smallholdings) reached retirement age in the period 1990–5; of these 150,000 had someone to take over their farm or holding, 200,000 had no one, while the remainder faced uncertainty. If the rural *vis-à-vis* the urban population is now relatively stable (27 per cent of the French population live in rural, non-suburban, *communes* numbering fewer than 2000 inhabitants), within this category peasant farmers count for barely one-third. See *Le Grand Atlas de la France rurale* (Paris: Éd. Jean-Pierre de Monza, 1989).

25 See Gervais, Jollivet, Tavernier (1977).
26 Hervieu, Vial (1970: 291–314).
27 These observations owe much to Bertrand Hervieu (1991 and 1993).
28 To take the title of a well-known study by Henri Mendras (1967).
29 Lipovetsky (1994).
30 Gradual obliteration as compared with the annihilation of collective memory that accompanied the totalitarian experience in eastern European societies.
31 Lambert (1985: ch. x).
32 Champion (1993).

8 The Chain Reinvented

1 On the case of Le Puy-du-Fou, see the remarkable article by Jean-Clément Martin and Charles Suaud (1992: 21–37).
2 For example, the highly successful reconstitution as living museums of early colonial settlements on the Massachusetts or Virginia coast (e.g. Old Sturbridge Village, Williamsburg); or the various practical lessons in history on offer, such as participation in a re-enactment of the Boston Tea Party.
3 Johnston (1992).
4 According to the definition given in Séguy (1971), see p. 183, n.18.
5 See Desroche (1969a, 1972).
6 Desroche (1974: 199).
7 Desroche (1973).
8 Desroche (1965).
9 Desroche (1974: 198).
10 The notion of a utopian voluntary group (in the sense of its possibly containing a utopian reference) was formulated by Séguy in 'Lettre à Jacqueline', no. 3' (1973–4). Two criteria define it: the voluntary recruitment of members, and a definition of aims, together with the means by which to attain them.
11 See Hill (1991).
12 Engels, *Socialism – Utopian and Scientific* (London, 1892), introduction.
13 See Séguy (1980b).
14 See Séguy (1984).

15 The literature is prolific, but see Creagh (1983).

16 See Hervieu-Léger (1983).

17 See Hervieu-Léger (1993).

18 See Löwy (1990); also Hewitt, 'Liberation Theology in Latin America and Beyond', in Swatos (1993: 73–91).

19 See Mary Jo Neitz, 'Inequality and Difference: Feminist Research in the Sociology of Religion', in Swatos (1993: 165–84).

20 Weber (1978: 444ff).

21 See Hervieu-Léger (1986: 349ff).

22 Hegel (1988: 114). The passage quoted occurs in the fourth part of a collection of manuscripts published long after Hegel's death and assembled in H. Nohl (ed.), *Hegels theologische Jugendschriften* (Tübingen, 1907). See also Hegel (1998).

23 See Hervieu-Léger in Swatos (1993: 128–48).

24 See H. Muller, *Jim Morrison, au delà des Doors* (Paris: Albin Michel, 1974).

25 Unlike the protest songs, represented by Bob Dylan or Joan Baez, which were clearly utopian in character, or even unlike groups such as Pink Floyd, whose songs expressly rejected western capitalist and *petit-bourgeois* modernity.

26 J. Hopkins, D. Sugerman, *No One Gets Out of Here Alive* (1981; London: Plexus, 1995).

27 In her study of the cult that has grown up around the pop singer Claude François, Marie-Christine Pouchelle amply demonstrates the significance of such 'minor' phenomena for an anthropology of contemporary culture. See Pouchelle (1983; 1990: 32–46).

28 Which meets with incomprehension, if not hostility, on the part of older generations who set greater store by commitment to society than by the emotional gratification of communal living, and who put a higher value on associating oneself with the common lot of humanity than on proclaiming one's religious difference.

29 See Hervieu-Léger (1987a: 218–34).

30 An illuminating example of such induction prior to a legitimating genealogy is furnished by Martine Cohen, describing the manner in which the Chemin Neuf community came gradually to identify with the figure of the Curé d'Ars. A chance encounter (some members of the group happened to be living close to Ars in 1977) led to an informal pilgrimage and to the growth of a vocation of listening and reconciliation within the community, whose work was among problem couples. The 'adoption' of the Curé d'Ars thus became a means of integrating their activity within a 'mission' of the Church, invested with historical authenticity, then of obtaining institutional validation of the community from the Catholic hierarchy, which received confirmation when the pope visited Ars in October 1986. See Cohen (1988: 102).

31 See Hovanessian (1992).

32 Cf. Glazer, Moynihan (1970).

33 Alexandre Popovic stresses the nebulous and mythical character of Islam

as represented by the Muslim population of the former Yugoslavia. Clearly, identification in this case implies not so much the reality of Islam in terms of a view of the world and a body of beliefs and practices as its effectiveness as an emblem (it having been the only legal vehicle for local nationalism under the communist regime) in forming an ethnic resistance to Serbia's expansionist aims. See Popovic in Michel (1992: 161–81).

34 See Smith (1981).
35 See Schnapper (1993: 159).
36 For an acute analysis of changing belief in a Belgian context, see Dobbelaere, Voyé (1990; 1992).
37 de Certeau, Domenach (1974: 11–12).
38 Michel (1988: 148).
39 Sixty-three per cent of Swedes declare themselves to be Christian 'in their way' in that, for most of them, God represents a 'higher force', though an impersonal one, and Christianity a set of moral values, while 9 per cent describe themselves as practising Christians and 26 per cent as non-Christian. See Eva Hamberg, 'Religion, Secularisation and Value Change in the Welfare State', paper given at the first European Conference on Sociology, Vienna, 26–9 August 1992. See also Gustaffson (1987: 145–81) and Ole Riis, 'Patterns of Secularisation in Scandanavia', in T. Pettersson, O. Riis, *Scandinavian Values* (Uppsala: Acta Universitatis Upsaliensis, 1994), pp. 99–128.
40 More meaningful here than a mere declaration of belonging, as is commonly given in France, where a large majority of the population are not churchgoers yet declare themselves Catholic.
41 Religious observance in Sweden, as in all Scandinavian countries, is below 5 per cent.
42 Susan Sundback, 'The Post-war Generations and Lutheranism in the Nordic Countries' in Roof, Carroll, Roozen (1993).
43 In particular, the Chrétiens-Solidarité group, led by Romain Marie.
44 Michel (1988) and 'Religion, sortie du communisme, et démocratie en Europe du Centre-Est', in Michel (1992).
45 Davie (1990).

Conclusion

1 In Peter Berger's *A Far Glory* (1992), the notion of pluralism is central to the restatement of his sociological and theological interpretation of modern religion.
2 Berger, Luckmann (1967).
3 R. Finke, R. Stark, 'Religious Economies and Sacred Canopies', *American Sociological Review*, 28 (1988), pp. 27–44; R. Stark, L. Iannaccone, entry for 'Sociology of Religion', in *Encyclopedia of Sociology*, ed. Edgar and Marie Borgatta (New York: Macmillan, 1992).
4 Iannaccone (1991: 156–77).

5   Peter Berger (1979).
6   I wholly agree with the analysis developed by Patrick Michel (1993), namely that all contemporary societies, both western and those of the former eastern bloc, are now 'post-communist societies, in the sense that they all have to come to terms with the sequel to the polarisation of ultimate references which informed attitudes and even mind-set'.
7   Touraine (1992: 216).
8   Ibid., pp. 224–5.
9   Giddens (1990; 1991).
10 This is best shown in Richard H. Niebuhr (1957) and has been subsequently taken up in the Anglo-American sociology of sects.
11 This is the case for renewal movements operating within traditional religions; but also, in our opinion, for other renewal movements which contain religious features, in the political arena particularly. It would be rewarding, for instance, to study the sectarianism of the Green movement in Europe.
12 Campiche, Bovay et al. (1992). See, in particular, Campiche's conclusions, pp. 267–79.
13 See de Certeau (1983) and Panier (1991).
14 For an analysis of the different ways in which young people affirm their belief, see Lambert, Michelat (1992).
15 The crisis of institutional regulation is seen particularly in the spread among charismatic groups of the spontaneous practice of reading scriptural texts. For a detailed account, see D. Hervieu-Léger, 'La Pratique de la lecture spontanée des textes scriptuaires', in É. Patlagean, A. Le Boulluec (eds), *Les Retours aux Écritures. Fondamentalismes présents et passés* (Louvain and Paris: Peeters, 1994), pp. 47–61.
16 Incidentally, one should be careful not to make too much of the divergence. The three religions of the Book have in their respective ways contributed to promoting the individuation of the relationship between a personalized God and the believer for whom he becomes personalized. One recalls the remark attributed to the first Shi'ite Imam: 'To know oneself is to know one's Lord.' See Corbin (1981).
17 Danzger (1989).
18 Willaime (1992: ch. 1).
19 Introductory address by Mgr Duval to the assembly of French bishops, *La Croix*, 28 October 1992.
20 Willaime (1992).
21 'Painless ethics', which is well described by Gilles Lipovetsky (1992), though there is no need to go along with all his conclusions about the end of moral obligation and devotion because of the pervasive influence of the ethics transmitted by the media.
22 Baubérot (1988) combines brilliantly an analysis of the causes of this threat to its survival and a plea for action to overcome it.
23 Lautman, 'Du désert au musée. L'identité protestante', *Autrement* (Paris), 115 (1990).
24 Frequently a very selective history: for instance, the travel guide drawn

up by the charismatic community of Emmanuel, itself much involved in the preparation and organization of the Czestochowa march, in which the French contingent numbered 2,000, evokes the memory of St Norbert, founder of the Premonstratensians, in its pages about Prague, but makes no mention of Jan Hus.

25 For a detailed analysis of the Czestochowa episode as an element in the strategy of reasserting Catholic identity, see Hervieu-Léger (1994: 125–38).

Select Bibliography

Abensour, M. (ed.), 1987. *L'Esprit des lois sauvages. Pierre Clastres ou une nouvelle anthropologie politique*, Paris: Éd. du Seuil.

Alexander, J., 1990. 'The Sacred and Profane Information Machine: Discourse about the Computer as Ideology', *Archives de Sciences Sociales des Religions*, 69–1, January–March, pp. 161–71.

Augé, M., 1982. 'Football. De l'histoire sociale à l'anthropologie religieuse', *Le Débat*, 19, February.

——, 1992. *Non-Lieux, Introduction à une anthropologie de la surmodernité*, Paris: Éd. du Seuil.

Azria, R., 1991. 'Pratiques juives et modernité', *Pardès*, 14, pp. 53–70.

Balandier, G., 1984. *Anthropologie politique*, Paris: PUF.

——, 1985. *Le Détour. Pouvoir et modernité*, Paris: Fayard.

——, 1988. *Le Désordre. Éloge du mouvement*, Paris: Fayard.

Barker, E. (ed.), 1982. *New Religious Movements: A Perspective for Understanding*, New York and Toronto: Edwin Mellen Press.

Bastide, R., 1967. *Les Amériques noires*, Paris: Payot.

Baubérot, J., 1988. *Le Protestantisme doit-il mourir? La différence protestante dans une France pluriculturelle*, Paris: Éd. du Seuil.

Baudrillard, J., 1988. 'Modernité', in *Encyclopædia universalis*, vol. 11, pp. 139–41.

Béguin, J., Tardits, C. et al., 1987. *Cent ans de sciences religieuses en France à l'École Pratique des Hautes Études*, Paris: Éd. du Cerf.

Bell, D., 1977. 'The Return of the Sacred? The Argument on the Future of Religion', *British Journal of Sociology*, 28, pp. 420–49.

Bellah, R. N., 1957. *Tokugawa Religion*, Glencoe, Ill.: Free Press.

——, 1970. *Beyond Belief: Essays on Religion in a Post-traditional World*, New York: Harper and Row.

——, 1975. *The Broken Covenant: American Civil Religion in a Time of Trial*, New York: Seabury Press.

Bellah, R. N., Hammond P. E., 1980. *Varieties of Civil Religion*, New York: Harper and Row.

Berger, P., 1967. *The Sacred Canopy: Elements of a Sociological Theory of Religion*, New York: Doubleday.

——, 1979. *The Heretical Imperative: Contemporary Possibilities of Religious Affirmation*, New York: Anchor Press.

——, 1992. *A Far Glory: The Quest for Faith in an Age of Incredulity*, New York: Macmillan and Free Press.

Berger, P., Luckmann, T., 1967. 'Aspects sociologiques du pluralisme', *Archives de Sociologie des Religions*, 23.

Bergson, H., 1977. *The Two Sources of Morality and Religion* [1932], Notre Dame, Ind.: University of Notre Dame Press.

Bertrand, M., 1979. *Le Statut de la religion chez Marx et Engels*, Paris: Éditions Sociales.

Boudon, R., 1988. 'Sociologie. Les Développements', in *Encyclopædia universalis*, vol. 21, pp. 211–14.

Bourdet, Y., 1976. *Qu'est-ce qui fait courir les militants?* Paris: Stock.

Bourdieu, P., 1968. *Le Métier de sociologue*, Paris: Mouton-Bordas.

——, 1971. 'Genèse et structure du champ religieux', *Revue Française de Sociologie*, 12–3, July-September, pp. 295–334.

——, 1980. *Leçons de sociologie*, Paris: Éd. de Minuit.

——, 1987. 'Sociologues de la croyance et croyances de sociologues', *Archives de Sciences Sociales des Religions*, 63–1, January–March, pp. 155–61.

——, 1990. The Logic of Practice, tr. R. Nice, Cambridge: Polity Press.

Bourdieu, P., Wacquant, L., 1992. *An Invitation to Reflexive Sociology*, Chicago: University of Chicago Press, and Cambridge: Polity Press.

Boy, D., Michelat, G., 1986. 'Croyances aux parasciences: dimensions sociales et culturelles', *Revue Française de Sociologie*, 27, pp. 175–204.

Brohm, J.-M., 1976. *Sociologie politique du sport*, Paris: Delarge.

Campiche, R., Bovay, C. et al., 1992. *Croire en Suisse(s)*, Lausanne: L'Âge d'Homme.

Castoriadis, C., 1986. *Domaines de l'homme. Les carrefours du labyrinthe*, Paris: Éd. du Seuil.

——, 1997. *The Castoriadis Reader*, tr./ed. David Ames Curtis, Oxford: Blackwell.

de Certeau, M., 1983. 'L'Institution du croire. Note de travail', *Le Magistère. Institutions et Fonctionnements, Recherches de Sciences Religieuses* (Special number).

——, 1985. 'Le Croyable. Préliminaire à une anthropologie des croyances', in H. Parret and H.-G. Ruprecht (eds), *Exigences et perspectives de la sémiotique*, Amsterdam: John Benjamin, vol. 2, pp. 687–707.

de Certeau, M., Domenach, J.-M., 1974. *Le Christianisme éclaté*, Paris: Éd. du Seuil.

Champion, F., 1989. 'Les Sociologues de la postmodernité et la Nébuleuse mystique-ésotérique', *Archives de Sciences Sociales des Religions*, 67–1,

January–March, pp. 155–69.

——, 1993. 'Religieux flottant, éclectisme et syncrétismes dans les sociétés contemporaines', in J. Delumeau (ed.), *Le Fait religieux dans le monde d'aujourd'hui*, Paris: Fayard.

Champion, F., Hervieu-Léger, D. (eds), 1990. *De l'émotion en religion. Renouveaux et traditions*, Paris: Le Centurion.

Chauvet, L.-M., 1989. 'La Notion de "tradition" ', *La Maison-Dieu*, 178.

Clastres, P., 1974. *La Société contre l'État*, Paris: Éd. de Minuit.

Cohen, M., 1988. 'Les Charismatiques français et le Pape', in J. Séguy et al., *Voyage de Jean Paul II en France*, Paris: Éd. du Cerf.

Coleman, J., 1970. 'Civil Religion', *Sociological Analysis*, 31–2.

Coles, R. W., 1975. 'Football as a "Surrogate" Religion?' *A Sociological Yearbook of Religion in Britain* (London), 8.

Constant, B., 1980. *De la liberté chez les Modernes. Écrits politiques*, texts assembled and introduced by Marcel Gauchet, Paris: Le Livre de Poche, coll. Pluriel.

Corbin, C., 1981. *Le Paradoxe du monothéisme*, Paris: L'Herne.

Creagh, R., 1983. *Laboratoires de l'Utopie. Les Communautés libertaires aux États-Unis*, Paris: Payot.

Danzger, H., 1989. *Returning to Tradition: The Contemporary Revival of Orthodox Judaism*, New Haven, Conn.: Yale University Press.

Davie, G., 1990. 'Believing without Belonging: Is this the Future of Religion in Britain?' *Social Compass*, 37–4.

——, 1993a. 'You'll Never Walk Alone: The Anfield Pilgrimage', in L. Reader, J. Walter (eds), *Pilgrimage in Popular Culture*, London: Macmillan, pp. 201–19.

——, 1993b. 'Believing without Belonging: A Liverpool Case Study', *Archives de Sciences Sociales des Religions*, 81.

Deconchy, J.-P., 1959. 'La Définition de la religion pour William James. Dans quelle mesure peut-on l'opérationnaliser?' *Archives de Sociologie des Religions*, 27, pp. 51–70.

Desroche, H., 1965. *Socialismes et sociologie religieuse*, Paris: Cujas.

——, 1968. *Sociologies religieuses*, Paris: PUF.

——, 1969a. *Dieux d'hommes. Dictionnaire des messianismes et millénarismes de l'ère chrétienne*, Paris and The Hague: Mouton.

——, 1969b. Retour à Durkheim? D'un texte peu connu à quelques thèses méconnues', *Archives de Sociologie des Religions*, 27, pp. 79–88.

——, 1972. *Les Dieux rêvés*, Paris: Desclée de Brouwer.

——, 1973. *Sociologie de l'espérance*, Paris: Calmann-Lévy.

——, 1974. *Les Religions de contrebande*, Paris: Mame.

Desroche H., Séguy, J., 1970. *Introduction aux sciences humaines des religions*, Paris: Cujas.

Desrosiers, Y. (ed.), 1986. *Religion et culture au Québec. Figures contemporaines du sacré*, Montreal: Fidès.

Dobbelaere, K., 1981. *Secularisation: A Multidimensional Concept*, London: Sage Publications.

Dobbelaere, K., Voyé, L., 1990. 'From Pillar to Post-Modernity: The Changing Situation in Belgium', *Sociological Analysis*, 51, no. S, S1–S13.

——, 1992. *Belges et heureux de l'être*, Louvain: De Boeck.

Dumont, L., 1983. *Essais sur l'individualisme. Une perspective anthropologique sur l'idéologie moderne*, Paris: Éd. du Seuil.

Durkheim, É., 1982. *The Rules of Sociological Method* [1895], tr. W. D. Hall, London: Macmillan.

——, 1984. *The Division of Labour in Society* [1893], tr. W. D. Hall, London: Macmillan.

——, 1995. *The Elementary Forms of Religious Life* [1912], tr./ed. Karen E. Fields, New York: Free Press.

Erlich, J., 1978. *La Flamme du Shabbath*, Paris: Plon, coll. Terre humaine.

Fenn, R., 1978. *Toward a Theory of Secularisation*, Storrs, Conn.: Society for the Scientific Study of Religion.

Fulton, J., Gee, P. (eds.), 1994. *Religion in Contemporary Europe*, Lewiston, Queenston and Lampeter: Edwin Mellen Press.

Gauchet, M., 1985. *Le Désenchantement du monde. Une histoire politique de la religion*, Paris: Gallimard.

——, 1989. *La Révolution des droits de l'homme*, Paris: Gallimard.

Gervais, M., Jollivet, M., Tavernier, Y., 1977. *Histoire de la France rurale*, vol. 4: *La Fin de la France paysanne*, Paris: Éd. du Seuil.

Giddens, A., 1990. *The Consequences of Modernity*, Stanford, Cal.: Stanford University Press, and Cambridge: Polity Press.

——, 1991. *Modernity and Self-Identity, Self and Society in the Late Modern Age*, Stanford: Stanford University Press, and Cambridge: Polity Press.

Gisel, P., 1990. *L'Excès du croire. Expérience du monde et accès à soi*, Paris: Desclée de Brouwer.

Glazer, N., Moynihan, D., 1970. *Beyond the Melting Pot: The Negroes, Puertoricans, Jews, Italians and Irish of New York City*, Cambridge, Mass.: MIT Press.

Glock C. Y., Hammond, P. (eds), 1973. *Beyond the Classics: Essays in the Scientific Study of Religion*, New York: Harper and Row.

Gustaffson, G., 1987. 'Religious Change in the Five Scandinavian Countries, 1930–1980', *Comparative Social Research*, 10, pp. 145–81.

Halbwachs, M., 1952. *Les Cadres sociaux de la mémoire*, Paris: PUF.

——, 1968. *La Mémoire collective* [1950], Paris: PUF.

——, 1971. *Topographie légendaire des Evangiles* [1941], Paris: PUF.

Hammond, P. E. (ed.), 1985. *The Sacred in a Secular Age: Toward Revision in the Scientific Study of Religion*. Berkeley: University of California Press.

Hegel, G. W. F., 1988. *L'Esprit du christianisme et son destin*, Paris: Vrin.

——, 1998. *The Hegel Reader*, ed. Stephen Houlgate, Oxford: Blackwell.

Hervieu, B., 1991. 'Les Ruptures du monde agricole', *Regards sur l'actualité*, 168, February.

——, 1993. *Les Champs du futur*, Paris: Éd. François Bourin.

Hervieu, B., Vial A., 1970. 'L'Église catholique et les paysans', in *L'Univers politique des paysans dans la France contemporaine*, Paris: A. Colin–FNSP, pp. 291–314.

Hervieu-Léger, Danièle, 1979a. *Le Retour à la nature. Au fond de la forêt . . .*

l'État (with Bertrand Hervieu), Paris: Éd. du Seuil.

——, 1979b. 'Les Utopies du retour', *Actes de la Recherche en Sciences Sociales*, 29, September, pp. 45–63.

——, 1980. 'Ebyathar ou la protestation pure' (with Bertrand Hervieu), *Archives de Sciences Sociales des Religions*, 50/1, July–September, pp. 23–57.

——, 1982a. 'Apocalyptique écologique et retour de la religion', *Archives de Sciences Sociales des Religions*. 53/1, January–June, pp. 49–67.

——, 1982b. 'Charisma, Utopia and Communal Life: The Case of the Rural Apocalyptic Communes in France', *Social Compass*, XXXIX/I, pp. 41–58.

——, 1983. *Des Communautés pour les Temps Difficiles. Néo-ruraux ou nouveaux moines* (with Bertrand Hervieu), Paris: Le Centurion.

——, 1986. *Vers un nouveau Christianisme? Introduction à la sociologie du christianisme occidental* (with Françoise Champion), Paris: Éd. du Cerf.

——, 1987a. 'Charismatisme catholique et institution', in R. Luneau, P. Ladrière (eds), *Le Retour des certitudes. Évènements et nouvelle orthodoxie après Vatican II*, Paris: Le Centurion, pp. 218–34.

——, 1987b. 'Faut-il-définir la religion? Questions préalables à la construction d'une sociologie de la modernité religieuse', *Archives de Sciences Sociales des Religions*, 63/1, January–March, pp. 11–30.

——, 1990. 'Renouveaux émotionnels contemporains. Fin de la sécularisation ou fin de la religion?' in F. Champion, D. Hervieu-Léger (eds), *De l'émotion en religion*, Paris: Le Centurion, pp. 217–48.

—— (ed.) 1993. *Religion et Écologie*, Paris: Éd. du Cerf.

——, 1994. 'Religion, Memory and Catholic Identity: Young People in France and the "New Evangelisation of Europe" ', in J. Fulton, P. Gee (eds), *Religion in Contemporary Europe*, Lewiston, Queenston and Lampeter: Edwin Mellen Press, pp. 125–38.

Hill C., 1991. *The World Turned Upside-Down* [1975], London: Penguin Books.

Hovanessian, M., 1992. *Le Lien communautaire. Trois générations d'Arméniens*, Paris: Armand Colin.

Hunter J. D., Ainlay S. C. (eds), 1986. *Peter L. Berger and the Vision of Interpretative Sociology*, New York: Routledge and Kegan Paul, pp. 143–58.

Iannaccone, Lawrence R., 1991. 'The Consequences of Religious Market Structure', *Rationality and Society*, 3(2), pp. 156–77.

Isambert, F.-A., 1966. 'La Fête et les fêtes', *Journal de Psychologie Normale et Pathologique*, July–December.

——, 1975. 'Les Transformations du rituel catholique des mourants', *Archives de Sciences Sociales des Religions*, 39.

——, 1979. *Rite et efficacité symbolique*, Paris: Éd. du Cerf.

——, 1982. *Le Sens du Sacré. Fête et religion populaire*, Paris: Éd. de Minuit.

——, 1990. 'Durkheim: une science de la morale pour une morale laïque', *Archives de Sciences Sociales des Religions*, 69, January–March, pp. 129–146.

——, 1992. 'Une religion de l'Homme? Sur trois interprétations de la religion dans la pensée de Durkheim', *Revue Française de Sociologie*, 33, pp. 443–62.

——, 1993. *De la religion à l'éthique*, Paris: Éd. du Cerf.

Izard, M., Smith, P. (eds), 1982. *Between Belief and Trangression: Structuralist Essays in Religion, History and Myth* [1979], Chicago: University of Chicago Press.

James, W., 1985. *The Varieties of Religious Experience* [1902], Cambridge, Mass.: Harvard University Press.

Johnston, W. M., 1992. *Postmodernisme et bimillénaire. Le culte des anniversaires dans la culture contemporaine*, Paris: PUF (translation of *Celebrations Today: The Cult of Anniversaries in Europe and the United States*, New Brunswick and London: Transaction Books, c.1991).

Kepel, G., 1987. *Les Banlieues de l'Islam. Naissance d'une religion en France*, Paris: Éd. du Seuil.

Kriegel, A., 1968. *Les Communistes français. Essai d'ethnographie politique*, Paris: Éd. du Seuil.

Lambert, Y., 1985. *Dieu change en Bretagne*, Paris: Éd. du Cerf.

——, 1991. 'La "tour de Babel" des définitions de la religion', *Social Compass*, 38–1, March.

Lambert Y., Michelat G. (eds), 1992. *Crépuscule des religions chez les jeunes? Jeunes et religions en France*, Paris: Éd. L'Harmattan.

Le Bras, G., 1956. 'Sociologie religieuse et science des religions', *Archives de Sociologie des Religions*, 1, January–June.

Lefort, C., 1986. *Essais sur le politique, xixe-xxe siècles*, Paris: Éd. du Seuil.

Lipovetsky, G., 1983. *L'Ère du vide, Essais sur l'individualisme contemporain*, Paris: Gallimard.

——, 1992. *Le Crépuscule du devoir. L'Éthique indolore des nouveaux temps démocratiques*, Paris: Gallimard.

——, 1994. *The Empire of Fashion* [1987], Princeton: Princeton University Press.

Löwy, M., 1988. *Rédemption et Utopie, Le Judaïsme libertaire en Europe centrale*, Paris: PUF.

—— (documents compiled by), 1990. 'La Théologie de la libération en Amérique latine', *Archives, de Sciences Sociales des Religions*, 71–3, July–September.

Luckmann, T., 1967. *The Invisible Religion: The Problem of Religion in Modern Society*, New York: Macmillan.

——, 1990. 'Shrinking Transcendence, Expanding Religion?' *Sociological Analysis*, 51–2, Summer.

Luhmann, N., 1989. *Ecological Communication*, Cambridge: Polity Press.

Maître, J., 1988a. 'Les Deux Côtés du miroir. Note sur l'évolution religieuse actuelle de la population française par rapport au catholicisme', *L'Année Sociologique*, 3rd series, 38.

——, 1988b. 'Horoscope', in *Encyclopaedia Universalis*, vol. II, pp. 577–9.

Martin, C., Suaud, C., 1992. 'Le Puy-du-Fou. L'interminable réinvention du paysan vendéen', *Actes de la Recherche en Sciences Sociales*, 93, June, pp. 21–37.

Martin, D., 1978. *A General Theory of Secularization*, Oxford: Blackwell.

Marx, K., 1977. *Towards a Critique of Hegel's Philosophy of Right: Intro-

duction in *Karl Marx: Selected Writings*, ed. David McLellan, Oxford: Oxford University Press.

McGuire, M., 1992. *Religions: The Social Context* [1983], Belmont, Mass.: Wadsworth.

McNamara, P., 1974. *Religion American Style*, New York: Harper and Row.

Mendras, H., 1992. *La Fin des Paysans* [1967], Paris: Colin.

Michel, P., 1988. *La Société retrouvée. Politique et religion dans l'Europe soviétisée*, Paris: Fayard.

——, (ed.), 1992. *Les Religions à l'Est*, Paris: Éd. du Cerf.

——, 1993. 'Pour une sociologie des itinéraires du sens: une lecture politique du rapport entre croire et institution. Hommage à Michel de Certeau', *Archives de Sciences Sociales des Religions*, 81–3, July–September.

Michelat, G., Potel, J., Sutter, J., Maître, J., 1991. *Les Français sont-ils encore catholiques?* Paris: Éd. du Cerf.

Moingt, J., 1990. 'Religions, traditions, fondamentalismes', *Études*, 373–3, September.

Mothé, D., 1973. *Le Métier de militant*, Paris: Éd. du Seuil.

Namer, G., 1987. *Mémoire et société*, Paris: Méridiens-Klincksieck.

Nesti, A., 1985. *Il religioso implicito*. Rome: Ianua.

Niebuhr, R. H., 1957. *The Social Sources of Denominationalism*, New York: Meridian Books.

Nora, P., 1996–8. *Realms of Memory: The Construction of the French Past* (ed. Lawrence D. Kritzman, tr. Arthur Goldhammer). New York: Columbia University Press, vol. I, *Conflicts and Divisions*, 1996a; vol. II, *Traditions*, 1996b; vol. III, *Symbols*, 1998 (translation of *Les Lieux de Mémoire*, vol. I: *La République*, 1984; vols II, III, IV: *La Nation*, 1987; vols V, VI, VII: *Les France*, 1992, Paris: Gallimard).

O'Dea, T. F., 1966. *The Sociology of Religion*, Englewood Cliffs, NJ: Prentice Hall.

O'Toole, R., 1984. *Religion: Classic Sociological Approaches*, Toronto: McGraw-Hill Ryerson.

Panier, L., 1991. 'Pour une anthropologie du croire. Aspects de la problématique chez Michel de Certeau', in C. Geffré (ed.), *Michel de Certeau ou la différence chrétienne*, Paris: Éd du Cerf.

Parsons, T., 1969. *Introduction* to M. Weber, *The Sociology of Religion* [1963], Boston: Beacon Press.

Pickering, W., 1984. *Durkheim's Sociology of Religion: Themes and Theories*, London: Routledge and Kegan Paul.

Piette, A., 1993. *Les Religions séculières*, Paris: PUF, coll. Que sais-je?

Pociello, C. (ed.), 1981. *Sport et société. Approche socioculturelle des pratiques*, Paris: Vigot.

Pouchelle, M. C., 1983. 'Sentiments religieux et show-business: Claude François, objet de dévotion populaire', in J.-Cl. Schmitt, *Les Saints et les Stars*, Paris: Beauchesne.

——, 1990. 'Les Faits qui couvent, ou Claude François à contre-mort', *Terrain*, 14, March, pp. 32–46.

Poulat, E., 1960. 'La Découverte de la ville par le catholicisme français contemporain', *Annales*, 16th year, 6, November–December, pp. 1168–79.

——, 1986. 'Genèse', in Marc Guillaume (ed.), *L'État des sciences sociales en France*, Paris: La Découverte.

——, 1987. *Liberté, laïcité. La guerre des deux France et le principe de modernité*, Paris: Éd du Cerf–Cujas.

——, 1990. 'La CISR de la fondation à la mutation: réflexions sur une trajectoire et ses enjeux', proceedings of the Twentieth Conference of the International Society for the Sociology of Religion (ISSR/SISR), August 1989, Helsinki, *Social Compass*, pp. 37–1.

Prades, J., Ladrière, P., 1990. (documents compiled by), 'Relire Durkheim', *Archives de Sciences Sociales des Religions*, 69.

Renaut, A., 1989. *L'Ère de l'individu*, Paris: Gallimard.

Richir, M., 1991. *Du sublime en politique*, Paris: Payot.

Rivière, C., Piette, A. (eds), 1990. *Nouvelles idoles, nouveaux cultes. Dérives de la sacralité*, Paris: Éd. L'Harmattan.

Robertson, R., 1970. *The Sociological Interpretation of Religion*, Oxford: Blackwell.

Roof, Wade C., Carroll, Jackson, Roozen, David (eds), *The Post-war Generation and Established Religion*, San Francisco: Harper, 1993.

Roussel, L., 1989. *La Famille incertaine*, Paris: Éd. Odile Jacob.

Russell, B., 1999. *Religion and Science* [1935], Oxford: Oxford Paperbacks.

Samarin, W. J., 1972. *Tongues of Men and Angels: The Religious Language of Pentecostalism*, New York: Macmillan.

Schnapper, D., 1993. 'Le Religieux, l'éthnique et l'éthnico-religieux', *Archives de Sciences Sociales des Religions*, 81.

Séguy, J., 1971. 'Une sociologie des sociétés imaginées. Monachisme et utopie', *Annales*, March–April, pp 328–54.

——, 1973–4. 'Lettre à Jacqueline no. 3', duplicated copy of a seminar at the École Pratique des Hautes Études (5th Section).

——, 1975. 'Situation historique du pentecôtisme', *Lumière et vie*, 125, November–December.

——, 1980a. *Christianisme et Société. Introduction à la sociologie de Ernst Troeltsch*, Paris: Éd du Cerf.

——, 1980b. 'La Socialisation utopique aux valeurs', *Archives de Sciences Sociales des Religions*, 50–3, July–September, pp. 7–21.

——, 1983. 'Sociologie de l'attente', in C. Perrot, A. Abecassis et al. *Le Retour du Christ*, Brussels: Presses des Facultés Universitaires Saint-Louis.

——, 1984. 'Pour une sociologie de l'ordre religieux', *Archives de Sciences Sociales des Religions*, 57–1, January–March, pp. 55–68.

——, 1986. 'Religion, modernité, sécularisation', *Archives de Sciences Sociales des Religions*, 61–2, April–June, pp. 175–85.

——, 1989. 'L'Approche wébérienne des phénomènes religieux', in R. Cipriani, M. Macioti (eds), *Omaggio a Ferrarotti*, Rome: Siares, Studi e richerche.

——, 1990. 'Rationalisation, modernité et avenir de la religion chez Max Weber', *Archives des Sciences Sociales des Religions*, 69–1, January–March, pp. 127–38.

Shils, E., 1981. *Tradition*. London and Boston: Faber and Faber.

Sironneau, J. P., 1982. *Sécularisation et religions politiques*. The Hague: Mouton.

Smith, A., 1981. *The Ethnic Revival*, Cambridge: Cambridge University Press.

Swatos, W. H. (ed.), 1993. *A Future for Religion? New Paradigms for Social Analysis*, London: Sage Publications.

Synan, V., 1971. *The Holiness-Pentecostal Movement in the United States*, Grand Rapids, Mich.: Eerdmans.

Terray, E., 1992. *Le Troisième Jour du communisme*, Paris: Actes Sud.

Tillich, P., 1955. *Biblical Religion and the Search for Ultimate Reality*, Chicago: University of Chicago Press.

Touraine, A., 1974. *Pour la sociologie*, Paris: Éd du Seuil.

——, 1992. *Critique de la modernité*, Paris: Fayard.

Troeltsch, E., 1977. *Writings on Theology and Religion*, ed./tr. Robert Morgan and Michael Pye, London: Duckworth.

——, 1981. *The Social Teaching of the Christian Churches* [1912], Chicago and London: University of Chicago Press.

——, 1991. *Religion in History*, Minneapolis: Fortune Press.

Tschannen, O., 1992. *Les Théories de la sécularisation*, Geneva: Droz.

Tylor, E., 1871. *Primitive Culture*, 2 vols, London: John Murray.

Veyne, P., 1976. *Le Pain et le Cirque*, Paris: Éd. du Seuil.

Vidich A. J., Lyman, S. M., 1985. *American Sociology: Rejections of Religion and their Directions*, New Haven, Conn.: Yale University Press.

Voyé, L., 1991. 'L'Incontournable Facteur religieux, ou du sacré originaire', *Revue Internationale d'Action Communautaire*, 26/66, Autumn, pp. 45–56.

Wach, J., 1955. *Sociologie de la religion*, Paris: Payot.

Weber, M., 1952. *Ancient Judaism* [1917–19], tr./ed. H. H. Gerth and D. Martindale, Glencoe, Ill.: Free Press.

——, 1978. *Economy and Society* [1922], ed. Guenther Roth and Claus Wittich, Berkeley and Los Angeles: University of California Press.

——, 1991. *Essays in Sociology*, tr./ed. H. H. Gerth and C. Wright Mills [1948], London: Routledge Paperback.

——, 1992. *The Protestant Ethic and the Spirit of Capitalism* [1905], tr. Talcott Parsons [1930], London: Routledge.

Willaime, J.-P., 1992. *La Précarité protestante. Sociologie du protestantisme contemporain*, Geneva: Labor et Fides.

Wilson, B., 1969. *Religion in Secular Society: A Sociological Comment*, Baltimore: Penguin Books.

——, 1976. *Contemporary Transformations of Religion*, Oxford and New York: Oxford University Press.

——, 1979. 'The Return of the Sacred', *Journal for the Scientific Study of Religion*, 18–3, pp. 315–32.

——, (ed.), 1981. *The Social Impact of New Religious Movements*, New York: Rose of Sharon Press.

——, 1982. *Religion in a Sociological Perspective*, Oxford and New York: New York University Press.

——, 1990. *The Social Dimension of Sectarianism: Sects and New Religious Movements in Contemporary Society*, Oxford and New York: Oxford University Press.

Yinger, T. M., 1957. *Religion, Society and the Individual*, New York: Macmillan.

Yonnet, P., 1982. 'Joggers et marathoniens. Demain les survivants?', *Le Débat*, 19, February.

Zylberberg, J., 1985. 'Les Transactions du sacré', *Société*, 1–4, June.

Index of Names

Compiled by Meg Davies
Registered Indexer, Society of Indexers